7.50

Also by Mark Svenvold

*Elmer McCurdy: The Misadventures
in Life and Afterlife of an American Outlaw*

Soul Data
(poems)

BIG WEATHER COUNTRY 2004 (M. D. Biddle)

Montana

North Dakota

Minnesota

Wyoming

South Dakota
■
Manchester

Yankton ■

■ Hadar

Nebraska

Norfolk ■

Omaha
Iowa

North
Platte ■

Grand
Island ■

York ■

Lincoln ■ ■ Bellevue

■ Hallam

Wilber ■

Hebron ■

■ Beatrice

Colorado

Lebanon

Belleville
■

■ Cawker City

Kansas

Dodge City
■

■ Wichita

■ Attica

■ Wakita

Missouri

Oklahoma

El Reno ■

■ Oklahoma City
■ Moore

Bridge ■
Creek

Norman

New
Mexico

Arkansas

Healdton
■

Gainesville
■

Texas

For those keeping score: In 2004, Kansas set records for the most tornadoes (124) and for the most tornadoes in a single month (66 in May). There were 600 more tornadoes than the twenty-year average for the United States. © M. D. Biddle

BIG WEATHER

Chasing Tornadoes in the Heart of America

MARK SVENVOLD

A John Macrae Book
Henry Holt and Company
New York

Henry Holt and Company, LLC
Publishers since 1866
175 Fifth Avenue
New York, New York 10010
www.henryholt.com

Henry Holt® is a registered trademark of
Henry Holt and Company, LLC.

Library of Congress Cataloging-in-Publication Data
Svenvold, Mark, date.
    Big weather : chasing tornadoes in the heart
    of America / Mark Svenvold.—1st ed.
        p.   cm.
    "A John Macrae book."
    Includes bibliographical references and index.
    ISBN-13: 978-0-8050-7646-2
    ISBN-10: 0-8050-7646-8
    1. Tornadoes—United States.   I. Title.
QC955.5.U6S75   2005
551.55'3—dc22   2004060753

First Edition 2005

Designed by Michelle McMillian
Map art © 2005 by Samuel Valasco

Printed in the United States of America
1   3   5   7   9   10   8   6   4   2

To Martha, Livia, and Jasper—the trifecta

A Klee painting named "Angelus Novus" shows an angel looking as though he is about to move away from something he is fixedly contemplating. His eyes are staring, his mouth is open, his wings are spread. This is how one pictures the angel of history. His face is turned toward the past. Where we perceive a chain of events, he sees one single catastrophe which keeps piling wreckage upon wreckage and hurls it in front of his feet. The angel would like to stay, awaken the dead, and make whole what has been smashed. But a storm is blowing from Paradise; it has got caught in his wings with such violence that the angel can no longer close them. This storm irresistibly propels him into the future to which his back is turned, while the pile of debris before him grows skyward. This storm is what we call progress.

—WALTER BENJAMIN, *Theses on the Philosophy of History, 1950*

Gosh, it's for the awe at what you are seeing.

—PIONEER STORM CHASER ROGER JENSEN, 1990

Contents

BIG WEATHER

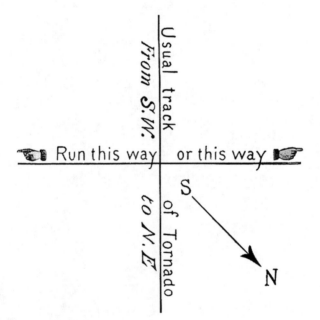

From John P. Finley, *Tornadoes,* 1887

ONE

Becalmed:
Dreaming of Yevtushenko

It somehow reminded him of his mortality.
—MELVILLE

I

Air is water's ghost, flowing, like water, through its seasons. In the spring, as every child in grade school knows, the northern hemisphere of the earth is tipped toward the sun, and the jet stream, that narrowest and swiftest channel of the river moving at speed aloft, drops southward, in a grand lasso, through Canada into the United States. A cold and dry air mass that has been hovering over the polar cap all winter thus barrels across the country. It would drop as far south as Texas and Louisiana, as it sometimes does, but for an epic collision with the only thing on earth that can stop it: the Maritime tropical air mass thrusting north from the Gulf of New Mexico. To the ensuing windswirl, and to the water metaphor that helps describe it, a different—and decidedly mixed—metaphor adheres: air masses advance and clash and retreat like armies, and then advance and clash again across shifting fronts and flanking lines through the months of April, May, and June.

The land beneath these colliding air masses is home to more violent weather than anyplace else on the planet: on average, 10,000 severe thunderstorms sweep over the continental United States annually, bringing with them 5,000 floods and 1,000 tornadoes. While tornadoes occur everywhere in the world, fully three quarters of them strike the United States over a region that encompasses all of the Midwest, most of the East Coast, and nearly all of the South. Some maps delimit a zone of greatest tornado frequency along an area beginning in South Dakota and extending southward to include most of Nebraska, Kansas, and Oklahoma and much of Texas—the legendary region of Tornado Alley. But there are several Tornado Alleys, perhaps the most significant being the big, right-hand turn at Oklahoma that reaches eastward through Arkansas, Mississippi, and much of Alabama. If these two alleyways were combined, from the Dakotas to Alabama, they would form a giant, listing "L," a soaked sock.[1] Distinctions can and will be made among states about their indigenous features, even about tornadoes, a sort of ill wind boosterism. Texas ranks first in sheer number of tornadoes, Kansas in the number of that rarest sort of tornado, the F5, so designated by the Fujita scale of magnitude: sixteen such monstrous tornadoes have hit Kansas over the last fifty years. Then there is the matter of the Palm Sunday Super Outbreak of April 3–4, 1974, the biggest in recorded history, which unleashed 148 tornadoes across 14 states as well as Ontario. At one point there were as many as fifteen different tornadoes on the ground simultaneously. Although most did relatively little damage, the Super Outbreak produced six F5 category tornadoes, two of which had damage paths longer than a hundred miles. The F4 tornado that swept through Monticello, Indiana, had the longest damage path at 121 miles.[2] This calamitous event, an historical and statistical anomaly in the extreme, is liable, in the manner of the proverbial five-hundred-pound movie executive, to draw attention away from a seasonal battle that rages nowhere else with greater apocalyptic fury than in the prairie state of Oklahoma. "Threat maps" estimating tornado probability invariably place Oklahoma in the center of an oblate zone of concentric rings, with Oklahoma City and its surrounding counties the bull's-eye. More violent tornadoes of magnitude F4 or higher strike Oklahoma than anywhere else on earth—nearly a hundred in the last fifty years.[3] Oklahoma City has been hit more than any city anywhere, 112 times by tornadoes in the last hundred years. On seventeen occasions, two or more tornadoes struck on the same day.

Yet these statistics, of course, are misleading. Most Oklahomans grow up, marry, raise children, and grow old, passing through the weeks, months, years, and decades—time lived on the human scale—without ever seeing a tornado firsthand. Fewer still are those directly affected by the destruction of a tornado. The cycles of tornado occurrence and recurrence play out on a time scale quite beyond the human frame of reference. For each spot on the Oklahoma prairie, a thousand years might pass between one tornado strike and the next, but climatologists who study the matter would consider a rate of one tornado per thousand years a veritable tornadic rush hour. Against the backdrop of statistical recurrence, entire generations come and go between tornado strikes, the memory of their destruction ebbing, receding into the historical vanishing point.

In an earlier era, the change of seasons on the prairie would have been unremarkable to anyone driving an Allis-Chalmers tractor, say, disking up his fields. Spring storms were facts, and the transition from winter to spring was a fact the way snow was a fact of winter—just a part of a farmer's lot, of deep interest because of its bearing upon one's livelihood: a good snow cover was good for wheat, because the moisture seeped into the ground, but it also increased calf mortality: ponds silted up and froze so that calves couldn't get to water. As wheat grew, so did the worrying. Too much wind could blow dirt and bruise the young wheat berries. A drought followed by a sudden down-pour could be disastrous. What was needed was a steady drizzle—and what was needed was a talisman or trick of some sort, as the days amassed and burned, to block the very thought of hail from entering one's mind. A beer or two at day's end might suffice. A prayer might suffice. A basement hobby: lapidary, or leather tooling, anything to stave off the worry. In recent years, however, spring has become a time of migration to the central plains for a certain species of visitor, as seasonal as any flock of geese streaking north on the flyways in staggered chevrons. And the locals had grown accustomed to spotting them, not that there was any great trick to it.

They arrived in expensive SUVs equipped with portable satellite dishes, ham radio antennae, custom hygrometers, twirling anemometers, and roof-mounted amber flashing lights. There were many different sorts of radios—two-way radios, ham radios, CB radios, police scanners, N.O.A.A. weather radios. They had purchased and installed lightning detection sensors and were equipped with on-board radar and laptops programmed with forecast-ing software and wireless Internet access. A few of them also included gas masks, chemical suits and gloves, fire extinguishers, just in case. Each contained a small arsenal of cameras, both still and video, film and digital, along with lenses and tripods and field glasses and backup supplies—extra video tape, extra film, extra backup cameras just in case. Hands-free headsets. Cell phones. Global positioning systems. Pagers. This new migratory species returned to Oklahoma, of all places in the world, like swallows to Capistrano, and it heralded something beyond the simple changing of the season, though few could say exactly what that was.

The boxy, oversized gadgetry of an earlier era was now portable, palmable. There was a precision and a musculature in the miniature, an earnestness in the array, and an inescapable whimsy in the Wi-Fi. A tiny alphanumeric pager no bigger than a matchbox and clipped to one's belt and capable of delivering our best guess as to God's next move—vibrating or chirping a Mozart sonata or singing an elbow-swinging version of "Hava Nagila" from a friend back in the city, or reciting a grocery list from a wife at home. Such was the state of technological advancement in the first years of the third millennium A.D. that Promethus seemed to have tapped a thunderbolt in order to light a cigarette. They brought DeLorme maps. Multicolored highlighting pens. Duct tape. Batteries. And on the seventh day, they saw that it was all very expensive. And so they installed car alarms and motion sensors in their homes. "Some are locks for the sensors on the car," one chaser announced on his web page. "Others are video security cameras. I can't list all of the security measures because it would defeat the purpose of having them."

They were weather dweebs, weather dorks, weather weenies, savants of all things meteorological, more likely than most to turn on the Weather Channel first thing—and then, more likely than most to start arguing with the Weather Channel about the forecast. They were, as they used to say of a certain type of social misfit, a bit touched—liable to vanish suddenly, to wander out of doors for days, then return just as suddenly, their pickup trucks pocked by hailstones, the wheel wells caked with mud, their clothes in tatters, their hair in disarray, their eyes like saucers, wearing a crazy, beatific smile—"tetched in the head," is how people used to put it. Upon their minds, it seemed, the mighty, big finger of God had descended, leaving them standing by roadsides, or in convenience store parking lots, quasi-autistic in T-shirts that said things like PROJECT VORTEX or STORM TRACKERS, or MODERATE RISK. They had a singular point of focus in the world, and a private language all their own, one filled with "capping inversions," "convergences on the dry line," and messages in cipher writ—"Woodward Temp 91.87/64 in Gage SSE winds. D/L just west. N winds DDC 85/64 in P 28."

They were liable, at any given moment, to drop what they were doing, call in sick to work, break off appointments, start their engines, and drive for hundreds, sometimes thousands of miles, in pursuit of big weather. Some took vacation time and ventured forth onto the plains. Thus came William T. Hark, a doctor from Richmond, Virginia, each year; and Ward Davenny, a professor and landscape painter from Carlisle, Pennsylvania; and from Greeley, Colorado, the self-described, self-published "Tornado Tim" Baker, author, with his daughter and navigator, Crystaline, of the young-adult novel *Tornado Chaser: Life on the Edge.* So did Betsy Abrams and Matthew E. Crowther, two of the most senior meteorologists at the Weather Channel, taking a little "vaykay," driving all the way up from Atlanta; and from St. Paul, Minnesota, the Twister Sisters, who are not actual sisters but meteorology student–entrepreneurs from the aptly named St. Cloud University, who arrived with two vans full of tornado tourists, some from as far away as Johannesburg, South Africa. They arrived from Europe, as did Christoph Gatzen, Jan Hoffman, Steffan Dietz, and Sebastian Unger, a quartet of German meteorology students; and Olivier Staiger, who when he was not chasing storms followed solar eclipses around the world. A very large number arrived annually from England and Australia. In an imaginary taxonomy, this itinerant group of amateur weather watchers might fall under the heading *Meteorologica migratorius,* those who had seen big weather and, like Saul on the Damascus road, had been changed at the core, their compasses forever realigned, pointing toward the center of this storm-tossed continent, drawn, each spring, like antinomian pilgrims, toward the unpromising state of Oklahoma. And their enthrallment with the Oklahoma sky, and the fact that they were just passing through, like visitors to some hardship post in greater Albania, allowed them to overlook a few things: the patchy suburban sprawl, the fast-food franchises stretching off to the horizon, the mobile-home dealerships, and the Baptist churches with colossal neon marquees positioned strategically alongside the Interstate announcing the arrival of the hereafter.

Some of them had decided to remain. They stayed on the prairie, which became their home range, and they, a rarer sort of bird—*Meteorologica vagabonda expatrius,* at loose ends in winter plumage—bussed tables or delivered pizzas. Or perhaps they took more extreme measures, such as enrolling in graduate school, for instance. But as spring approached, they would hover over their isobaric charts, their MM5 printouts, and their Day One Convective Outlooks, and tap out notices and square off with one another on Internet discussion groups. Some of them were scientists, a sub-species of expatriate weather people, drawn by professional orientation: cloud physics, computer science, severe local storm research, or the burgeoning field of private-sector meteorology, and they accepted jobs at universities best known for football and right-wing religious fundamentalism. For these scientists, the laboratory was the Oklahoma sky outside their windows—and for a storm researcher, nowhere else in the world was the sky so volatile, so visible, so likely to produce storms to study. They measured and weighed and scanned and recorded that sky, they surrounded tornadoes and recorded their telemetry, and they made miniature versions of that sky, which whirled inside supercomputers. They were on a quest as old as the notion of time itself, and more elusive and of greater value still than any alchemy, for they were trying to poke and prod and cajole their way into the future—to construct and construe it, to see the future for themselves, and to say in advance—not by prophecy or augury, but by virtue of sound scientific principles—what would happen there.

Others still were part of a remarkable subgroup involved in local media coverage of severe weather. They formed a community of professional weather wonks, field workers, drivers, technicians, reporters, men and women placed in front of a camera in their rain slickers, storm spotters and hangers-on, sent at a moment's notice in foul weather gear, a *Meteorologica celebratoria,* to capture images that fed a broadcast market phenomenally interested in stories of severe weather. Some had attained a certain measure of regional notoriety, like the storm chaser for KWTV, Channel 9, the redoubtable Val Castor, with that name like something out of a Fantastic Four comic book. On a big weather day, all of them—the media people, the scientists, the recreational storm chasers, the teenagers skipping school, the emergency management officials, the storm spotters—arrived in flocks, blending together like a roadside exhibition of disposable income lingering for a bald, unguarded moment on the prairie. They represented a late phase of American consumption; some had spent tens of thousands of dollars per chase car, plus hundreds of dollars per season in fuel, and motel rooms, and cases of Diet Coke and bad coffee and Crackerjacks and truckstop food, and hours upon hours of country-western songs. They descended en masse upon some little bit of nowhere in the middle of the North American prairie—near Salina or Seiling, or Slapout—to gather by the hundreds, sometimes blocking traffic for a country mile while cattle lifted their heads in puzzlement. They'd stop, set up their tripods and their portable Doppler radars, while the wind blew in great gusts, and the storms did the fearful things that storms do, and they, wherever they came from, and for whatever reason—for the mere thrill of it, or in the name of science—found themselves hopping up and down and hollering at the sky.

What were they after? Storm chasing admitted a confusion, a complex, of motives. The easy answer—they wanted to see a tornado—of course begs the question. A tornado represents many things, beginning with its own extreme unlikelihood. Every tornado represents a supreme, if momentary, trouncing of the second law of thermodynamics, the glum law of entropy that states that all things move from order to chaos. Tornadoes move the other way, from a chaos of cloud swirl, from a mixture of lines of force, density, temperature, lift, speed, and convergence, a set of initiating conditions whose exact ingredients are still unknown, to a near perfect level of order and organization, capable, paradoxically of delivering immense destruction, an order that creates widespread disorder, confusion, and chaos. The storm chasers came, in short, because every tornado is a perfect storm, a wonder occurring oftener than once every hundred years. They came because over a thousand such perfect storms strike North America every year, and because this frequency, itself a fluke of geography and topography, raised the chance of actually seeing this miracle with one's own eyes, of looking, and staring in wonder, at a tornado.

They came for the same reasons people choose to encounter other natural wonders—to experience the dislocating sense of the sublime, to feel small in comparison with something large and powerful, to plunge oneself into an experience so outsized as to bring the rest of life's contours, momentarily, into relief: so, soldiers say, after combat, things shimmer, the leaves in the trees suddenly sparkling with a presence rarely felt in ordinary life. But unlike other, natural wonders—Niagara Falls or the Half Dome of Yosemite—a tornado can occur anywhere. In this regard, it is something like the whale in *Moby-Dick,* a holy terror of unfixed address, liable to rear its head at any point upon the wide ocean of the world. A tornado is like the whale, but more terrifying in its aspect. It takes no biomorphic form. There are no eyes that see, no mouth or ears to hear, no head or limbs to suggest a kinship, however distant, with human anatomy. A tornado is all geometry, and thus more potent; it is not the bearded god of cathedral paintings, lounging on a cloud, but the god of the Alhambra's arches, the god of geometry, mathematics, the god of the asymptote, repeating itself infinitely. The god of paradox, that seems both to exist and not exist. The god of mysterious substance, a word that has meant, at different times in its usage, both something and nothing, both the tangible and the intangible, the body and the spirit.

And a tornado is like a whole lot of nothing bearing down upon your house. The substantive facts of wind in a tornado, for instance—velocity, vorticity—are most often measured indirectly, in the wreckage left behind. The thing itself, however—the thing that comes into your neighborhood and rips your house apart—contains an emptiness, an eye of sorts, that is insubstantial. Driven and fueled by the parent storm above, the windswirl of the tornado can create an ear-popping pressure drop over an extremely steep gradient of 100 millibars. Air, we often forget, has weight and density. The weight of the atmosphere, all fifteen miles of it, presses down upon you at all points so that it feels insubstantial, but if you were to experience a sudden drop in air pressure of 100 millibars, that absence, created by wind vectors swirling within a tornado, could rocket you upward as if you'd been shot out of a canon—you'd be launched by an emptiness, a nothing, a tornado.

So they came for the wonder of it, for a bit of self-induced awe. Some, like the Twister Sisters, had discovered hidden markets, inviting guests to travel the region in search of an encounter with big weather. For those less disposed to direct encounter, the local and national media sent their intrepid reporters into the storm, harvesting schadenfreude. For some, big weather became an occasion for volunteerism and community service. Acting as a sort of home guard, storm spotters placed themselves in harm's way, radioing reports of tornadoes, or pea-sized hail, or torrential rain to their local emergency management offices. Big weather provided a baseline sense of "reality," of perspective, of "weather citizenship," a chance to empathize with communities imperiled at a distance, but surviving. Destruction brought people together, made people aware of the things that really mattered in life. For others, big weather was a reminder, a recapitulation of a different sort, a dramatic enactment of God's larger plan, out of Revelations, to destroy the world in order to save it.

Most sought a sort of mastery—the scientists surrounded the tornado with radar trucks, gathering information that could be studied later at leisure, while others came like primitives to stand near their quarry, to capture something of its spirit in images—for unlike a hurricane or other storms, a tornado fits within a frame. And so they came to position themselves, standing on the prairie with a tornado glowering in the background like a molten angel, a fire that held the gaze. They brought their Nikon cameras the way Indian warriors brought coup sticks to battle, to touch the enemy, that potent and potential undoer, and to bring their exploits back home as trophies. Big weather as big medicine.

II

My interest in big weather arose by chance. One afternoon, in the untroubled spring of 2000, I was driving east under the voluble, shifting sky in Oklahoma when behind me, closing hard, came a darkening of the world. By the time I'd finished eating a burrito at a local roadhouse, towering columns of convection were billowing upward like geysers toward the uppermost reaches of the atmosphere, five to six times higher than the Grand Canyon is deep; that high, the jet stream scythed each column flat and pushed the crystallized air miles in front of the storm. It was just this sort of "overshooting anvil" that often made me marvel, as a child in Montana, when hail seemed to fall out of a clear blue sky.

Outside the restaurant, I noticed that the gust front—displaced, supercooled air plummeting downward off the steadily rising mass of condensing cumulonimbus clouds, or thunderheads—was creating little cyclones in the parking lot and soon began bouncing my rental van all over the road. Thousands of feet above, an epic collision was taking place as warm, moist air from the Caribbean Basin and Gulf of Mexico mixed it up with cool, dry air from the Arctic, each stream of air flowing opposite the other, and fueling the storm taking shape around me. In my rearview mirror, a moving wall of rain loomed, gobbling up whole sections and townships. I craned my head for a better look. All around me, wheat fields brilliantly lit by the sun were throwing off light in battered waves: coppery swirls and half-acre pockets of wind-clobbered, un-ripened Key lime green. With a black sky coming on, it all seemed less like a landscape than a swirling, enveloping *predicament,* so I charged ahead toward the town of El Reno, to take cover in a cheap motel.

When I pulled into the parking lot, two cowboys standing next to a pickup truck were talking quietly, sipping Buds, and watching the sky to the west flash with lightning. The wind had picked up noticeably. I unloaded my rental van and turned on the television. The weatherman was waving his hands, pointing in sweeping arcs at a regional map that displayed, at different levels of detail, radar images of the approaching storm, whose vortices fairly glowed with intensity. Just then, the television emitted a series of attention-getting beeps directly into my room, and a news bulletin from the National Weather Service began scrolling at the bottom of the screen. The warning reserved its strongest, most dire predictions for Caddo, Washita, and Canadian counties, where, within the last half hour, storm spotters had seen three tornadoes touch down, accompanied by golf-ball-sized hail that was shredding the countryside with straight-line winds clocked at 75 miles per hour. SEVERE PROPERTY DAMAGE LIKELY, the warning said, and the unlucky residents of Caddo, Washita, and Canadian counties, now just coming home from work or sitting down to dinner, were being urged, rather unambiguously, to TAKE COVER IMMEDIATELY.

Charged as he was to rouse potentially imperiled viewers from the television-assisted unreality of the drama unfolding before them, a weatherman could hardly be blamed for a little arm-swinging hyperbole. Two years earlier, in 1998, Oklahoma had been hit 146 times by tornadoes, a record in the fifty years that the National Weather Service had been counting. On May 3 of the following year, a uniquely violent storm system sent seventy-six tornadoes spiraling down from the sky in six and a half hours, plowing through central Oklahoma and Kansas, blowing people out of their homes and from under freeway overpasses and killing forty-eight of them. The outbreak destroyed livestock, wrecked 10,000 cars, trucks, and vans, caused $1.2 billion worth of damage. It included the single most damaging tornado in recorded history. It was the seventh most closely followed news event of 1999, and I was among its audience, watching from the protection of my New York City apartment as CNN and the Weather Channel broadcast live footage of tornadoes plowing through farmland and headed straight toward a city of half a million people; the Weather Channel anchor, receiving the live feed from Gary England at Oklahoma City's CBS affiliate, KWTV, was palpably alarmed; England, the hero of the moment, was in a fugue state, ordering viewers in the path of the tornado to take cover. "If you're not underground," he said at one point, "you're not going to make it." Over the next few hours, his reporting would save hundreds of lives.

Meteorologists that night tracked eight separate tornadic monster storms, or "supercells," each of which dropped dozens of tornadoes. Two of them presented the extremely rare and dangerous convergence of multiple, violent tornadoes threatening a densely populated area of 608 square miles. The first supercell, later identified as Storm A, moved across the southeastern portion of Oklahoma City. Storm B ran parallel and to the northeast about twenty miles away. Together, the two supercells produced thirty-four of the fifty-eight tornadoes that struck central Oklahoma before moving on to Kansas and Missouri, where another eighteen violent tornadoes were reported late the same evening. A tornado from Storm B flattened the town of Mulhall, population 200. Soon after it struck, emergency crews were forced to evacuate the area when a second and much larger tornado passed through. The recurrence interval—the time that can be expected to elapse between tornado strikes at any given spot—is usually estimated in that part of the world at sixteen hundred years, but that evening in Mulhall, a veritable cataract of time, inconceivable on the human scale, had shrunk to minutes. Across the region, supercells exploded and were given labels that moved, alarmingly, toward the middle of the alphabet—Storm C, Storm D, Storm E,

Storm G, Storm H, Storm I. But it was to the south, with Storm A, that a tornado of the highest magnitude had begun to form: a wedge-shaped, long-tracking F5, estimated to be a staggering half mile in diameter, with winds in excess of 300 miles per hour, that stripped sod from the ground, peeled asphalt from the road, and obliterated houses, then, as an afterthought, erased their very foundations. In the Oklahoma City suburb of Moore, whole swaths of subdivisions vanished. Eight thousand homes, nearly three times more than in any other single tornado in U.S. history, were damaged or destroyed, leaving one eyewitness mumbling in disbelief to a CNN reporter: "No one. No one has ever heard of this. No grandfathers have seen anything like it."

A year after the May 3 outbreak, I was sitting in an Oklahoma motel watching my own storm on television, caught between alarmist naiveté and an unwillingness to embarrass myself in front of the locals. In the glow of late-twentieth-century television production values, an ironic distance had firmly established itself between the tornadoes whirling around outside and the soft, rustling calm of my air-conditioned room. Shouldn't I, in fact, "take cover, immediately"? Were people killed by their own ironic exceptionalism? First they were shuffling around in their pajamas, eating a bowl of cereal, say, probably watching the storm on television as one might sit through a fall fund-raising drive—with the perverse pleasure one gets from ignoring the barrage of entreaty and imprecation, the winning appeals to reason and good judgment, the reminders to do right by oneself and by others—while warning sirens wailed in the distance, the windows rattling, curiously, as if a freight train were approaching. Then, *blammo*. Would the last thing I saw be this motel room with its fake paneling, its freakish, oversized table lamps the shape of cooling towers, its smell of Lysol, its plate-glass window staring into the grille of my van? And still I wondered whether I should, (a) order a pizza, or (b) try, in some manner, to save myself.

I checked my two cowboys, still leaning imperturbably against their truck, T-shirts aflutter, tipping back their beers; then I visited the motel office and asked the woman behind the desk whether she had a basement. She looked at me blankly and said, "No, we don't have a basement." This was as close to a vision of state character as I had come, nonchalance lassoed to an ethos straight from the oil fields, an indifference to the concept of harm, an impatience with anything that smacked of self-preservation, a tendency to view issues of safety or health as the preoccupations of wussyboy easterners. While the television meteorologists warned of dire things to come, the manager of my cheap motel sailed under a different flag, the unspoken, unofficial flag of Oklahoma, which in my mind included among its votive images a thunderbolt illuminating a glistening plate of baby back ribs. The unofficial breakfast: a cigarette stubbed out in a doughnut. The unofficial motto: "No, we don't have a basement."

Back in my room, the weatherman was talking with the hyperactive zeal of a track announcer at Saratoga. There was hail at Corn, almost three inches in diameter; hail was hitting Colony, to the east, followed by a tornado that had made a track two and a half miles long. Tornadoes were sighted outside of Eakly and west of Binger, all of them coming down the backstretch straight for El Reno. My own private apocalypse was bearing down on me, yet I was hooked to the television screen just like the viewers whom broadcasters kept glued to their television sets to watch the end of days in Anthony Burgess's *The End of the World News.* I wanted to see how it all played out, but then I looked outside again: my two cowboys and their pickup had vanished.

That settled it. I knew it was unwise to venture out *into* a storm, but what if, as a polite visitor to Tornado Alley, I simply got out of its way? The map on the TV showed the storm moving roughly northeast. I loaded up the van and headed north toward a single patch of blue sky, stopping twice after darkness to see where I had been: the entire southern sky was forking and strobing with lightning like a city being carpet-bombed. Three hours and a hundred miles later, I had outflanked the storm system and was coming up to inspect what was left of El Reno. The place was drenched but intact, as if put through a car wash. The following morning, I pulled the curtains open to a gentle spring breeze, the grille of the van ticking in the rising heat of a new day. I squinted upward. Blue on blue, streaked with wisps of cirrus and the contrails of jets plowing the upper atmosphere.

I blinked into that sky and the sky blinked back like a wan and cheerful amnesiac, chirping away, recalling nothing of the drama that had held me in its grip so completely the previous night. The room, now flooded with light, argued against my memory of the storm, which seemed to grow fugitive and suspect by the minute. I blinked again. The sky's amnesia seemed contagious. There was no mention of the tornado in the *Daily Oklahoman*. The waitress at breakfast looked blankly at me when I asked her about it. My memory of the night before—*What was it, anyway?*—seemed outvoted by unanimous consent of sun and sky, a sky that betrayed an absolute allegiance, along with the rest of the bustling world, to the business of getting on with whatever was next. "You ready to order?" my waitress asked, tapping pen to pad. It was as if my wild night in El Reno had never happened.

I won't say that I began looking into the matter of the storm of May 26, 2000, which I took to calling "my storm," in order to prove that the whole evening had not been an extended hallucination. A storm had occurred. I had the odometer mileage on my van to prove it. But certain other questions needed answering. Had I behaved foolishly or wisely in fleeing my storm? I knew that a car was one of the worst places to take refuge from a tornado, but in a phone conversation with a man named Keith Brewster, a senior research scientist at the Center for the Analysis and Prediction of Storms in Norman, Oklahoma, I learned that because I had, technically, evacuated the area, I had not necessarily made a bad choice. He was careful to add, however, that although I successfully fled the danger in El Reno, I could easily have driven directly into the path of a newly forming storm to the north.

My behavior followed a typical pattern of what risk management officials, geographers, epidemiologists, and other experts in the human ecology of severe weather call "risk reception and response." The swirling dust in the parking lot of the burrito joint, the darkening of the sky behind me as I drove to Oklahoma City, the thunder as I checked into the motel in El Reno—these were "environmental cues," which prompted what experts call "queueing behavior," the gathering and storing of additional information about the storm from different sources. As soon as I turned on the television, which began emitting the audio and scrolling video tornado warnings, I became a "warning user," or "stakeholder," engaged in a variety of forms of "confirmation behavior," a blanket term used to describe the many ways we dither before we die. From a risk management perspective, the issue in tornado mortality and morbidity is one of "warning compliance." Yet for me to have complied in El Reno would have involved climbing into the bathtub and hauling a queen-sized mattress over my head, which seemed a little preposterous at the time. This was the "normalcy bias" kicking in—the sneer of the motel clerk, a local, shaming me, an unschooled visitor, into denial; the white noise of the air conditioner washing out any uncomfortable rumbling outside; the television, despite the announcer's warnings, whispering that this was all someone else's problem; and my two cowboys, or "stakeholder peers," implacably sipping their beer. All of this added up to about half an hour's worth of waffling before, in a state of "hypervigilance," I reached my "decision threshold" and fled. The people killed on May 3, 1999, by the F5 tornado at Bridge Creek had thirteen minutes between the time when the first warnings were issued and when they died.[4]

Then there was the gee-whiz factor of Oklahoma weather itself, a jaw-dropping response to its colossal scale. I had encountered a sky that seemed so large—so terrifyingly real—it had completely involved me in the way that fire involves a house. It had made me feel danger. It had reacquainted me with unfamiliar verbs. It had made me *dash*. It had made me *flee*. And yet my sense of imperilment was completely out of proportion to the episode's place on the continuum of springtime storms on the prairie and to the weather in general. According to the National Weather Service Forecast Office in Norman, Oklahoma, my storm had generated three tornadoes and caused nearly a million dollars' worth of property damage across three counties—but this was, by Oklahoma standards, of negligible size, almost beneath comment.

I didn't realize it at the time, but the prairie sky and the land that lay beneath it had realigned something in me as in so many others, had drawn me, in a more general sense, into the sky's many spheres—from "topo" to "tropo"—and into the many puzzlements that surround our relationship with this common, communal element of wind and weather. The weather reminds us, in ways that can be felt upon the skin, that we are alive, together. Even Dostoevsky's Underground Man, from the darkest part of modern consciousness, reluctantly shares the weather, suffers through it, refuses to rejoice in its limitless supply. The weather is the social equivalent of the sympathetic nervous system: talk of the weather preempts conscious thought, starts any conversation. It's the thing that goes without saying. It's the "it" in "It's snowing." We do not accord it agency, but when it takes the form of a tornado and lands on our head, we call it an act of God. Its recurrent patterns have given definition and identity to cities, states, and regions. We call that climate. Like those tiny, anonymous figures, meant to suggest scale, in the paintings of Bierstadt, Cole, and Church, we stand alongside it in our mind's eye, divining the spark of an American sublime.

Then there was the effect that talk about big weather had on other people at, say, cocktail parties. As my interest in big weather grew, I made plans to return to Oklahoma. I had the great luxury of answering the question "What are you up to?" with a simple declaration: "I'm going tornado chasing in Oklahoma." Never mind that it was December. I blurted out my little fact, and steered the conversation weatherward, and, in time, made my wife and closest friends leery of ever speaking to me again. In truth, I liked the way people responded. It made me feel suddenly, unexpectedly, interesting. A little crazy. A little daring, like a correspondent dispatched into a war zone. Soon enough, late one spring afternoon at the beginning of the third millennium, in a rented Dodge Grand Caravan, heading north up the Oklahoma Interstate 35, I sat alongside Matt Biddle, who would be my chase guide for the month of May, 2004.

III

May is universally acknowledged to be the peak and pinnacle month in chaserdom, high season on the plains. It was a view bolstered by decades of anecdotal experience and well over a hundred of years of climatalogical study. If you had a month at your disposal, and your aim, for good or ill, was to see a tornado, you'd choose the month of May, and you would station yourself in the bull's-eye of central Oklahoma, and the seasonal low pressure troughs would sashay from the Rockies into the high plains, and the moisture would come screaming in on a low-level jet from the Gulf, and the CAPE—the convective available energy—would be off the charts, like a powder keg, and the surface winds would be backed, and the upper-level shear would guarantee long-lived supercells, and you would hit the Mid-way Market on your way out of town, loading up with Mountain Dew and Skoal tobacco, and you'd set off for some godforsaken target area out near Woodward, say, on the Oklahoma Panhandle, just south and east of the triple point, and wait for the towering cumulus cloud to break the cap and start firing off the dry line.

That was the plan, in any case, the expected pattern of action, but in early May 2004, things weren't going well in the storm department. A high-pressure ridge had parked itself over the Plains. Weather systems moving in from the west were bumping into this ridge and being shunted north, so the southern Plains had remained bone dry. Down in the Gulf there was moisture but no wind, which suppressed the movement of the Maritime air mass inland. Pulse storms, feeding off moisture transpired from the sea of wheat and corn that was the middle of America this time of year, moved in isolation over places with seafaring names like Grand Island, Nebraska, but when it came to storms of the sort that people like to chase, the first half of May was an absolute and comprehensive bust. The long days of weather clemency that first week began to blend together into laundry days, and days spent in the History of Science Collection at the University of Oklahoma's Bizzell Memorial Library, and days spent wondering about Yevtushenko. The calm weather, if it persisted into a second week, threatened to bring to fruition a meeting I'd actually planned, in a desperate bid for backstory, with a representatives from the State of Oklahoma's Storage Tank Remediation Division to discuss ground seepage.

I went off one day with Matt Biddle to visit the *Twister* Museum in Wakita, Oklahoma, about two hours north of Oklahoma City, near the Kansas border, in the middle of nowhere. The *Twister* Museum is one of those oddball places that spring into existence as if in answer to a silent prayer for relief from the mind-numbing monotony of the landscape. The flatter the landscape, it seemed, the more these roadside curiosities began to appear, like so many marvelous oases. Thus Kansas, which had been the subject of a recent quasi-scientific study undertaken by geographers from Texas State University, who determined, once and for all, that Kansas was, indeed, flatter than a pancake[5]—thus, Kansas was home to the Barbed Wire Museum, in LaCrosse, and the World's Deepest Hand-Dug Well, in Greensburg, and the World's Largest Ball of Twine, in Cawker City. Like these, the *Twister* Museum was the sort of place that tried to screen off its loneliness in the universe with a veil of kitsch. Something had happened here once, and then nothing had happened, and then nothing had continued to happen for a very long time, and—more or less—nothing would most assuredly ever happen here again, save for THIS GIANT BALL OF TWINE, and so forth. It was the sort of place one went when things weren't going well in the storm department.

Matt had just completed his written and oral exams for a doctorate in geography at the University of Oklahoma. Wakita was where the natural-disaster movie *Twister* had been filmed in 1995. Universal Pictures, like an extravagant circus, more or less took over the town of 300, built up and knocked down buildings, shipped in its own catered food, deployed trucks and tents and a small army of gadgeteers with lights and dollies and tracking cables, and generators, and an arsenal of other expensive cinematic equipment, plus a pack of angry production assistants to keep it all running on schedule, barking out orders. They were professional assholes, confident in the effect that fat rolls of hundred-dollar bills had on the locals. When the shooting was done, they allowed the residents of Wakita to sift through the mess they'd made of the town and take what was left. Much of the film detritus made its way into the *Twister* Museum.

For two weeks Matt had worked with the B Unit film crew, guiding them close to a few tornadoes and thunderstorms. Strangely, the movie that single-handedly brought tornadoes and tornado chasing into the public consciousness contains not a single frame of an actual tornado: everything is computer generated except for the cloudscapes that Matt, along with chase partner, Mark Herndon, helped the B Unit find, the actual, bona fide natural world becoming a backdrop to the film credits that roll by, an afterthought. As a memento, he'd been given one of the hundred or so "flying probes," a kind of eyeball with wings, which, at the climax of the movie, are released into the howling tornado from "Dorothy," the experimental canister that is placed in the path of a monster tornado in order to measure its depth. Matt had, subsequently, lent this *objet du cinéma* to Linda Wade, the volunteer curator of the museum, where it had remained for a number of years. Now, in the spring of 2004, Matt wanted it back.

I'D FIRST MET Matt four years ago. The El Reno affair had brought me to the Storm Prediction Center, where I'd been given a brief tour of the facilities and was even allowed to sit in the operations room and listen as forecasters discussed the weather. Joe Schaefer, the director of the SPC, had led me out the door into the late afternoon sun, where people were leaving work for home. Across the parking lot sat a beat-up maroon El Camino, in front of which stood a scruffy character in sunglasses, a hockey jersey, and two-day stubble. He was leaning on crutches, eating from a bag of potato chips.

"Matt," Joe said, introducing me, "you look like hell."

Matt explained that he'd just returned from a trip with a television crew from *National Geographic,* who had hired him to bring them to a tornado. It had been a successful chase, for Matt, at least. But the television crew had stopped so often for food and bathroom breaks that they fell far behind, and were out of position when an F3 tornado finally roared through Siren, Wisconsin.

"It was about a thousand yards off my rear bumper," Matt said.

He shifted his weight. His left leg seemed locked in place, as if he were wearing a full-length cast. I said good-bye to Joe and talked for a while longer with Matt, who gave me his phone number.

He was still on crutches when I arrived to chase storms with him in 2002. What I had thought was a cast turned out to be a prosthetic leg, connected above the left knee by a strap and locked rigidly into place. Matt had suffered all his life from a rare congenital bone disease, "a syndrome," as he explained in medical parlance, "of major orthopedic anomalies of unknown etiology," which Matt was quick to point out was a fancy way of saying "a genetic accident of some sort that didn't appear to be hereditary." He'd had major orthopedic surgery as an infant, which included the amputation of his left foot. As a boy in Ohio, he refused a wheelchair and instead signed up for hockey. He'd had at least a hundred minor surgeries and twenty-five major ones, four of which, occurring in his early twenties, included multiple disc removal and fusion, and the implantation of so many titanium rods and cables that "an X-ray of it looked like the Mackinaw Bridge." After the first of these four major orthopedic operations, he developed a staph infection that nearly killed him. Once he'd recuperated, he continued to chase, fighting off for many years chronic fevers and chills and other debilitating side effects of osteomyelitis. Finally, in 1998, he consented to have his left leg reamputated.

Hockey remained a passion. In the spring of 2002, after a long day's chase, we'd inevitably wind up in a tavern, where he'd badger the bartender until he tuned the television to the Stanley Cup Finals. Matt's boyhood team, the Detroit Red Wings, were playing. He'd been chasing tornadoes for fifteen years and had lost count of the number of tornadoes he'd intercepted, though he remembered the big ones, some of which, that spring with his wife, Mamie, several months pregnant, presented possible names for a baby girl. Of all the potential names, Allison, after the F5 in Allison, Texas, was the strongest contender. "Too big to videotape," Matt said. "You couldn't get it all into the frame."

Matt had been driving a research vehicle for a team of scientists on May 3, 1999. "It took me five years of dedicated storm chasing before I saw my first tornado," he recalled (Marshall, Oklahoma, 1991), "and on May third, I saw fourteen tornadoes in a single day, some of them violent. I saw the F5 that went through Oklahoma City." Because his most spectacular tornado spotting days seemed, counterintuitively, to correspond so often with the bland-sounding Storm Prediction Center pronouncement of "moderate risk," Matt had attached the phrase to his own storm-chasing consulting company. In the heady days of the late 90s, when movie producers and television executives regularly called upon his services, Moderate Risk had a website and something of a regional following among storm-chasing enthusiasts, who would follow Matt in the beat-up El Camino around the countryside.

"They were weather groupies?" I asked.

"It was all because of that stupid movie," Matt said, referring to *Twister.* Released in 1996, *Twister* was the year's second highest grossing film in the United States, prompting a spate of magazine and newspaper articles and giving birth to a genre of tornado video. First came the *Twister*-inspired videocassette collections: *Chasers of Tornado Alley,* produced by Prairie Pictures, and the Tornado Project's *Tornado Video Classics* series. The Weather Channel weighed in with *The Enemy Wind*; then came the Learning Channel's *Storm Force: Tornadoes,* which prompted another gush of independent disaster videos—*May's Fury, Twisters: Nature's Deadly Force,* and *Twister: The Dark Side of Nature.* Storm chasers could sell a well-composed, in-focus image for as much as $200 per second. But then came a shift in style and sensibility to Duchampian ready-mades: amateur videos, with poor production values, made by ordinary folks—not by chasers but by the unfortunate few who got chased, who happened one day to look out their back door and see a howling tornado bearing down upon their house. "Today," according to one observer of the trend, the taste was more toward "the thrilling, shocking, 'Cops'-like video—handheld and all jerky, with the focus going in and out, and a lot of screaming." In these "voyeuristic environmental porno flicks," as *Time* magazine called them, one can hear real fear in voices that shout, "Get back down in the basement!" even while the person shouting ventures onto the patio for a better shot of the approaching monster. While earlier videos left no doubt that the main star and object of mythic potency was the tornado itself, the new form of "torn porn" supplanted the tornadoes with a human document—an unguarded moment of transparent stupidity, unglossed by artifice. Connoisseurs of the form identify these clips by the incidental comments made during the filming—"Get Away from the Window!" or "God, I Hate Oklahoma."

By the close of the last decade of the twentieth century, the tornado—or the people caught in the paths of tornadoes—had arrived, filling a niche market in weather mongering. Hard on its heels came the Discovery Channel's *Raging Planet* series, beginning in 1997 with a tidal wave and continuing the following year with a string of disaster hits: "The Hurricane," "The Earthquake," "The Lightning Bolt," "The Fire," and "The Flood."

The public appetite for big weather remained keen, which was partially why I was with Matt this spring. I wanted to follow him as he moved through this subculture, which, he found, had undergone so much change that our passage through it came to seem like a farewell tour. I would grow dependent upon Matt's expertise and accustomed to the many different sides of his personality: the scientist, the laconic wit, debunker of myths, the cowboy in his El Camino, the guide to the weather and culture of the prairies. But I never grew accustomed to what it took for him to move around, to make his way in the world. On crutches, with his left leg locked in place, he struggled to go from his office on the OU campus to his car. But "struggled" is wrong: there was no struggle, just ordinary determination applied without comment to an extraordinary disadvantage. Sometimes, he'd invite the subject in—after a day's chase and a few beers, say, after Tie Domi of the Toronto Maple Leafs skated away from the action of a playoff game and leveled the

New Jersey Devils defenseman Scott Niedermayer with an unprovoked elbow to the head. Then Matt would lean into me and say, "That's what I miss most about hockey—the violence." What distinguished Matt from other storm chasers was more than the countless operations he'd endured. He carried an abiding, Ahab-like desire for vengeance against a force much larger than himself; call it the swirl of chance and fate, the bad hand he'd been dealt; call it God, the whirlwind, appearing out of the chaos of clouds, spiraling down upon a sea of prairie wheat. He would wince at the radio evangelists who fill the Oklahoma airwaves. "All I want from God is respect," he once told a magazine writer in one of many post-*Twister* interviews. "Looking at the signs," Matt said, "his destiny for me is not to exist. So, He can just get a new damn plan."[6] The pure violence of hockey had years ago given way to another pursuit; the sides of his El Camino bore decals from successful sorties, little tornadic insignia with dates and place names like signs of conquest on the fuselage of a P-38. "Chasing," Matt said, "is love *and* spite." In the months to come, he and his wife would hold in their arms a beautiful, perfectly formed baby girl. Her name surprised me at first, but spoke volumes. What was it, after all, that one sought for one's child if not the very thing one lacked, and here she was, in person and in name—*Faith*—babbling softly, to what was there, and to what was not there, and to what was yet to come.

Our time together in May 2004 involved a loosening or jettisoning of old affiliations, it seemed. On our drive to Wakita, Matt had placed something on the van's dashboard. I picked it up. It was a piece of punched-metal script that spelled out "El Camino," the only relic of Matt's old chaser-mobile, which he'd sold recently to a junkyard. It surprised me a little, the shock I felt, so attached had Matt become in my mind to his old ride, but he was looking back, taking stock, tossing things out. The "flying probe" movie prop from *Twister* was small enough, it seemed, like the El Camino plaque, to remain a keepsake.

Off the interstate, I turned onto a stretch of red clay and headed west into the sun. Matt asked me to pull over. Outside, I walked a few yards down the road to get a feel for the middle of nowhere. The engine ticked and the prairie wind parted my hair. The sky was a colossus, a Rothko painting, a vast blue field of color without stitch or contrail or wisp of cirrus, whelming over the young wheat that sashayed in every direction as far as you could see, clear to the horizon, where it met the wronging tide of unrelenting blue.

On WX-Chase, an Internet discussion group, everyone was keeping up a stoic front about the calm weather. Still, one could read in the conversation, drifting back and forth about chase equipment and software and famous storms from bygone days, the unmistakable signs of frustration about what was now labeled the Death Ridge. One chaser, stranded under sunny skies in Council Bluffs, wrote: "The past week has been the most dreadful early May pattern that I have personally had the misfortune of experiencing."[7] Another wondered, "Can we . . . rise from the dead soon?"[8] Into this sardonic mix came a message that, by comparison, seemed almost chirpy. "My friend, Alissa, is leaving from Jacksonville, Florida, tomorrow to go chasing," a man from Gainesville wrote. "How are the forecasts looking?"[9]

"Tell her to bring a book, maybe several," came the response.[10]

As for Yevtushenko, back in April, before I'd left New York City, I'd sent him an e-mail introducing myself and requesting an interview. The great Russian émigré poet had, in his home country, read to audiences of twenty thousand; in January 1972, he had read his poetry, along with Stanley Kunitz, James Dickey, Richard Wilbur, and Senator Eugene J. McCarthy, to an audience of five thousand in Madison Square Garden. Yevtushenko was a spectacular contrast to the buttoned-down trio of Great Swinging Poets on the bill that evening. Indeed, his rank as an international figure was of the sort for which an "audience of five thousand" seemed a little on the smallish side—was, in fact, perhaps the smallest unit of measurement for a personality so largely and extravagantly wrought. Unfortunately, in post-seventies America, it wasn't always possible to scare up an audience that big, and so, over the years, Yevtushenko had stormed the American university system, "dressed outlandishly in silver suits," as one NYU student recalled of a Russian survey course she'd taken in the early 1990s. Yevtushenko had "stalk[ed] back and forth across the front of the lecture hall, [taking] time to detail his own history as a poet, especially the delights of hearing 'Bobby' De Niro read his classic 'Babi Yar.'"[11] The night before I flew to Oklahoma, Yevtushenko had attended a gala at the Russian embassy in Washington,

D.C., ostensibly in honor of Alexander Pushkin. According to *The Washington Times,* Yevtushenko "launched into his own verse, set to 'Lara's Theme' from the score of *Dr. Zhivago,* then waltzed with an actress doing her best to tra-la-la along to the melody." The paper reported that Mr. Yevtushenko had organizers find someone, "'young, tall, and beautiful—it doesn't matter if she can sing.'"[12] For Yevtushenko, it seemed, it was just another evening spent declaiming and dancing and carrying on with a beautiful actress in front of an audience of 250 people, including members of the U.S. Supreme Court. To say that Yevtushenko was flamboyant, in other words, was like saying that Carmen Miranda had a nice hat. If he was prone to self-display, he was also not afraid to shoot from the hip at the powers that be. It was Yevtushenko, after all, who, in the 1970s told Leonid Brezhnev to lay off Aleksandr Solzhenitsyn.

Now he was living and teaching in Tulsa, Oklahoma, and I couldn't help but wonder what Yevtushenko might have to say about, among other things, the weather of the prairies. It seemed like a good question, a reasonable question, but I'd heard nothing from him. My first day in Norman, I'd called the English Department at the University of Tulsa; the secretary did not know where Yevtushenko was but said that she'd fax him my interview request. Fax him my request? That seemed strange. The skies remained clear, sunny, and calm; I busied myself with other things, such as underground storage tank remediation, but my mind kept returning to the great poet. Not wanting to make a nuisance of myself, I held off for a few days. On Friday I called, only to learn that Yevtushenko had been moving and packing things away in flurry to leave for Russia and had told the secretary that he'd see her again "in the fall." I hung up, then dialed right back, offering to drive to Tulsa to take Yevtushenko to the airport, to lift his bags. I had a van, I said. But I was too late, the secretary replied, sweetly. Yevtushenko had left the country the day before.

And there it was, suddenly born into the world, into the bright light and merciless calm that had beset Oklahoma since I'd arrived, a freshly minted word—"yevtushenko": a verb that meant to stall, to avoid, or to dodge with or without the help of intermediaries. One might say that someone had yevtushenkoed someone else, for instance, or that someone had really given me the old yevtushenko. There was, moreover, a nice bit of onomatopoeia in the

Matt Biddle and daughter, Faith.
Norman, Oklahoma, 2005.
© Kelly Herndon

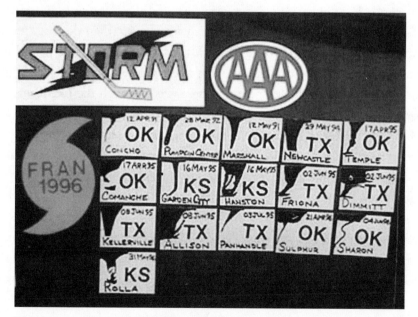

The insignia on the side of Matt's Camino illustrating tornado intercepts, one hurricane, and an abiding passion for hockey. © M. D. Biddle

four syllables—*yev-tu-shen-ko*—which sounded like loose change jingling in the pocket of someone running to catch a plane, someone who had success- fully shucked and jived and made himself inaccessible, by flying off to Rus- sia, for instance. But as the second week of May rolled in, as I sat through my appointment with the Underground Storage Tank Remediation Division of the Oklahoma Corporate Commission, with sunny skies overhead, and somewhere in Kansas the World's Largest Ball of Twine waiting for me, it seemed then that I was being yevtushenkoed by forces larger, even, than Yevtushenko.

I found a certain solace in knowing that I wasn't alone in all this. Others had been becalmed in a silent sea, a *Meerestille,* as German sailors in the days before steam power called this oceanic predicament—worse, some said, than a storm, which at least gave one something to do. But without wind, as Coleridge says in the *Rime of the Ancient Mariner,* without breath "nor motion, as idle as a painted ship upon a painted ocean," on the becalmed prairies, nothing that one knew about the weather by means of radar or satellite imagery would change the weather. Here was the anti-storm, weather as non-weather, the "light airs and calms" of Captain James Cook's dull passage in January 1771 between Java and the Cape of Good Hope, when his men scrubbed between decks with vinegar, then died of "fevers and fluxes," day after stultifying day—this was the inverse of weather, which is to say that it was the opposite of what one wanted. "This was as it should have been," wrote Joshua Slocum, as he passed through the Doldrums, or horse latitudes, in June 1898, near the end of *Sailing Alone around the World.* "For, after all the dangers of the sea, the dust-storm on the coast of Africa, the 'rain of blood' in Australia, and the war risk when nearing home, a natural experience would have been missing had the calm of the horse lat- itudes been left out." Slocum could almost taste his home port of Cape Hat- teras, but a calm sea, "smooth and monotonous," stood between him and his journey's end. His response revealed an admirably stoic turn of mind that could find justice in a calm sea. "The term of her probation was eight days," he wrote. "Evening after evening during this time I read by the light of a candle on deck." Mine was not a flickering candle over a flat sea after a long journey's end but a wan probationary limbo, the commencement of a journey that circled back upon itself each day and came to rest at home port, the Sooner Motel. The Doldrums threw one back upon a psychological reef that made one stop and look around, uncomfortably, at things other than the weather. Something had gone terribly wrong in the world, for instance. Folly of the sort one never imagined possible in one's lifetime. As one stood at a Texaco station, pumping expensive gasoline into a rented minivan not because one needed to but because one could, the lines of connection between one's small folly and the larger folly of the world momentarily, testudinally, swam into focus, then vanished.

Others besides myself awaited a change in the weather. It was a wide and diverse group. There were two scientists in particular—Howard ("Howie") Bluestein and Joshua Wurman—who, with their separate, cooperative (but more or less competing) research teams, were the Ted Williams and Mickey Mantle of tornado field research that spring. There was a chaser named Tim Samaras, working for *National Geographic* magazine, who was attempting to deploy a highly specialized weather probe of his own design directly in the path of a tornado. There were probably hundreds of other chasers, who were spending the first two weeks of May in bars across Oklahoma, Kansas, and Nebraska. There were the Twister Sisters, who were preparing for the long drive to Norman. There were hundreds of meteorology students across the country cramming for final exams and making preparations to drive to the center of the country. There was a IMAX filmmaker named Sean Casey, en route from Los Angeles in an armored truck he called the Tornado Intercept Vehicle, or TIV, which he planned to drive near enough to a tornado to get spectacular IMAX footage. There was Steve Green, a stock-car racer from North Carolina who was still in his garage putting the finishing touches on a $300,000 customized car that he planned to drive directly into a tornado next month. And there was a cabdriver from Las Vegas who had never seen a tornado and had no intention of seeing one but had recently finished a movie script called "Tornado Fighters" that envisioned a team of scientists subduing violent tornadoes with exploding rockets. All of us were surprised, finally, by a cloudless sky, and instructed by it in weather's absolute indifference and in our absolute helplessness before it.

TWO

Weather Talk

The afternoon knows what the morning never suspected.
—SWEDISH PROVERB

Twenty thousand million years ago, or so, there came a generalized commotion, every particle of matter tumbling over itself to get away from every other. From this chaotic beginning, a suspicious, improbable, unnatural thing arose: the earth and its atmosphere, "possessed," in the words of the naturalist Lyall Watson, "of the outlaw qualities of regularity and organization."[1] And then—skipping ahead a bit—the formation of a consciousness that conceived and remembered, held and hoarded, in language, a sense of the weather and the wind as a wonder, a thing felt on the skin, and felt within, as proxy to the spirit, to creation and divinity. Eventually the gods were sent off, trailing in their wake the catcalls and withering laughter of the *philosophes,* and, in August 1755, down a muddy road near Annapolis, Maryland, galloped Benjamin Franklin, in pursuit of a passing tornado until he found himself alongside it. Brandishing his whip, he "tried to break this little whirlwind," striking frequently through it again and again. As he followed the twister, he noticed that it raised "the old dry leaves with which the ground was thick covered, and making a great noise with them and the branches of the trees, bending some tall trees round in a circle swiftly." He then saw "the trunks and bodies of large trees inveloped in the passing whirl." Franklin followed the tornado for nearly a mile until falling tree limbs made him "more apprehensive of danger." It was both high adventure and a scientific experiment of the first order—a first tornado chase carried out by one of the founding fathers, no less, riding at speed, upon the fastest form of human conveyance then available to him, in pursuit of big weather.

After a few turns of the odometer, as it were, deep into the second week of May 2004, something happened in the prevailing wind patterns of the upper atmosphere over the North American continent. The "death ridge" of high pressure that had becalmed the region was replaced by a series of deep troughs of low pressure that began generating storms of the kind more characteristic of May.

An explanation for the change in the weather might have begun by asking you to imagine viewing the earth from directly above the North Pole. If the earth were an apple, and the atmosphere with its pressure gradients were somehow miraculously made visible, you would see that atmosphere sloping poleward, toward a dense and steady low-pressure air mass over the North Pole. But because this is an atmosphere—a fluid movement of air rotating at speed around an axis—it would not resemble an apple's perfectly symmetrical, shouldering slope toward the stem. Rather, turn the apple around to see the lobes and troughs that form its base. Those are better approximations of the ridges of high pressure and troughs of low pressure that descend from the North Pole in regular, westerly-trending patterns known as Rossby waves, after their discoverer, Carl-Gustave Rossby. (Rossby, a Swedish-American meteorologist from the famed "Bergen School," taught meteorology at MIT, founded the first school of meteorology in the United States, and was the first weatherman to make the cover of *Time* magazine: December 17, 1956). As polar air meets warm tropical air, the depth of these waves crests and troughs increase. The warm ridge over the central Plains had been just such a pattern, more or less blocking any severe weather system that moved eastward.

The best forecasters in the world could not have told you precisely when the ridge would clear out; they could only say, paraphrasing Heraclitus, that in the fullness of time, things were bound to change, and the high pressure ridge would shove off. "The surface high pressure ridge weakened," explained Stephen Corfidi, for instance, a lead forecaster at the Storm Prediction Center. "The ridge was replaced by a more-or-less semi-permanent trough. This was because the jet stream pattern changed . . . from one which featured confluence [wind streams merging together] over the northern Plains, to one which featured nearly straight westerly flow across the Rockies." That westerly flow of air created a huge trough of low pressure on the downstream, or lee, side of the mountains. Smaller low pressure troughs within this "lee trough" then migrated from the foothills of the Rockies, ushering in a new regime.

But to recite all this is like reciting a story line rather than a plot. Some burglars broke into the Watergate Hotel complex. That was a story once covered in the newspapers. But the plot—what *caused* the break-in—lay hidden from view for a long time. Similarly, Corfidi's discussion of the change in the weather sounded suspiciously like a story line, a description of events, as he fully acknowledged. "If you ask *why* the upper air pattern changed . . . I'm afraid that you'll have to consider the whole topic of chaos."

In fact and in myth, the weather and the universe are rooted in "that old confusion," as a common prayer book from the sixteenth century describes it with uncommon accuracy, "wherein without order, without fashion, confusedly lay the discordant seeds of things."[2] Hesiod's *Theogony,* which predates the first book of Genesis, describes and gives a name to this first early state: Chaos, first of the gods, father of night and of day, creator of Aether, the bright upper air, fathering our sense of "the elements," of "space," "the expanse of air" that swirls in orderly, recognizable patterns. Recognizable enough to engender the entire body of weather folklore, from "Red sky in the morning, sailor take warning" to "Trout jump high when rain is nigh," but troubling, too, as such forecasting schema failed more often than not. In the *Inferno,* Dante places Chaos (unpersonified) at the circle just below the noble pagans. As far down as things go in Hell, it could have been worse, of course, than the Second Circle. For Dante and his audience, indeed for the contemporary reader, Chaos is a synonym for the damnable quality of randomness. Those who have given over their reason to random, impulsive behavior—to lust and wantonness—Dante places for all eternity in a swirling windstorm. Over time, our understanding of storms and of chaos would deepen. Chaos would no longer mean "randomness"; the word is now applied to those comprehensible realms known as nonlinear systems. Economic systems and population growth are examples, as is the weather. But near the end of the twentieth century, the science of meteorology had advanced to its own

Heisenbergian moment—call it an apprehension, a realization of the existence of certain nonnegotiable barriers to knowledge about these systems and of the limits to our ability to predict what would happen in them. Chaos in this sense was first fully articulated in 1961, by an MIT meteorologist named Edward N. Lorenz. Each storm that moves through the atmosphere moves in predictable ways, to be sure, but weather predictions are based on the measurement of weather conditions at some idealized "present moment"—idealized because it would be impossible to measure and account for every parcel of air in the earth's atmosphere. Estimates are used. Numbers are rounded off. But in nonlinear systems, as Edward Lorenz pointed out, the devil was in the details. Small deviations in initial conditions led to radically diverging outcomes. Thus, predicting exactly what a storm will do, describing details that actually affect human affairs—where and when a storm will form; exactly where it will go; how much rain or hail it will produce; whether or not it will produce a tornado; whether, when it dies, a severe downburst will descend from its core—each of these particulars has a set of "first causes" all its own, a source and provenance that, according to Lorenz, are ultimately beyond our capacity to predict.

Ideologically, Lorenz's work was a bucket of cold water thrown upon a dream of absolute knowledge that had built up a big head of steam for the last three hundred years. Envisioned first in 1814 by the French mathematician Pierre-Simon Laplace, the dream was a fantasy of a clockwork universe in which everything—past, present and future—was known and forgone. It was nature known through and through, completely under human control, demystified, rendered useful. Chaos theory showed that every storm points back to an inscrutable cause, and, at least metaphorically, points to that first beginning, the Big Bang, where from the very start, we now say with greater modesty than Laplace, the nonlinear rushed forward, the discordant seed of unknowing was first planted.

TODAY, CHAOS, EITHER as a theory of the weather or as the first condition of the universe, the egg from which Brahma is said to have emerged as light, the Buddhist *svabhavat,* the Icelandic *ginnungagap,* heart and hidden first cause of all things—chaos would have to wait. Matt had called. We were leaving at noon. We had fuel and batteries and film to buy. Sandwiches to make. Chaos may have been at the center of all this, but, like the weather one moved through, or under, or within, it went without comment. Mostly there was order and pattern to what we were doing—departure times, maps, target areas.

We were headed to Woodward on the "northwest passage," State Highway 270, which leads to the sagebrush of the Oklahoma Panhandle. Matt cracked open a bottle of Diet Coke and pointed to a scattered line of altocumulus— cotton balls on parade. "It's moving more to the east than I'd like to see," he said, grimly. Matt leaned heavily toward the fatalistic, like a narrator in a Russian novel, but would often *unsay* some dark pronouncement, allowing hope to slip through, as he did now, under his breath, of the uncooperative clouds: "It's not that big of a deal." Among chasers, Matt's was a common way of viewing the weather, a line of defense against the fact of chaos, a posture borne of disappointments too numerous to recall, a pessimistic stew with just a hint of pessimism's opposite number, an emotion that dared not speak its name. I wondered whether chasers, who were prone to acronyms, had a term for it. Nothing I came up with seemed to fit: DOWN, for instance, which, in my mind, stood for "depressed, or weather negative," was suffix- friendly but too complex, as was WAMPUM ("weather always makes people unhappy, mostly"), which, though true, was inept. CRAP ("constant reason applied pessimistically") came closer to the character trait I was groping to name, but did not bear repeated use, and GRIM! ("Getting reamed in mete- orology!"), despite its kinship with an actual acronym in use among fore- casters (BOHICA: "Bend over, here it comes again") was, in any case, still a bit over the top. I settled, finally, on MOPE, which came closest to describing the proportions of hope and despair that made for a generalized condition. MOPE stood for "minimal optimism, pessimistically engaged."

MATT WAS SITTING in the driver's seat, where he would remain, it seemed, for the next three weeks, looking at the sky, listening to the radio, pointing out the odd detail. "Watonga," he said, as we entered that town for fuel and snacks, "where part of *Rain Man* was filmed. . . . They have a cheese factory here." These two facts were uttered without malice or boosterish pride. There

was detachment, but also sympathy, as if his observation were a form of vale-
dictory address: "Onward, Watonga," I imagined the speech going. Fate and
destiny work from the outside, the way gods enter and exit the Odyssey, the
way tornadoes raked this landscape each spring, like a reverse lottery, the
way location scouts swooped into towns like Watonga or Wakita in search of
some illusory American backdrop, some stretch of Main Street that could be
immortalized. But, of course, fate also works from the inside, for the individual or the community, as in a Greek play, or, say, the construction of a
cheese factory. Matt was a connoisseur of this sort of detail and admired
Watonga's attempt, however improbable, at making its way in the world.

As we loaded up with sodas and pulled back out onto the highway, Matt's
view of our prospects seemed to have shifted again: "Too bad the liquor
stores are not open yet. I have a feeling we'll need it tonight . . . to console
ourselves." The thought floated in the cab for a moment like a balloon, a
funny little spell that he was casting. I fiddled with the radio, searching for
an update to the recent severe thunderstorm warning, something on the
radio besides country music.

"They should put out a bad music warning," Matt said.

Riding in the backseat was Austin Ivey, a young OU graduate with dark
hair and round features made boyish by a baseball cap. Austin had met Matt
while earning his degree in geography, and though he'd been chasing a few
years, he was still what might be called storm hungry. He came bearing some
useful electronic gizmos—a laptop hooked up to a GPS unit, for instance—
and he knew the meteorological lingo, but he seemed like a young tribal initiate, a hunter proficient at taking down small game but still in search of his
first epic encounter. Given the opportunity to chase with Matt Biddle, he'd
driven up for the weekend all the way from Los Alamos, New Mexico. He
was setting up his laptop and listening abstractedly as Matt complained
about the music.

"Try the local Watonga station," Austin suggested.

"What, for a cheese forecast?"

With his jeans, a Detroit Red Wings hockey jersey, dark hair and sunglasses framing an angular face and graceful nose, Matt looked like a Bulgar-
ian nobleman overcome by enthusiasm for the NHL. It was early—two
o'clock on a Wednesday afternoon—but a rush was already under way. The

word was out, and chase crews from television stations zipped past us. Television trucks and vans swooshed by, horripillating with antennae and satellite dishes, each patched directly into the databanks of home television stations in Kansas, Oklahoma, and Missouri, each directed by Doppler radar and a celebrity meteorologist—Mike Morgan, with the NBC affiliate KFOR, Channel 4; or Rick Mitchell at ABC affiliate KOCO, Channel 5; or the venerable Gary England at CBS affiliate KWTV, Channel 9—each giving instructions over the phone to his driver or receiving and transmitting live over the airwaves "updates" of the developing storm. The insides of these vans fairly hummed with circuitry. They glowed with digital display. They crackled with the clipped conversation of junior-grade meteorologists on two-way radios discussing CAPE, low-level shear, and convergence on the dry line. The vans' exteriors, emblazoned with bright logos like coats-of-arms, expressed fealty to the home station.

Ours was a journey that engaged the metaphor of the hunt, moving through a habitat of sorts, with its seasonal migrations of monster storms. As hunting went, it was a particularly cerebral endeavor, the mostly masculine, practical application of meteorological knowledge on a field that was, at the largest, "synoptic" scale, as big as the North American continent. I first noticed this sense of the synoptic scale as we were driving northwest to Woodward and Matt began talking about winds coming off "the front range." We were moving through a landscape unbroken by any range that I could see. Still, I looked around, just to make sure. All was flat in every direction. The range in question, of course, was the Rocky Mountains, hundreds of miles west of us, beyond the earth's curvature, yet as close and familiar in Matt's mind and as crucial in their influence on the day's events as if they were right in front of us. They were for Matt so commonplace a feature that they literally went without saying; that is, they took the more generalized and practical appellation of things that are more or less obvious because of their proximity, the way Chicago residents call the vast waters of Lake Michigan "the lake." The synoptic scale of reference, from the Greek meaning a general or comprehensive view, was where the bulk of a chaser's decisions were made—while key pieces of the weather were still nascent collections of air masses, convergences of vectors and gradients on weather maps displayed on computer screens. At the synoptic level, anything that

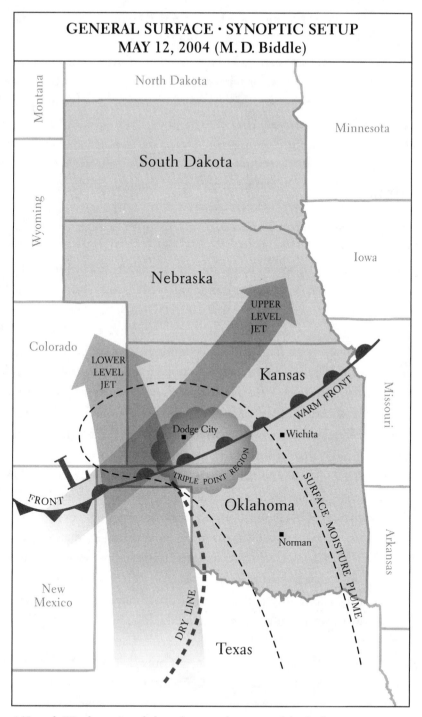

GENERAL SURFACE · SYNOPTIC SETUP
MAY 12, 2004 (M. D. Biddle)

Montana

North Dakota

Minnesota

South Dakota

Wyoming

Nebraska

Iowa

Colorado

UPPER
LEVEL
JET

LOWER
LEVEL
JET

Kansas

Missouri

WARM FRONT

Dodge City

Wichita

L

TRIPLE POINT REGION

FRONT

Oklahoma

SURFACE MOISTURE PLUME

Norman

Arkansas

New
Mexico

DRY LINE

Texas

A Tornado Watch was issued along the warm front, east of the dry line. © M. D. Biddle

happened today in Oklahoma or Kansas would be profoundly influenced by certain winds blowing off the lee side of the Rockies, creating a pattern of low pressure near the earth's surface that would help initiate storms. The largest feature involved a warm front that lay across Colorado, the Texas and Oklahoma panhandles, and central Kansas, running roughly northeast but curling north at both ends. The next synoptic feature of importance involved the surface low off the Rockies, which tracked eastward along the front like a curtain moving along its guides across the Texas panhandle until hitting a snag at Woodward, Oklahoma, where it billowed east like a question mark. Where this surface low intersected the warm front, a giant, bow-legged Y formed, like a splayed wishbone. Into this open Y rushed the Maritime air mass.

At the mesoscale, or middle range, from about fifty to one hundred square miles in area, the Y-shaped intersection of the warm front with a large boundary known as the dry line was called the triple point, a convergence of air masses rotating cyclonically, or counterclockwise, around a surface low, near Woodward. That morning I had attended a weather briefing at the University of Oklahoma's School of Meteorology, where a cluster of graduate students had gathered in Howie Bluestein's office on the thirteenth floor of the Sarkey's Energy Center. Bluestein sat at his desk, the rest of us hunkered in around him, and discussed the mesoscale "setup," the pattern of convergences for today that looked so promising.

"The five-hundred-millibar flow is going to be forty knots," Bluestein said, referring to the speed of the winds aloft, at about two and a half miles above the surface. "That's just outrageous," he added. According to a computer model at the National Center for Environmental Prediction, the winds near the surface would be easterly near twenty knots. ("That's awesome," someone in the room said.) Bluestein went on: "In Kansas they're going to be southerly. Along this retreating moisture boundary." He pointed to an area of low pressure west of the Texas panhandle. "So I would go to Woodward first."

Having a target area, of course, meant only that one had narrowed the playing field a little. The storm itself, when it emerged, could be anywhere within a vast hatchwork of longitude and latitude, section and range, needle and haystack. A storm could fire and drop a half-dozen tornadoes in an hour, but if, in your painstaking effort to get it right, you'd targeted the wrong part of the state, you'd miss the whole show. Being "out of position" was perhaps the most common frustration of the inexperienced chaser. The storm you'd chosen would evaporate, and then on the horizon, a monster storm would explode, the radio reporting tornadoes dropping from sky, and for the next few days the local news would be playing clips of all that you missed.

Tornadoes occur at the "storm scale," which is an entirely different sort of ball game. Small though they are relative to the mesoscale and synoptic scale forces surrounding them, storms are immense structures, which required a special orienteering savvy. Towering five to ten miles high, often sprawling across several counties, a storm is composed of many different constituent parts, moving rapidly in three dimensions, and often too large to take in. All of it is working as a single process in time, creating its own mini-environments, or boundary layers, which rise and fall, emerge and then vanish. Storms move in cycles of expansion and contraction and complex flow. Not everyone has the talent to think in three dimensions, to think quickly, to respond to subtle promptings of the storm swirling about one's head. In fact, many meteorologists remain content to stay at home with their large-scale maps and their radar overview. But many enjoy the challenge of driving into a big mess and then spelunking their way around from the inside of a quickly changing behemoth, moving and maneuvering within the storm, and coming to understand it the way a mouse, caught amid the blaring of trumpets, the stomping of elephants, and the roaring of lions, might suddenly apprehend the pattern of a three-ring circus, and scramble safely to the side for a fantastic view of the show.

All this is what we were hoping for as we stood in Bluestein's office around a computer screen. Before the weather briefing ended, Bluestein switched to a view of the southern Plains taken from a satellite orbiting 22,000 miles above the earth's surface. It was a black-and-white image with the states of Oklahoma, Texas, Kansas, New Mexico, and Colorado neatly outlined.

"Look at that." Bluestein sounded genuinely impressed.

"That looks beautiful," someone said. Oohs and ahs filled the room. The clouds, as I saw them, were messy, disorganized bunches splayed across the center of the continent. John Constable, the early-nineteenth-century English landscape painter, once said that understanding the weather involved as much time and dedication as learning how to decipher Egyptian hieroglyph-ics. Bluestein carefully traced a long line of cumulus clouds just north of Woodward and stretching in a graceful northeasterly curve into Kansas. There, the messy clouds aligned themselves in order like beads on a rosary, where the warm front met the surface low coming in from the west.

"If you can get a storm forming along the retreating portion of a front," he said, moving his pointer over most of the Oklahoma Panhandle, "and if the storm can propagate well to the right and move due east, it will be a real honker."

Back at Matt's house, I found Matt and Austin leaning into a computer screen. They were looking at a "forecast product," the term for the models and other predictive tools produced and distributed by the National Weather Service. This product was a map of the surface features for today that showed the synoptic setup, the lazy-Y confluence of cold front, dry line, and Gulf moisture all turning around a surface low that Bluestein had been viewing in his office. Where these large synoptic features intersected was the "triple point," an area of interest from fifty to a hundred miles across, where storms would first fire. Matt put his finger on the screen.

"We want to be just east of this surface low," he said, indicating the bil-lowing southern leg of the lazy Y, "and we want to be on the north side of the dry line bulge." Matt liked the positioning of the warm front; it curved down from Colorado, sagging like a swayback horse into the Oklahoma Panhandle, then turned northward away from the general storm direction, which would be slightly north of east. "If the front orientation is parallel to the storm movement," he explained, "you end up with training storms with squall lines and heavy rain. And we don't want that."

The problem here, of course, was not a lack of information. At nearly every truckstop, you could spot chasers drawing information from wireless Internet connections or from their cell phones. Others used local libraries to access the Internet. Data abounded. The problem was how to interpret it. This was, in fact, the ongoing problem of weather forecasting—the very thing that made the science of meteorology, despite its high-tech profile, list heavily toward the suspect realms of anecdotal experience, toward the realm of the hunch, the educated guess, the coin toss. For meteorology, unlike most of the sciences, was grounded in—and by—humility, its entire history a concession to the abiding fact that, weatherwise, nobody knew for certain what was going to happen next.

Attempts to predict the weather date back as far as one can go in Western Civ.: to the Assyrian kings of the second millennium B.C.E., whose cuneiform tablets include the earliest surviving record of the struggle for meteorological mastery. The *Enūma Anu Enlil* is a collection of seven thousand celestial omens that correlate the motions of the heavens with events down below, including weather. "If Jupiter stands in Pisces," one omen warns, "the Tigris and the Euphrates will be filled with silt." "If the moon is surrounded by a halo and the Bow star stands in it," another advises, "men will rage, and robberies will become numerous in the land."[3] Babylonian "astronomical diaries" from the sixth century B.C.E. record meteorological observations and predictions over an astonishing six hundred years. The Greek Pythagoreans of the fifth century B.C.E. developed the notion of cosmic harmony—of a profound, causal relationship between the heavens and the earth. The end of one of the earliest Greek texts, Hesiod's *Works and Days,* reads like a prototypical *Old Farmer's Almanac,* interweaving practical weather advice with moral and ethical instruction. Aratus' *Phaenomena,* from the third century B.C.E., set astro-meteorology to verse, and is an often cited instance, along with the work of Homer, Hesiod, Lucretius, and Virgil, of the degree to which the ancient world fully entrusted the preservation of its meteorological endowment to poets. Stone tablets, "parapegmata," discovered at Miletus by nineteenth-century German archeologists and dating back to the first century C.E., were used like calendars for astro-meteorological forecasting. Important days and seasons—and the corresponding agricultural instructions—could be tracked by means of a movable peg. How the parapegmata may have worked is not entirely clear—they were not exactly weather maps; what remains impressive about them is the ageless human impulse to bring the weather to heel. Just as geographical maps bring distances beyond the visible horizon under the purview of a single encompassing glance, so the parapegmata try to render the moving, shape-shifting clouds in stone.

Benjamin Franklin, the eighteenth century's best-known student of weather, used newspaper accounts of a big storm in 1743 that prevented his observation of a lunar eclipse to correctly surmise that published wind directions, which were southwesterly in Philadelphia and northeasterly in Boston, reflected not separate storms blowing in different directions but aspects of a single storm system moving from the southwest to the northeast. Franklin was, in essence, the first to guess that storms had structure and behaved in predictable ways. His observation transformed the field of meteorology. In 1802, Luke Howard, an amateur meteorologist in London, delivered his lecture "On the Modification of Clouds," arguing that science could be applied to weather. His taxonomy of clouds, six Latinate descriptive categories from "cirrus" to "cumulostratus," was to meteorology what James Hutton's 1788 *Theory of the Earth* was to geology. Hutton inspired Lyell and Darwin; Howard inspired Admiral Sir Francis Beaufort, of the Beaufort scale of wind intensity. In 1845, Joseph Henry, secretary of the Smithsonian Institution, suggested that the new technology of the telegraph be used to provide weather reports and to help with forecasting storms. By 1870, the U.S. Signal Service was producing daily weather maps for the country, and Sergeant John P. Finley was investigating significant storms, including tornadoes. Finley understood that severe storms were, above all, a problem of human ecology—the study of the interaction of the physical world (nature) with the human-behavioral world (culture). "Formerly . . . violent [storms] left no mark upon the treeless and uninhabited prairie," he wrote in 1887, ". . . but now the farm-house and the village dot the plain, and the hardy laborer has forced his way with his family into the depths of the forest." By the late 1880s, Finley had assembled from the mass of westward-settling farmers a volunteer army of more than 2,000 "tornado reporters," who observed and documented tornadoes and related severe weather. Using the telegraph, Finley became the first person to assemble timely data from regional reporters and issue weather "alerts," stating explicitly which areas were in danger and for how long. These alerts were the precursors of the "watch box" used today by the SPC. Strangely enough, Finley's efforts led to a ban on use of the term "tornado" in public announcements. The panic that the very word was thought to produce seemed, in the minds of many, to outweigh any actual tornado threat.

The ban, whether or not it was wise public policy, at least seemed to acknowledge a deep-seated fear, a pressure point of sorts, in the collective consciousness. That fear had an ancient provenance. Archeologists believe that five thousand years ago the inhabitants of Stonehenge honored the storm god by digging ditches parallel to the tracks of tornadoes. The Old Testament is shot through with terrifying whirlwinds. In his *Meteorologica,* Aristotle describes a "spiral [that] sinks to the earth and . . . with it the cloud . . . [that] carries off by force anything it meets." He correctly proposed, by way of explanation, a collision of opposing winds. Pliny the Elder, in *The Historie of the World,* describes what he calls a vortex, which "snatcheth up whatsoever it meeteth in the way aloft in to the skie, carrying it back, and swallowing it upon high." The tornado figures, as well, in the legends of North American Indians. The Blackfeet called it Windsucker; the Seneca saw it as Dagwa Noenyent, a giant that crashed through the forest. Kiowa myth tells of a medicine man who creates a great horse, Red Wind, whose swirling motion is meant to cool his people. But the horse gets loose and runs amok. The medicine man banishes Red Wind to the sky, from which place, every now and then, the horse descends with a vengeance. The Osage, the great tribe of the Plains, called the phenomenon, simply, the Big Wind.

"Tornado" appears first in English in a 1556 account by the explorer Richard Hakluyt of a tropical storm's "terrible thunder and lightning, with exceeding great gusts of raine, called *Ternados.*" The term and its alternative forms—"turnado," "tournado," "tornado"—does not exist in Spanish or Portuguese, but, according to the *Oxford English Dictionary,* may have been a mistake for the Spanish word for thunderstorm, *tronada.* This would explain why "tornado" at first seems to have signified all manner of "lowd blasts, stinking showers, and terrible thunders," as well as squalls and other unexpected violent gusts. Later appearances seem more specific, as in Captain John Smith's rendering, a century after Hakluyt, of "a gust, a storme, a spoute, a loume gaile, an eddy wind, a flake of wind, a Turnado." This same manifestation made it into Increase Mather's *Illustrious Providences* (1684), the first written record of a tornado in the United States, in Cambridge, Massachusetts: a thick black rotating cloud, inside which "there seemed to be . . . a pillar . . . about eight or ten feet in diameter . . . like a screw or solid body" that tore down trees and lifted up large stones.

After the great experimenters of the Enlightenment, and after the motion of all vortexes—from a hurricane to a dust devil swirling in a fallow field— had been named in 1835 for Gaspard Gustave de Coriolis, who first recognized their essential congruity; after the debates of the 1840s between James

Espy and William Redfield about the origins of storms and the characteristics of tornadoes; even after the far-reaching experiments of John Finley, the practical application of meteorological discovery has been shadowed and hampered by human fear. From 1890 onward, when Congress transferred the duties of weather observation and warning from the Signal Corps to the newly formed Weather Bureau, the challenge of accurate weather prediction has run headlong into the challenge of effective communications—of conveying degrees of weather danger to a skittish public. Few meteorologists speak with confidence about this second problem, a matter of rhetoric, where hard science bumps into the suspect terrain of human nature: ignorance, outmoded habits of thought, Luddite sympathies, old wives' tales, the congeries of cultural biases and myths, all mired in a slough of doubt and skepticism regarding weather reports. This was what the computer geeks at the Storm Prediction Center called, politely, since my tape recorder was rolling, "the human interface problem."[4]

But in the corridors of the Storm Prediction Center, the human interface problem had been temporarily set aside. As part of my tour, I was led to a glass case containing isobaric charts, at the bottom of which were the signatures of Air Force Captain Robert C. Miller and Major Ernest J. Fawbush. On May 20, 1948, a tornado had struck Tinker Air Force Base, causing $10 million worth of damage. Fawbush and Miller were subsequently assigned the problem of tornado prediction; such was the state of the science, the state of their expertise, and the state of the weather that within five working days they spotted a second storm nearly identical to the first. The two officers were astonished—and a bit daunted. The odds of a second tornado outbreak hitting the same place within the same week were no better than 1 in 20 million, but Fawbush and Miller stuck to their charts, and on the evening of March 25, 1948, they issued the world's first correct prediction of a tornado.

Across the street from the SPC was the National Weather Service Forecast Office, and beyond that, a small nondescript outbuilding from which weather balloons are released into the sky. The ascent of balloons in Norman is part of an international cooperative ritual, synchronized to Greenwich Mean Time: twice a day, at similar weather stations around the world and at roughly the same instant, hundreds of identical helium-filled sounding balloons are released, rising swiftly into the upper reaches of the atmosphere to assay and beam back in real time the global mood. Meteorologically speaking, nothing within the purview of the SPC or the NWS office occurs in isolation. Each molecule of vapor touches every other molecule, so that, weather-wise, as in a literal reading of karmic doctrine, what comes around goes around.

The balloon soundings and other meteorological readings join the data sets and climatalogical records in computers at the NWS office and in the SPC, where they become the initiating conditions that whirl in computer models poking into the problem of the future. Weather makes for a terrifically complicated problem in fluid dynamics, for air is freighted with invisible turbulences, laminar flows, viscosity and shear and vorticity. The study of air movement is one of the most complex fields in physics. The SPC operations room is crammed with monitor screens of different sizes, like a Cubist collage with radar images flickering above the heads of three men sitting at three separate computer stations. A mesoscale forecaster was watching the central Plains states, which that afternoon were dozing away, becalmed, with a lazy column of moist air moving up like smoke from a Texas barbecue. A second forecaster had his eye on a cluster of storms forming in Arizona and New Mexico.

"Still some good cells there. At least visible just north of Phoenix," he told the room, which remained silent but for the ambient hum of machines and the clicking of computer keys.

The third forecaster was shoveling takeout spaghetti into his mouth while winds blew off the Rocky Mountains onto the Plains. At that time of year, the backflow off the Rockies is a regular occurrence, known locally as a Chinook wind, like an afternoon freight train highballing east. The question was whether any of this wind would become severe. If so—if, in the opinion of these three men sitting in a windowless room in Norman, Oklahoma, the storm in the Rockies would soon present a danger to life and property— then, by government mandate, they would issue a storm watch. This was the exclusive role of the Storm Prediction Center. While the forecasters were mulling this over, a line of thunderstorms was setting up over Ohio to clobber the mid-Atlantic states. The lead forecaster was tracking both systems, like a captain on the bridge of a ship the size of the continent.

"Looks like the stuff up north of Scranton might have irregularities."

More clicking, more evaluative silence. Someone said it was a no-brainer.

Someone else agreed. Thus, in the interest of public safety, with a final phone call to the regional office of the National Weather Service, and with one or two keystrokes of a computer, a severe storm watch was issued from this bunkerlike facility on the central prairie—a watch that would soon begin scrolling at the bottom of television screens a thousand miles away, warning the residents of eastern Pennsylvania of high winds and potential flooding.

The state of Oklahoma has at its disposal an observational system called the Mesonet that effectively hard-wires every ten square miles, compiling and analyzing in real time a vast array of meteorological data from the ground up. The state's resources are supplemented at the federal level by the National Weather Service, the Center for the Analysis and Prediction of Storms, the National Severe Storm Laboratory, and, at the heart of it all, the Storm Prediction Center. Data from the Mesonet is fed into computers at the SPC, which in turn try to guess what the weather will do next. The computers use climatological data and experimental software, but the true heart of the decision-making process, the secret to its success, lies in the conversation that takes place between the men and women in this room, who could tell you a lot about storm fronts and storm-scale rotation and wind shear; they could *parameterize* conditions and write forwarding sets of equations until the cows came home; they might write dissertations on the environments of tornadic and nontornadic mesocyclones and talk until dawn about CAPE and about backflow blowing off the Rockies, but, of the hundreds of storms that blow across the state each year, and for reasons that go deep into the heart of chaos theory, the scientists with their Ph.D.s, parallel computers, and data banks cannot explain why some storms blow over like an angry, chained-up dog, while others run wild, dropping tornadoes out of the sky. "We don't know why storms tornado," said Paul Janish, a "techniques development" meteorologist at the SPC. Janish is responsible for new technology at the center, and while the building seems crammed with computers, their use to explicitly predict tornadoes was something he set far into the future. "It's beyond us," he said. "We won't be able to do that for a long time."

"Pueblo Colorado gusting thirty-seven knots," someone says. "Just a typical afternoon."

"There's a line of thunderstorms running through Charlotte."

"There's a line dropping out of New Mexico."

"I'm not very impressed. The flow is so weak. They're just gusting out."

The center has five junior-level assistant mesoscale forecasters, ten mesoscale/outlook forecasters, and five lead forecasters. There have only ever been thirty lead forecasters at the SPC, and the five who are currently working shifts are as famous in the meteorological field as rock stars. Some have meteorological phenomena named after them—the Corfidi vector is named for Stephen Corfidi—that are used around the world. Most of them are hired from local offices of the National Weather Service or promoted from within the SPC, advancing to the point where, at the height of their field, they cover twenty-four hours a day, in three shifts, perpetuating what must be the world's longest conversation about the weather.

At the end of my tour, I was shown the office of Dave Imy, lead forecaster and operations branch chief, who entered the room at a good clip, then sat down to address me. He was bald, with a beaky nose, wiry and a little wired— just off an eight-hour shift in the operations room, ready for anything. He seemed to have been born ready. As he looked across his desk, it suddenly seemed particularly on task to ask this top-gun meteorological man-in-charge a question about the day's weather.

Imy jumped into the answer at full speed, as one accustomed to dispatching the next of many simultaneous tasks, like an air traffic controller or a short order cook during a dinner rush: "We had a risk of severe weather from Texas, Oklahoma, northward into Kansas," he said. "We added to that outlook some severe weather to Columbia, to the South Carolina/Georgia area, as there was a what we call a MCV, a mesoscale convective vortex, which actually developed from convection that occurred overnight in Arkansas and moved into Alabama and Mississippi, and it appeared that as it moved into a very unstable air mass it would develop into thunderstorms that would become severe."

A lumbering storm had survived the cool overnight passage across Arkansas and was now heating up to make for an ugly day in Alabama and South Carolina. As he spoke, Imy began to slowly rock back and forth, as if absorbed in prayer.

"Another area of concern was out toward eastern New Mexico. We had a dry line that set up over the eastern part of the state, a warm front that was moving northward through Texas and Oklahoma, and a very moist and unstable air mass across Texas. Simultaneously, in a different part of the country, we had a trough, an upper-level area of low pressure, that was moving from California and Arizona and would be sweeping east-northeastward toward New Mexico late that afternoon. As that system approached, we expected thunderstorms to develop across eastern New Mexico and eventually develop overnight with severe storms across the Texas Panhandle, western Oklahoma, and into Kansas."

My innocent question about the day's weather had required a response that sounded vaguely like the catalogue of ships in the *Iliad*. And with each day came a brand-new epic to comprehend. This was my first apprehension of the scope of Dave Imy's problem, the SPC's problem, our problem: the weather's grinding, relentless change; the weather's embodiment of the Heraclitean truth that runs so contrary to human sensibility—the world's crushing momentum, its complete indifference to the dream of permanence or to human cycles of wakefulness and rest. It was a burden identified early on by the Weather Bureau's first director, Willis L. Moore, who complained to Congress in 1870 that the pressures of the job had led many a forecaster to a state of nervous collapse. Never would there be a time when the weather stopped doing what it did, stopped its shape-shifting parade, took a vacation, or paused for a moment to take a load off. And if it became your Homeric lot to grapple with this unceasing quality, as Imy did, to apprehend if not control it, then you, too, might start rocking in your chair.

In Tornado Alley, weather talk became a way of negotiating the flood of weather data streaming from places like the SPC at the speed of light. Although the local television networks seemed to square off for the best possible coverage of severe weather, at the business end of this battle—"on the ground"—the troops crossed enemy lines as a matter of course, gabbing, sharing equipment and information. At every gas station or parking lot along a storm chase, one could see complete strangers engaged in conversations laden with meteorological argot; whose effect was the usual one of joining together those who are fluent and excluding all others.

Once in 2002, at a gas station in Kremlin, Kansas, I got out to stretch my legs. Two SUVs, bristling with antennae, had also made a pit stop. Steve

Miller, from Channel 8 in Tulsa, was talking on his cell phone in the bright sunshine. Another meteorologist was phoning in a storm update to the Tulsa station. Miller walked over and introduced himself, and when Matt said his name, Miller took a half step back and said, "So *you're* Matt Biddle," then offered Matt the use of the equipment in his truck.

It was of many such moments during my time with Matt, a momentary glow of celebrity from someone whom Matt would describe as suffering from "severe storm syndrome." I accepted Steve Miller's invitation on Matt's behalf and struck up a conversation with a young man named Hans, who had spilled out of the Tulsa van. Normally, of course, the weather would be a handy, likely subject for small talk between strangers at a convenience store in the middle of Kansas, a universally safe subject, understood by all, entry point to other things. Here, it was an aim and end in itself, with its own phrases of significance, which flowed from Hans, quietly but excitedly. He mentioned something about an air mass at the 700-millibar level and then eyed me, meaningfully. All I could do was nod agreeably, as if to say that, when it came to air masses at the 700-millibar level, anything was possible.

Today, as we embarked upon the first chase of 2004, Matt was traveling light. He'd brought with him a small bag that contained a couple of cameras and a small pair of binoculars. Into the driver's side door handle, he had slipped a portable radio—a police, fire, and storm-chase scanner capable also of receiving emergency broadcasts from the National Weather Service. The alphanumeric pager on Matt's belt received MCDs, mesoscale convective discussions, pithy discussions about the outlook for severe storms written by SPC forecasters.

Austin was our information ace in the hole. Matt could use his cell phone to download information from the Internet to his laptop. His GPS map could plot our location as we traveled, and provide valuable routing information when things got hot and heavy. At twenty-three, with a bachelor's in geography from the University of Oklahoma, Austin now worked at the super-secret labs in Los Alamos, doing computer mapping of human behavior. His current project involved maps and counterterrorism, plotting the location of the indoor/outdoor populations in the country for "exposure assessment." Using the "Consolidated Human Activity Database," or CHAD, Austin was creating a mapping program that could tell you how many people would likely be out of doors in downtown Manhattan at three P.M., for instance, when a terrorist might release poisonous gases. Storm chasing seemed a happy antidote to these more sobering calculations.

We moved through a low-level cumulus field that Matt said would wax and wane and probably diminish as the day progressed. I asked Matt to describe the situation for the day. He set down the foam cup that functioned as his spittoon. "We have a fairly typical setup for spring," he said, "where the probability for severe weather is high. The tornado potential is not outrageous, but it's certainly there. Low pressure should form in the extreme northeastern Texas Panhandle, with a cold front trailing northwest from it, and a dry line trailing south of it." He glanced in the rearview mirror for a moment. "We are going to play an area to the east and south of the low, looking for isolated supercells. The key factor is whether we get enough winds aloft to give us a good shear profile to create rotating storms."

We drove for a couple of hours through sunny skies with fields of altocumulus that soon began training along a line, the west side of which remained clear and blue. "That seems to be the dry line," Matt said, meaning the boundary that separates the hot dry air moving in from the Rockies from the warm, moist air of the Gulf. From Oklahoma City, we'd been driving through a Maritime air mass, the main characteristic of which was its instability: it was warm, laden with moisture, and inclined to rise. This tendency to rise, the buoyancy or lift, was being blocked, however, by a capping inversion of dry air that lay about a mile above the earth's surface and would prevent the formation of storms. As the day progressed, the earth would heat up and begin eroding the capping layer from its base upward until the late afternoon, the warmest part of the day. At that point, the dry line, which moved from west to east, often combined with the surface heating and other forces to break through the capping layer. That's when an explosive burst of unstable air at peak temperature would rush the gap, forming a chimney of rising warm air moving through a surrounding environment of increasingly cold air aloft. Within this boiling column, rising at 20 to 30 miles per hour, condensing air released heat in great quantities that sustained the tower's ascent. Water droplets rose and fell thousands of feet, freezing, thawing, growing into hail, turning back into rain, the change of phase from liquid to solid releasing even more latent heat and driving the tower as high as 50,000 feet, where it would hit the tropopause, every storm's glass ceiling, and flatten into an anvil. Below the anvil, frozen pellets of hail circulated. A strong updraft would keep a pellet suspended, adding layer upon laminate layer of ice, until its weight overcame the storm's capacity to hold it aloft and it fell to earth. The more powerful the feeding updraft of the storm, the longer hail could remain suspended, which was why hail size was a good indicator of storm strength. Beneath the hail, droplets in the cloud tower consolidated into rainfall. The combined effect of rainfall and hail created a downdraft at the forward flank of the storm. When it hit the earth, it flattened just as, far above, the anvil flattened at the tropopause, the downdraft spreading like a pancake over section and township, kicking up great clouds of dust as it moved over plowed fields, often with such force that it generally clobbered and overwhelmed the storm's own incoming fuel source, the updraft, after which the storm dissipated. But if the prevailing upper-level winds happened to be blowing faster than the track of the storm, and in a different direction, then this "shear" would position the downdraft phenomena at some far remove from the storm's fuel source, enabling the storm to feed through the night on Maritime air for hundreds of miles.

Matt drove us right up to the dry line and pointed at it. On one side, to the west, the sky was blue and cloudless. On the other, little puffs of cumulus were popping up all over the place on an arc that ran roughly southwest. Nearly every other statement Matt would make about smaller-scale surface-level boundaries, I had to take on faith because, frankly, I saw but rarely understood what I was seeing. There were exceptions, of course. Matt might point out the shadow of an anvil, which neatly divided the windshield, my side of the van in shade and his side of the van in sunshine. This was a "thermal boundary" that could influence the way the storm played out. But there were "moisture boundaries" and "frontal boundaries," and "gust fronts and outflow boundaries," each of which was too big to take in and was more or less invisible, or made itself felt indirectly. We'd be driving down the road and suddenly the windshield would fog up. Matt might put his hand out the window and say, "Ah, we're moving into the inflow." Reading a storm was mostly about making sense of what was seen, at the storm scale, but it was also a kind of Braille, and we were the proverbial blind men deciphering an elephant from the strange and conflicting information at our fingertips.

We stopped for a few minutes in Woodward, where Austin tried unsuccessfully to establish an Internet connection on his cell phone, so we headed for the local library to get new satellite information. Just then Howie Bluestein's road crew swung ahead of us, so we followed them thirty miles toward the Kansas border. At four P.M., Matt's weather radio began screeching, which was followed by a tornado watch issued from the Storm Prediction Center in Norman for most of south-central Kansas.

"They're boxing the warm front," Matt said, referring to the SPC's decision to issue a "watch box," soon to be displayed for millions of viewers on the Weather Channel and on every television station in the region as a parallelogram running slightly north of east across central Kansas and encompassing at least 30,000 square miles. By issuing a Tornado Watch, the SPC had raised the level of alert by an order of magnitude above the standard Severe Thunderstorm Outlook. It was like a dramatic escalation in the first act of an immense and movable opera. Nobody in this audience doubted that we were headed for big things; *how* big was the dramatic arc. It wasn't just chasers who felt the suspense building. There was a thrum of anticipation at the sudden emergence of a TV and radio micromarket coterminous with the watch box issued by the SPC. Announcers were interrupting regular programming, priming the pump. In the next few hours, the oncoming storm would become a free public entertainment, a low-tech reality show the size of central Kansas. Emergency management officials for communities within that vast area could now issue standby notices to teams of volunteer storm spotters, who would soon be dispatched to predetermined viewing posts, very much like a home guard, where they would await the oncoming storms but also issue live reports that would be relayed over the airwaves into thousands of listening households, with occasional breaks for advertising revenue, for as long as the storms lasted.

For the moment, however, the weather was fair. Bluestein pulled over at the intersection of Highways 34 and 64, just west of the Cimarron River. It was 4:41 P.M.

"There's deeper cumulus up north," Matt said, referring to the cumulus towers beginning to form in Kansas. He craned his neck. To the west, the sky was an immaculate blue. Directly in front of us, to the north, clouds were bubbling all over the place. They would build, then collapse. "I believe we're right on the triple point," he said at last. In front of us, Bluestein had deployed his research vehicle's X-band radar. Austin and I got out of the van to look around.

The air was hot and dry, the sun beating down intensely. There were about ten cars at this intersection in the middle of nowhere. A cherry-red SUV with a satellite dish caught my eye. It belonged to a man who introduced himself as Billy Griffith from Dumas, Texas. The satellite dish, he explained, allowed him to hook up directly to the Internet, and, what was more important to Griffith's livelihood and status as a chaser, to feed captured video clips directly to regional television stations for immediate broadcast. Inside the SUV, Griffith had a bank of transmitting and receiving modems, a satellite positioning system that allowed him to send the video clips, and two deep cycle marine batteries to power all the gear. "What's that?" I asked, pointing to a rear-facing light at the back of his truck. "That's what you call a ten-dollar Wal-Mart special," he said. It was a strobe light: he switched it on when he pulled off the road, to make the SUV more visible to passing cars. But it was hard to imagine how anyone could fail to see the vehicle driven by Billy Griffith. With its half-dozen antennae, twirling anemometer, and satellite dish, it was a meteorological man-of-war. Last, he showed us his laptop, on which he had installed the kind of fancy professional forecasting software that made chasers linger in a weak-kneed moment of transport. We said good-bye and walked away. "Man," Austin said under his breath, "he must have twenty thousand dollars' worth of gear on that truck."

Back at the meteorology camp, Bluestein had instructed a colleague to set up an infrared camera to read the temperature of a nearby cloud base. Bluestein squinted into the sunlight. "Is that a possible high base funnel right there?"

There was a murmur of excitement from his grad students as they spotted the little rotating curlicue in the clouds. A high base funnel was a good indicator of low-level shear; this hopeful sign, according to MOPE protocol, required a counterbalancing response: "It's probably the only funnel we'll see all day," someone said.

"Howie," a grad student asked, "shall we tell Mike to start the dance?"

But it was too early in the day, and there was too much going on in the sky. A rain dance, or a propitiatory storm dance—whatever "the dance" happened to be—seemed best reserved for more quiescent times. "No," Howie said with a smile. "Not yet. Maintain cool-osity."

I stood next to him for a few minutes as we watched a tower of cumulus build; he maintained cool-osity, cautious pessimism, his own version of MOPE.

"It looks nice," he said at last of the towering cumulus, "but it's not going to do it."

A bit later: "We have some crepuscular rays," meaning the way sunlight was scattered in the clouds above us into rays that seemed to converge upon a point, like furrows in a plowed field. Crepuscular rays have been known down the ages as an indicator of moisture in the upper air. But this hopeful sign was crushed a moment later:

"That thing got sheared over," he said of a cumulus tower that began to topple. "It's El Croako."

And so it went, like the play-by-play of a baseball game, with Bluestein coaching third, reading the arcane signs of the unfolding drama, pacing the narrow margin of the state highway from the radar truck to the infrared camera a few yards down the road, grad students milling around like team-mates chattering in a dugout, everyone engaged in his own idiosyncratic mode of waiting for the crack of the bat and the game to break open. I walked away from the caravan, across Highway 64 and up an embankment to a nearby oak tree, where I looked north beyond the Cimarron River. A killdeer complained overhead. Prairie flowers were in full bloom. Big trucks whooshed by, and the wind carried the sound of the radar truck's generator, like the drone of a suburban lawn mower. Then a horn honked. It was Matt, signaling me to come back to the van.

"The posse's moving out," he said as Bluestein and his crew zoomed past. We followed, crossing East Moccasin Creek. Matt had seen Howie's shear funnel and had also noticed a horseshoe vortex—a rotating column of air stretched over an isolated updraft.[5] "Whenever I've seen something like that, more than half the time I've also seen tornadoes," he said. Guarded though this was, it was the most optimistic utterance I'd heard from Matt all day, and of course it called for a compensatory observation.

"There's an orphan anvil right over there to the southeast," Matt said, meaning an anvil without an updraft base beneath it, no column of rising cumulus, just the storm's decapitated topmost feature. "Not a good sign," Matt added.

"They're trying," he said finally, meaning the clouds to the north and south, pushing up against the cap. "It's a garbled mess. They'll continue to struggle, but if they form, they'll be severe."

Because we would be driving through the broadcast area of any number of radio stations in Oklahoma and Kansas, all of them struggling fiercely for market share of an audience that was uncommonly interested in up-to-the-minute coverage of the weather, Matt had the radio on, occasionally reaching for a forty-ounce Big Gulp of Diet Coke ("With caffeine. Otherwise, why bother?"). Beside the Big Gulp was an unopened sixteen-ounce bottle of Diet Coke for backup. In his other pocket, he carried a can of Skoal chewing tobacco—long cut, mint. The nicotine of the chewing tobacco and the caffeine of the Diet Coke suppressed the appetite, he said, and kept the mind alert for when things got interesting.

Things did get interesting in the late afternoon, when the storms around us reached full boil and the last important choices had to be made. Right now there were two areas of interest: one that was forming about thirty miles to the northwest, and one directly overhead that didn't impress Matt in the least.

"The base is too high," he said. "It's elongated and disorganized. It looks like crap." The choice seemed clear. Matt was troubled, however, by a logistical concern: the important part of the day was just beginning, but we only had a third of a tank of gas. The nearest station was Medicine Lodge, about six miles north. As we drove up over a rise on the prairie, Matt noticed a large sheet of precipitation, loaded with hail, threatening to cut off our route.

Hail exacted a price on chaser vehicles. It busted windshields and left deep pockmarks in the metal—some chasers simply attached wire mesh cages for protection. For a rental van contractee who knew better than to mention to the rental company how I was going to spend my month in the fair states of Oklahoma, Kansas, and Nebraska, hail could only mean trouble at the end of the trip.

"We can make it," Austin said.

Hail struck the van loudly, at first like someone popping a balloon, and then like someone taking a nine-iron to the vehicle, the noise completely out of all proportion to the size of the hailstones. It was a wincing, stomach-tightening drive to Medicine Lodge.

Thanks to his sunglasses, Matt's countenance seemed as unperturbed as an Aztec mask. Some people are like that—a crisis becomes a way of bringing the complex world to heel. The bigger the storm got, the more implacable Matt got, like an inverted emotional thermostat. As hail cracked against the van, he seemed to enter a zone of serene alertness, his mouth packed with chewing tobacco, the calm unbroken even as lightning struck the ground nearby. The bolt created a field of electricity that radiated outward in every direction, traveled through the antenna that was attached by a magnet to the top of the van, and passed through the cord that led to Austin's laptop.

"Ouch! I just got shocked," Austin said.

"St. Elmo's fire," said Matt, as if from the bottom of a well.

At last we made Medicine Lodge, where we pulled into a filling station just as the hailstorm reached its peak. I stood outside pumping gas, listening to hail ricochet off the station awning. When I climbed into the van, the scanner that Matt had clipped to the visor suddenly began a sustained screeching, followed by the strange, electronically generated, disembodied voice of Igor, the Stephen Hawkings–like computer-generated voice of the National Weather Service, announcing a tornado warning. Igor had been decommissioned a few years ago in favor of a much more "human"-like voice, but today, he was making a strange reappearance.

We had entered the final act. A Tornado Warning, the highest level of alert, had been issued on the storm to our northwest, where spotters had reported a tornado on the ground. We headed north into brilliant sunshine again, the fields all around us ablaze in sunlight—young wheat and corn blowing against a backdrop of darkened sky toward a fat, towering column rising straight up and fanning out a massive anvil. That was our storm, moving easterly at twenty-five miles an hour.

"We'll catch it," Austin said.

Our southern approach, in the rain-free part of the storm, left us a clear, unobstructed view of the meso-cyclone, a vast circulating column that seemed to descend from the cloud base nearly a thousand feet toward the ground. Some chasers call the meso-cyclone "the mother ship"—and, indeed, approaching it felt as if we were steering a dinghy alongside some intergalactic transport. From this colossus, the biggest object I had ever seen in my life, Matt spotted a funnel cloud emerging. It was lying down on its side and was just about to go vertical. If a tornado formed, it would pass within a half mile of us and directly in front. We pulled over to watch the show. With the exception of a single car and a pair of chasers leaning against their vehicle, cameras at the ready, we had the view to ourselves.

The reason we had the view to ourselves, of course, was that the storm to the south, the less promising storm, the storm that looked like crap, was producing a series of strong tornadoes—five in all—that would make regional and national news for several days to come and set chasers chattering away on the Internet: "Wowie Zowie!" one chaser exclaimed. "[This] made up for all the dismal chases of the previous two weeks!" Bluestein would call it Tornadofest 04. It would sweep through and destroy parts of Barber and Harper Counties, Kansas, leveling houses in Attica and Sharon, and hoovering up parts of Medicine Lodge, exactly where we had been minutes earlier. Austin spotted it first. My eyes followed his gaze down the road to the southern horizon, ten miles distant, where I saw the outline of a massive vortex descending all the way to the ground.

It was the first tornado I'd seen with my own eyes, and it was like seeing the Statue of Liberty for the first time—*from a plane.* My first impulse was to get closer. I wanted to see it. I wanted to see it up close. I wanted to jump in the van and drive south, and I wasn't the only one who wanted this.

"I think we should get on *that* storm," Austin said, pointing to the tornado on the ground. "The surface winds right here are not that good."

Both of us were trying to be polite, but Matt was leaning up against the driver's door, unmoved. "The really good winds are blowing way up over your head," he said. "You can't feel them here."

"I know," Austin said, his voice trailing off. He was pointing his camera to the south and rocking on the balls of his feet, looking through the viewfinder. Matt, with an occasional glance to the southern storm, kept his focus on the meso-cyclone in front of us. Too often, he'd told me once before, chasers got caught up in the moment. And when chasers stopped thinking and acted on impulse alone, they gave themselves over to Dante's second circle. In the hierarchy of chaserdom, those who drove around after storms without understanding the meteorological basis for their decisions were known as "yahoos," "Jethros," bumpkin-esque thrill seekers who tended to be dangerous, even reckless drivers, passing when they shouldn't, coming to sudden stops in the road, disregarding everything but their own wanton rush to get on the action. In the popular idiom, yahoos tended toward caricature: one imagined a pickup truck with a gun rack, three paunchy, bestubbled guys in baseball caps sitting shoulder to shoulder, a six-pack clinking at their feet, the truck, a Rebel flag on the grille, screaming down the highway playing Lynyrd Skynyrd at full blast. They were redneck, bass-fishing, loudmouthed idiots who got teary-eyed about hunting dogs and about what happened to Dale Earnhardt Sr., at Daytona. The trouble with the caricature wasn't just that it was completely inaccurate. The trouble was that the caricature made it difficult to notice how anyone, at any time, could suddenly become a yahoo, could devolve before your very eyes into the worst sort of chaser imaginable, simply by turning off his brain and surrendering to the impulse to hit the accelerator hard and simply *go,* merely because he could. Matt never made a move without knowing why he was moving, and he spoke to Austin with deliberation, calmly talking him down from a ledge.

"You're not going to feel any wind right here," Matt said again, "because we're in the hook. You're not going to feel the good inflow. The inflow is way over there." He pointed to the east.

Austin, his back to Matt, had zoomed in on the tornado to the south. He was practically climbing into the lens to get a better look. He was smiling, but he was wincing, too. "I'm just looking at that tornado down there," he said.

"I say let's give this storm another minute or two," Matt said. "If the storm to the south is going to cycle through and drop multiple tornadoes, we'll be able to intercept it. If it's not, well, we're not going to get it, anyway."

There was no answer to this, of course. We couldn't be in two places at once. And, anyway, Austin had walked away from the van.

"I feel the RFD winds kicking in," Matt said. The "hook echo," or back eddy of the storm, had passed, and now we were feeling the rear-flanking downdraft, zooming up from behind like the windswirl from a passing truck. RFD winds were thought to be crucial in the development of tornadoes; indeed, the horizontal funnel cloud soon tilted toward the vertical and hung there like a Christmas ornament, but then, in a whisper, it dissipated.

We followed the storm system for a while, hoping it might regroup, but soon, the entire thing split apart and fizzled out; we headed south.

As we closed in on the southern storm, even I could make out what was happening: a towering supercell, which had remained at a distance like a Himalayan peak, soon loomed directly overhead, and we drove underneath its base into a shadow world, with its own shadow fields and shadow farms and sad little shadow towns with shadow laundry hanging loose upon the lines. The alarm for this world was sounded over the National Weather Service radio frequency in a machinelike voice that had never known human sorrow or desire, a voice that did not speak but rather emitted a long string of uniformly shaped pellets—the syllables of a shadow language, cooled to absolute zero. From this, one was meant to infer that danger was near. We stopped once at a propane storage yard to watch a lowering in the clouds. Matt leaned heavily out of his open window, his hand in the air, feeling the wind.

"I don't know," he said, bringing his hand in and sitting back down. "God, it's kind of disorganized."

We continued south, toward Harper, Kansas, but we were losing light. Already it was dusk. For the first time in several hours, I felt myself settle back into my seat: we had entered the denouement. The dramatic arc of the day had shifted slightly but irrevocably into another mode altogether, the post-storm mode of busting, skunking out. All day the radio's weather coverage had helped us track our storm's progress and to make routing decisions, but now, with darkness closing, there was nothing left to do but listen to a drama that was taking place somewhere else.

"We just entered the city limits and, boy, it's just raining to beat the band here," one Kansas spotter reported, live on the air. "Water is splashing up from the front wheels of the mobile unit."

"We do have a—[sneeze]—excuse me—We *do have* a lowering of the clouds *not even a hundred yards from me.* I can see some rain and some trees bending."

It was easy to laugh at this sort of "remote broadcast," with the intrepid, rain-spotted storm spotter in foul-weather gear, sneezing into his microphone and filing a report on "rain and some trees bending." Easier still to imagine a whole region leaning into this selfsame form of free public entertainment. One could do worse than to eavesdrop on this home guard of volunteers calling out "Rotation in the clouds," and "Pea-sized hail," scaring the bejesus out of each other. Out of the encompassing prairie darkness came split-second, stroboscopic views of boiling cumulus towers, panoramas of canyons, crags, and massifs, stacked high into the troposphere. The heavy hitters of late-night religious radio were also out in force, the voice of evangelical ministry drumming up business across the static of time and space, an electric organ warbling somewhere in the background. I was jacked up on Mountain Dew and hopping between stations, which created an unusual effect, the fire and brimstone of the preachers commingling with the storm reports, while outside, fire in earnest—lightning from the storm, each bolt six times hotter than the surface of the sun—forked from cloud to cloud.

"Do you mind if we listen to this?" I asked.

Matt shrugged. "Sure. But maybe not for all night."

"And ye shall go before Him," the radio preacher intoned, working up a full lather, "in the spirit that cowereth the lion, that brings the hearts of the fathers for their children, and the disobedient to the wisdom of the just."

It was a three-hour drive back to Norman. Near Attica, Kansas, which had been hit hard by a tornado, we were slowed down by roadblocks. A wet local sheriff by a barricade waved us onto a detour, the lights of his cruiser flashing red and amber in the steady rain. The local radio DJs were breaking up the regular playlist and joining the spirit of the evening, in which "Riders on the Storm" by the Doors found its melancholy way back into the rotation. For decades, that song had been overplayed on radio stations across America, but now I seemed to hear it as if for the first time—a basic blues pattern slowed down and cleverly set in a heart-creasing minor key that made hopelessness seem like something to be embraced. Jim Morrison's long-lost voice arrived like a dark, voluptuary counterbalance to the seesaw battle between God and Satan on the revivalist stations.

The three of us had been quiet for a long time, blundering along a two-lane back road in the middle of Kansas trying to find the way back onto a main arterial, when Matt suddenly leaned forward.

"What the hell is *that*?" he said.

Our headlights shone on a boxy, wide-bodied vehicle that filled the van's windshield. It lumbered along and took up part of the oncoming traffic lane like a piece of slow-moving farm equipment, or a tank. In fact, it had a turret on top, and its wheel wells were covered, so that it seemed to float through the darkened landscape and morph into vaguely recognizable shapes that I struggled to name. Now it seemed less tanklike than boatlike. Was it a Civil War battleship—*Monitor? Merrimack?* Or was it a crazy parade-float combination of the two? It was silver and constructed, it seemed, entirely of duct tape. It had a flat flank and was windowless but for narrow side slits on the driver and passenger sides, like the sort of windows through which airline pilots give the thumbs-up sign to the ground crew. It had a two-piece, dagger-like windshield, also like a jet or a dragster. On its sides were numerous tornado insignia. This was the IMAX filmmaker Sean Casey, in the Tornado Intercept Vehicle.

"His brake lights are out," was all Matt had to say about the TIV, as we passed it and found our way back to Norman.

THAT WAS THE first of many chases in the month of May. The following day, Matt, Austin, and I drove south into the Texas Panhandle on a desultory chase that took us past Archer City, Texas, and then to Gainesville, for barbecue. The outlook had been of minimal interest, but we'd gone anyway, still smarting from being skunked the day before, and because one never knew what might happen. I suppose if we'd seen yesterday's half dozen tornadoes in Kansas, as nearly everybody in the chaser universe had, we might have slept in and done laundry. But we hadn't. So we drove almost four hundred miles round-trip to see a shelf cloud. We saw a few other things, too. At the end of the day, Matt spotted a chaser with Michigan plates easing onto the shoulder of the road. He had had a twenty-hour drive from Michigan, Matt estimated, all for a day like this, in which nothing much had happened. "He's probably pulling over to have a good cry," Matt said. On the way back, I called Sean Casey, who suggested we meet for a drink at the Library, a bar in Norman, and watch the Lakers game, to which Matt agreed. He wanted to get a closer look at the TIV. There was now just the matter of the two-hundred-mile drive back to Norman. "What's the difference," Matt said as we reached the city limits, "between a storm chaser and someone who drives around like an idiot for hundreds of miles?" Nobody said a word.

I knew at the outset that even experienced storm chasers didn't always find what they were looking for. During a recent three-month season, from April to the end of June, Matt had taken part in a field experiment that included a team of very experienced chasers based in Norman who successfully intercepted tornadoes nine times in sixty-two attempts, logging over 21,000 miles in the process—the equivalent of traveling seven times between New York City and Los Angeles, intercepting one tornado for every 2,375 outward-bound miles. What seemed to make Matt wince about the Attica debacle, however, were two rookie mistakes he'd made. First, he had lost track of our fuel level so that at a critical juncture we were forced to find gas in Medicine Lodge. Second, and more important, when the tornado warning came out for the northwest storm, he simply reacted to it rather than thinking it through. "I chased the warning," Matt said, shaking his head in disgust. We should have incorporated the warning into an overall strategy that might have also included a glance at radar and satellite data; instead, we jumped in the van and sped north like a trio of yahoos.

Matt simmered away, shaking his head occasionally, and took the blame upon himself. It was all completely unnecessary. I'd seen more big weather that day than I had in nearly a lifetime. At the Library, beer and basketball offered themselves as consolation. I dropped off Matt and Austin, cleaned up a bit at the Sooner Hotel, then headed to the bar, where the TIV sat like a beached, musclebound canal barge on a residential street beneath swaying linden trees.

Sean was wedged into a booth next to Joshua Wurman, founder and director of the Center for Severe Weather Research, a nonprofit research institute funded by the National Science Foundation and the National Center for Atmospheric Research in Boulder, Colorado. Wurman was the inventor of the "Doppler on wheels" trucks, or DOWs, which had until recently been based in Norman. To Wurman's right was Herbert Stein, a broad-shouldered, handsome man in his mid-fifties with a lantern jaw, close-cropped silver hair, and a glint in his eyes. He seemed always on the verge of a joke—indeed, he had a ready supply, and a gift for impromptu hilarity, which was often delivered, unexpectedly, over the two-way radios used by the DOW team. He was a connoisseur and prolific practitioner of meteorological double entendre, and he had an encyclopedic if not eidetic memory for nearly every DOW deployment in the last ten years. He looked like a retired lumberjack, but he spoke fluent Meteorology and had become, over the years, an indispensable member of the DOW crew. With Stein's many accomplishments—his knowledge of electronics, his ability to repair equipment on the spot, his chasing instincts, his training as an emergency medical technician—he was, perhaps, especially prized for his ability to lead with a light hand, each day, a group of flighty, distractible undergraduate meteorology students as they headed incredibly expensive scientific equipment directly into the teeth of very dangerous storms. "He's our institutional memory," Wurman would say to me, later, out of Herb's earshot. For his part, Herb looked at me and asked, "How tall are you?"

I said I was six foot three, and there ensued a few other height-related banalities—filler, throw-away conversation, like talk about the weather in other circles. But it seemed to mildly irritate Sean Casey, who was sitting across the table drinking a beer and watching the basketball game. "Oooh," he said, "listen to the tall people with their tall-people talk."

It was the fourth quarter of an NBA semifinals game between the San Antonio Spurs and Sean's team, the Los Angeles Lakers. A win would give the Lakers a 3–2 advantage in the best of seven series, but the Spurs had chipped away at a substantial Lakers lead until now, in the closing minutes, it was anybody's game to win. Wurman and Stein had become sudden San Antonio fans, teasing Sean mercilessly, though it was clear that these two science dorks couldn't have cared less about the game and were mostly enjoying the rare opportunity to watch Sean squirm. Sean, who was not tall, was in turn venting a little frustration in Herb's direction. It evaporated instantly during a television time-out, whereupon Sean ordered a round of beers for the table and turned his attention to me. I was watching him take a deep dip of Skoal. He was in storm geek attire, T-shirt and shorts, with a two-day stubble on his face, which was a dark oval. His black, close-cropped hair was just beginning the long, slow process of recession at the temples, like a pair of retreating glaciers. He was an otherwise cool customer, a California smoothie with a long fuse and a sharp, understated wit, who cracked wise softly about his two companions, with whom he'd been chasing for the last four years.

"At first, Josh didn't want his crew to hang out with me," Sean said, sipping his beer, "because he was afraid that, in doing so, they'd go feral."

One of a half-dozen tornadoes near Attica, Kansas, on May 12, 2004, obliged the crew of a DOW radar truck to "reposition"; that is, flee. © Herbert Stein/Center for Servere Weather Research

Jana Lesak, undergraduate meteorology student and driver of DOW 2. © Jana Lesak

He put a pinch of Skoal in his lower jaw and grinned like a dark-eyed apostle. "It's a habit I picked up here on the prairies."

Herb recalled the time, during a post-chase party the previous year, when Sean broke out an electric razor. He woke up the next morning with a red Mohawk. At a roadblock in the Dakotas, Sean climbed out of the TIV looking like a character from a Mad Max movie and handed the policeman his driver's license, issued by his home state of California. "Oh, that explains everything," the roadblock cop said, waving him on.

Matt appeared at our booth and said hello to Josh and Herb, both of whom he had known for years. "You were on the northern storm?" Herb asked Matt of the debacle two days earlier. Matt nodded his head. "Too bad," Herb said.

"So you saw it all?" asked Matt.

"Oh, yeah. Five, maybe six tornadoes." Herb said. "We got the one that went through Attica."

"Stop it," Matt said. "You're driving a dagger straight through my heart."

The game resumed and Matt left us to talk with a few chaser friends in the corner. The San Antonio Spurs appeared to have eliminated the Los Angeles Lakers in the NBA playoffs. Tim Duncan had made a clutch shot to put the Spurs ahead by one point with the clock stopped and less than a half-second to go in the game. Time-outs were called. Out came the charts and play diagrams. Finally, a quick pass to Kobe Bryant, who instantly launched the ball toward the net. Time expires just as the ball leaves Bryant's fingertips. I know this because the sports news shows played the clip repeatedly after the fact. The ball leaves Bryant's hand, the clock ticks to zero, but the ball is soaring, still alive, a long, graceful arc, and sinks into the basket for two points, winning the game, again, and again. Sean jumped up and pumped his fist in the air as the bar crowd erupted. I walked over to Matt, who turned from his conversation with his chaser friends. He had a smile on his face.

"We weren't the only ones who got suckered into that northern storm," he said. He mentioned Charles Edwards, owner of Cloud 9 Tours, Charles Doswell III, a retired national service storms laboratory scientist-turned professor from OU who practically invented the taxonomy of storm propagation, and Gene Rhoden, whom Matt had identified a year earlier, when I was looking for people to interview, as one of the top five chasers in the country. Gene had been drawn north but had recovered in time to see the show in Attica. The fact that Gene had nearly missed seemed to take some of the sting out of getting skunked. Suddenly the bar crowd erupted again. We both looked up. The local weather news was playing a clip from the storm two days ago that showed a house in Attica, Kansas, being lifted in one piece, like Dorothy Gale's farmhouse in *The Wizard of Oz,* then soaring and spinning about a hundred feet in the air before it exploded. The bar crowd cheered again. The news channel played that clip repeatedly.

"This happens out here after every big storm," Matt said, shouting into my ear over the din. "There are so many chasers, and the television stations get so much footage . . ." His voice trailed off. There was another roar from the bar as the Attica house lifted off the ground and exploded again in slow motion.

"It's like sports," Matt said, with a shrug.

THREE

Children at Play

first met Sean Casey in January, having heard about him on the chaser grapevine. Nobody seemed to know who he was exactly, this "guy," in his tanklike vehicle; in the interest of full disclosure, it must be said that whenever Sean was the subject, there was a fairly brisk trade between the noun "guy" and adjectives such as "crazy," "idiotic," and "ridiculous." He was "the crazy IMAX guy," "the idiotic guy in the tank," or, in the most elaborate version, "the ridiculous guy driving the car that looks like it belongs to Jed Clampett." The word was that the "guy" was apparently trying to drive his vehicle into a tornado while filming the whole experience with an IMAX camera. It was such an odd, barrel-over-the-falls ambition that I couldn't pass up the chance to meet the man. After a few phone calls to the IMAX corporation, which knew nothing about him, I found a kindly production assistant who'd heard about the project and whose information ultimately led me to a tiny back lot behind Graphic Films, an independent production company specializing in IMAX nature films and owned by George Casey, Sean's father, in Culver City, California. In the hallway of the tiny office building, I found Sean, a bit frazzled and wearing aqua-colored, grease-impregnated overalls. He led me to a storage room in the back that seemed to be his domain. It had an "unfinished basement" feel, like a teenager's hangout—a farrago of exposed wood, electrical wiring, film canisters, a fuse box, tool boxes, office furniture, and, sitting incongruously in an anteroom next to the water heater, a state-of-the-art AVID digital editing machine. The experience was like walking through a junkyard and finding a purring Ferrari. Sean's was a cultivated repo man aesthetic—grease and gaskets, rebar and plate steel, blowtorches and industrial-strength grinding tools lying around in complete disarray, this in the service of some of the highest-end filmmaking in the business.

In one of the editing rooms of Graphic Films, a freelance editor was putting the final touches on *Forces of Nature,* a film that would be released that year in IMAX theaters across the country and that included segments on volcanoes, earthquakes, and tornadoes. It had been several years in the making, and it involved location shots around the world and interviews with vulcanologists, seismologists, and meteorologists. Joshua Wurman appears in the film. Sean was cinematographer for the project, filming from helicopters in Montserrat and following Wurman and the DOW trucks across the Plains. During the first several chase seasons, before the construction of their armored vehicle, Sean and a friend named Greg Eliason, a line producer for *Forces of Nature,* had driven a minivan, using experienced chasers such as Gene Rhoden and Jeff Piotrowski to guide them to the right storm. The day I visited Graphic Films, Sean grabbed a short feature about a chase with Greg two years earlier, near Aberdeen, South Dakota, and slipped it into the AVID editing console. Sean and Greg appear in the foreground, standing next to their van, Sean hunkered over a bulky IMAX camera, Greg next to him, using his hand to keep raindrops off the lens. In the distance a tornado approaches. Over the howling inflow winds, you can hear Sean shouting to Greg, who dashes back to the van to get a different lens. "That's the heavy voice of a storm chaser in the heat of battle," Sean said.

"How close is that tornado?" I asked.

"That's still pretty far away. I'd say about a mile," Sean said.

On this occasion, Sean had secured the guide services of Gene Rhoden, but neither he, nor his car, nor anyone else can be seen.

"At this point we got separated from Gene," Sean explained. "The minute we saw this tornado we left him behind and headed directly toward it. Gene doesn't like to get as close as we like to get."

And for good reason. Surprising little is known about tornadoes, as compared with other natural phenomena. The definition of a tornado is, scientifically speaking, vague, its climatology virtually unknown.[1] We know about as much now, with respect to tornadoes, as we did about human anatomy at the beginning of the fifteenth century, before Vesalius. We poke and we probe and "we know one when we see one," but the tornado's most basic aspects we find hard to pin down. The man widely regarded as the founder of contemporary tornado science, Dr. Tetsuya Theodore ("Ted") Fujita, defined a tornado as the fastest quarter mile of wind over any given section of terrain, which doesn't exactly bring the beast into focus. A commonplace definition—"a violently rotating column of air in contact with the ground and extending from the base of a thunderstorm," say—while serving a purpose, is almost entirely qualitative, as most meteorologists who study severe local storms would agree.[2] An accurate, encompassing, quantitative definition does not yet exist. Neither does there exist a quantitative, scientific compilation of tornado types—a tornado taxonomy, as it were. Of the vortex or "core flow region," the area bounded by the strongest winds, next to nothing is known. Extending outward from this is the tornado's "near environment," a zone ranging in size from a few hundred yards to over a mile, which also remains, more or less, terra incognita. Practically speaking, it is a place where violent things happen very fast, very unpredictably, and from any direction. Beyond the matter of debris—tree trunks, refrigerators, pickup trucks—landing on your head, the tornado itself can suddenly intensify, or change direction, or split into a hydra of satellite vortexes, or clone itself— or do all these things simultaneously. It can lull you to sleep, stretching into a long, narrow rope, the signature of a dying tornado, but at this stage, it is prone to radical pendulumlike shifts in speed and direction that can send it charging toward you at seventy miles per hour.

In the next frame of the video, Sean and Greg are again outside the van, but now they are within three hundred yards of the approaching tornado. Nobody willingly gets this close to break out a camera. It is a zone of almost complete uncertainty. Already, a satellite vortex can be seen forming to the left of the main tornado. Yet Sean, at least in his narration of the video sequence unfolding for me in his office, remained nonchalant: "Now the tornado has gotten a little sappy looking," he said, "the lower end is obscuring the top, and it's kind of a mess."

Sappy looking? Kind of a mess? It was a mode of ridicule that I'd noticed out in the field among chasers, a form of mockery lofted upward toward the prized object, a way of talking it down lest it get too full of itself. Often such chaser talk sounded like someone heckling a sunset. For good or ill, Sean had clearly assimilated the art, to the point of disparaging a tornado that could easily have killed him, even though, for the moment, it was weakening. It was a defensive verbal buffer, the best way, perhaps, of approaching Goliath; later, if things played out the way they should—and they would, of course; nobody had yet died chasing tornadoes—then you could continue with your plans, you could narrate your close encounter with the serene detachment that Sean Casey brought to nearly everything he did, and you could make your plans to meet the monster again in the spring.

But if the tornado was, indeed, sappy looking, the parent storm above it ensured that it would not remain so. In a few moments, it would prove this beyond a doubt. Perhaps the point of belittling a tornado was that if you were going to throw yourself into the bear's cage, the bear should at least cooperate and *look* menacing. If it didn't, well then, *fuck it.* It was *sappy.*

It was impossible to watch the footage that followed and not feel that the people in and out of the frame—Sean, Greg, and the unfortunate soul holding the video camera—had chosen to enter a place of specific size and circumference, and of a specific historical moment, that was completely owned and possessed and contained by whatever god or law you wanted to believe in—the god that shakes the mountains and the god that shudders the rafters—Lord Shiva, or Kali, or Jesus, Son of Man, descending "in the clouds of heaven with a power and a glory"[3]—the lord of the chamber and the roulette wheel and the gun barrel; the god of Chaos, of the second law of thermodynamics; the god of the gladiator ring, or the bullring, or of Dante's Second Circle of hell; the god of the mistake and stupid accident, the lord of all blunders and bewilderments to which Sean Casey and his two friends had handed over their fate.

What happened next was this: a downdraft threatens to blow them flat onto the ground. The tornado is getting too close. Maybe another one is forming above them. ("Now it's starting to get dangerous," Sean Casey allowed.) They rush to the van, but they have locked themselves out. They have locked themselves out of the van, and Sean is yelling. Greg searches his pants pockets, then starts looking around for something to smash the windows; as I watch this, it occurs to me that this is how people die. Not because they are sucked up and shredded by a giant, house-sized blender in the middle of South Dakota, but *because they forget their car keys.* Now we are in the moment. What to do? The moment of arrival. The moment of sacrifice. The miraculous, battlefield moment of clarity. What would you do? Sean *never* carries an extra set of keys. But out from his pocket, in his hand, they appear. Mud blowing sideways splatters the van as they escape, fishtailing down the muddy road.

Sean popped the video out of the console and looked at me. "That," he said, "was a real good day."

It stayed with me, that highlight reel near Aberdeen, South Dakota, the first thing that Sean Casey had wanted me to see about his life. It was a way of pointing, I later understood, of showing me the target, the goal, which was not so much the tornado as what the tornado provoked—the intense moment of clarity just before Greg decides to break the windows of the van. Then the escape. Then, perhaps, later, a new rule added to the campaign. A new rule that fairly glowed with the burnished touch of hard-won experience, like a talisman: *Everybody gets an extra set of keys.* Perhaps, along with this new procedure, added to the many others similarly earned and feeding the whole enterprise, experience becoming a kind of armature, perhaps there emerged a kind of song that could be heard only after such a thing, and only by those who'd experienced it. Tornado survivors almost always want to talk. They want to tell you what it was like, but they can't. They launch into the story, but very soon you can see in their faces how language fails. In a found poem by Heather McHugh, a tornado survivor comes close, saying: "It was over maybe once. Then it was never over." But what if *that*—whatever it was—became something you didn't just "survive," or "endure," or "get beyond," but instead something you actually sought out? Maybe it was something that you actually enjoyed—*that battlefield moment of clarity*—the way some war veterans, upon returning home, turn their backs on the quotidian rituals of civilian life and take up bow hunting with a vengeance, or simply vanish into the woods, leaving deadly tripwires behind them for anyone who might follow. What if, using a movie screen that was eight stories tall, you could convey, in some measure, the song—a medley of that small, metallic taste of fear in the mouth, the squirt of the adrenal glands, and a rumbling in the ground? And what if, as an unforeseen side effect of this Oz-like orchestration, you, the cinematographer, the author of the experience, settled some long-standing grudge and got bigger by proxy—taller—larger than life?

Outside, on a raised gravel bed built into the side of a hill: armature in earnest, the hulking form of the TIV, a modified Ford 450 heavy-duty truck that had been stripped down to the chassis, then wrapped with quarter-inch steel. At some point, Sean had realized that the days of rented minivans were over. If he wanted to get close to the beast, it was time to get serious. "We built up from the chassis—putting a quarter-inch plate as flooring, putting I-beams on top, then from that we used quarter-inch tube steel throughout the frame, then between the tube steel we welded eighth-inch steel." All told, the TIV weighed 14,000 pounds—seven tons. Each wheel well was covered with a wide, flat piece of eighth-inch plate steel, hinged at the top and with a handle at the bottom for lifting. I grabbed the handle on a front wheel flap but it was too heavy to lift with one hand. The TIV took three solid months, seven hours a day, to build—to weld together, to install bulletproof Lexan windows, to add a four-link hydraulic suspension, and to wire the electrical system, which ran the hydraulics and the engine. The working conditions were less than ideal.

"This used to be a two-foot-wide gravel space," Sean said of the back lot. "So I had to excavate to the hillside, going about another eight feet, then take all the excess dirt and pile it around here." He pointed to the pad built into the hill. "Then I built a retaining wall, and a garage with a gate entrance. The very next day, after completing the garage, one of the neighbors went into the city. A building inspector came out and said that it all had to come down. The whole idea was to build something so the neighbors wouldn't be bugged by the grinding sounds." Sean looked up the hillside at the houses above him. "Now when I grind," he said, "I grind with a certain glee."

After the garage came down, Sean worked outside under a tarp. People came in after dark and stole equipment. He put up barbed wire. "This one guy keeps coming back here and going to the bathroom," he said. "So I have this ongoing war of attrition with some bums and some kids who steal stuff. It's kind of like car camping—trying to do serious welding while car camping out in the wilderness."

In the first week of May 2003, a big tornado outbreak swept through the Oklahoma City area. Sean was racing to complete the TIV. "The minute I was finished, we hit the road. We stopped for fuel, and the vehicle wouldn't start. There was something wrong with the electrical system, so we spent our first day in a repair shop in the Central Valley." Things didn't go smoothly after that, either. First the hydraulic suspension gave out. "Hydraulic pistons aren't made to take the abuse of always holding a load, or always taking the road shots. They're used for smooth, steady movements, like what you see tractors or backhoes doing, not for being jostled a hundred times a minute." Somewhere near Great Bend, Nebraska, an electrical fire started in the back of the TIV, where four twelve-volt batteries were stored. "All the cables were on fire," he said. "There was smoke coming out of the dash." The half-inch Lexan windshields scratched and warped easily. The lights of oncoming traffic shattered into blinding spidery patterns, which made for terrible night driving. There were a hundred other pesky mechanical problems throughout the first shakedown season that required Sean's constant attention, to say nothing of the several fundamental design flaws that he hoped to address during the time I saw him that winter. The first involved the design and construction of the swiveling turret, to replace the removable side panels from last year. In a turret without a cannon, Sean would use his IMAX camera to shoot tornadoes from any angle. He climbed inside the TIV and popped his head through a circle of heavy-gauge steel.

"Devising this was a huge headache," he said. "I finally decided to build a big ring that sat on bearings. It's called a turret race." He began to describe the process of fabricating the turret race so that it would turn smoothly, even when 300 or 400 pounds of equipment were placed on it; as he spoke, the spiteful hillside neighbors, the larcenous teenagers, the defecating bums, the traffic flowing by on Cahuenga Boulevard, the rest of the world—all seemed to vanish in the particulars of the task at hand.

"*This* is going to be more polished, then I'm going to get new bearings and *these* are going to be seated *inside* so that *these bearings* are only sticking out a *half-inch. This rim* will now be down *there,* so it will have a lower profile. *Then* we make another ridge out *here* to keep out the rain, put a flange over *that,* then you have guides to hold *this* down. So if you hit a bump off the wind, you won't actually *take the sway.*" It was like an emphatic little poem from high school metal shop, a song about cutting and shaping and polishing and aligning and milling and truing an intractable material like steel into a shape that fit one's purpose, that said, in praise of the material, what the signs say at construction sites: "Steel is real."

The hydraulic system Sean would exchange for an air-bag suspension, the kind used by semitractor trailers and buses. He would add an escape hatch and cut a door on the passenger side. And the windshields would be replaced with a scratch-resistant tempered-glass/Lexan laminate. And he would carry his own portable welding and grinding equipment, so that he wouldn't have to sweet-talk a machine shop owner every time something snapped or needed refitting. There was a list of at least a dozen more major repairs or retrofits that needed attention, and countless minor details. I contemplated Sean for a moment and imagined him driving this gigantic silver tank into a small service station in Kansas and then emerging from his turret.

"Maybe you should come out wearing helmets?" I said.

"I'll show you the helmets," he said. "We had bicycle helmets last year, but they looked really uncool. We need to look cool in this vehicle, so we have black snowboarding helmets now. They're the sleekest-looking things in the operation."

The desire to look cool while emerging from a tank was something I hadn't considered. Coming from Sean Casey, a man in his mid-thirties, it was voiced through a scrim of irony, proffered for my amusement, a gesture toward the aesthetic imperatives of an eleven-year-old boy, say, who has sent away for a tank advertised in the back pages of *D.C. Comics* and is waiting impatiently by the mailbox, a sleek black snowboarding helmet snugly strapped under his chin. But it seemed also to be offered in recognition of the soundness (if not the momentary triumph) of that same perspective upon the humdrum world. It was the perspective of a person in a position to engage in a life of serious play, a life spent not in an office or a boardroom, with quotas to fill or deals to close, or a family to support, but a life given over to a perpetual summer camp, filled with ambitious backyard projects like the fabrication of a seven-ton armor-plated tank. Serious play combined the earnestness of the eleven-year-old with the protective ironies of adulthood, so it was not always easy to tell which perspective was in charge, especially when the child in question was sipping a beer or cutting plate steel with a blowtorch. Both seemed equally in the fore. They didn't cancel each other out, like a mere contradiction, but, like any true paradox, serious play created a third thing that told a truth about the world, a truth about any serious endeavor in science or art. For the moment, it was Sean Casey building and retrofitting the TIV, and then deciding that, when it came to the details of tank accoutrement, it only made sense to go all the way and look as cool as one could.

How all this was maintained was another question. "Maintained," as in "financed," "funded," "preserved against the eroding effects of adulthood." The answer lay in his father, George.

Everything about Sean spoke to a life that had been lived, from its earliest moments, on the margin. Graphic Films, for instance, was a marginal enterprise in a rarefied medium, whose cinematic subjects were almost exclusively out-of-your-seat natural disasters writ large on an IMAX screen, the movie equivalent of a carnival ride.

In 1956, after his discharge from the Army, George Casey became interested in making documentary-style recordings—first-person "you are there" LPs that focused on the lives of military personnel. *The G.I. Experience in Germany,* made in the early 60s, was such an offering. Film documentaries, such as *Vietnam with the American Fighting Man* (1965) soon followed. These views of war from a grunt's-eye view sold well in Army posts and at Navy and Air Force stations back home. Indeed, Casey demonstrated a nose for discrete, marginal markets—the first being in the posts and bases where service members brought their modest pay into the PX's (Army "post exchanges") and BX's (Navy and Air Force "base exchanges"). These government stores tended to feature off-brand, after-market inventories of retail items that nobody in their right mind would buy in the civilian world—clothing that had fallen out of fashion and government-issue forms of diversion. Who would have dreamed that there could be a market for what came to be known as military sound-off recordings—featuring Army grunts marching in unison while a drill instructor—like some sort of pioneering jar head rap artist—barked out an often bawdy, sometimes obscene, call-and-response cadence? Casey found and filled this unlikely niche with dozens of sound-off albums, boot camp documentaries, and compilations like *Music of the Army* and *Music of the Navy,* which one imagines being played loudly, against the welter of the world, in the homes of retired admirals and generals. By the time Sean was four years old, George Casey had diversified the military recordings portfolio into a second, similarly unheralded market in natural disaster. He purchased an inflatable viewing theater that sat around 300 people, called it the Omni Dome, and booked himself into state fairs and carnivals across the country. He had joined the mother of all marginal realms, the American carnival circuit.

Sean remembered traveling as a young boy with the Omni Dome. The family's bread and butter, for crowds that showed a preference for big, bright things that exploded, was a feature on erupting volcanoes. One early memory that seemed to sum up the family's carny life was Sean walking up to a miniature Doberman Pinscher that had been sitting by himself, and then, at his mother's urging, stealing him, more or less. They called the dog Clyde, and he became Sean's road companion. "There was a lot of hunter-gatherer, stuff-getting," Sean recalled, referring, probably, not so much to larceny as to the creative, ad hoc, carny way of patching their lives together and keeping things going. In the early 70s after purchasing a half-interest in Graphic Films, George Casey began making feature-length disaster films using IMAX technology, a 70mm film negative that increased the negative's size by a factor of nine and could project a steady, crisp moving image that was eight stories tall and one hundred feet wide. The viewer's field of vision was entirely surrounded, and with a sound system that matched the size of the screen, an IMAX film became a powerful simulation chamber by which a viewer seemed to "experience" rather than simply "watch" a film. Sean graduated from high school in San Diego, went to college, took a year off, then went to work in a cannery in Soldatna, Alaska. He worked fourteen-hour days and lived in a tent city amid gambling and drinking and guns and knives. In 1980, after the eruption of Mount St. Helens in Washington State, Sean's father spliced together a bunch of footage from the event, built a viewing theater and a gift shop close to the rain-bespattered town of Castle Rock, near the disaster site, and assigned Sean to manage both the theater and the gift shop. Thousands of people came, many of them retirees in recreational vehicles, and nearly all wanted to purchase some sort of memento of their Mount St. Helens visit. With *The Eruption of Mount Saint Helens* and its sequel, *Ring of*

Fire, and several other cinematic odes to the volcano, George had discovered his signature subject.

Sean became proficient with the IMAX camera and shot sequences for a number of his father's nature films. Sean climbed into a cage with scuba gear and filmed Great Whites for *The Search for the Great Sharks.* Once, submerged inside a cage, he watched, as a Great White began a large orbit around the cage, passing directly in front of him and then vanishing into the murk, then cruising back into view, turning this into a series of passes around the cage. Sean began to train the camera at the spot where the shark would reappear on its circuit, panning as the shark approached and passed in front of the cage, then vanished again. Presently, the shark appeared from the murk as before, then once again cruised by the cage, and again vanished from view. Then nothing. No shark. Sean looked up from the viewfinder—and then he turned around. The Great White was poised directly behind him. It had lulled him into an expectation, and then cunningly broken the pattern. "They're tricky," Sean said.

He was charged by grizzly bears on the Katmai Peninsula in Alaska, and he filmed a pod of feeding humpback whales while cruising among them in a Zodiac. "They start singing at a high pitch, which triggers a defensive mode in their prey. The lead whale then blows a bubble net, which drives the ball of bunched-up fish to the surface. Then the rest of the pod, following the lead whale, explodes to the surface, with their mouths extended wide. We placed microphones in the water, and when the lead whale's song ended, we knew we had about six seconds before they began rocketing upward all around us." Once, he saw a thirty-ton whale heading at speed from the depths directly underneath him. The whale swerved from the Zodiac at the last second. "They knew exactly where we were," he said.

Sean's was a career, it seemed, of close encounters, of seeking proximity to large and dangerous things, an adventurer's career. That's it, I thought. He was an adventurer. He sought out dangerous things to film and then screened them in a large format, so that we could have the experience indirectly. If his father's subject had been volcanoes, Sean would make his own mark, and in *Forces of Nature* (2004), he'd finally discovered his metier. Tornadoes asked the most of you. They were the most unpredictable, the most difficult, and probably the most dangerous thing on earth to film up close.

"*Forces of Nature* covers three subjects in forty minutes," Sean said. "When you subtract the opening and the ending, you have thirty-six minutes of running time, which, divided by three, leaves only twelve minutes each to cover volcanoes, earthquakes, and tornadoes." When it came to tornadoes, however, "twelve minutes didn't really tell the story."

He mentioned an earlier IMAX film called *Storm Chasers,* which, according to Sean, missed the mark. "They were out chasing and filming for four years, and they got one tornado, from about two miles away. It was a pretty tornado, but I don't think it really captured the whole feeling of the chase. And that's the challenge for us. We're trying to get the feeling of what it really is to chase tornadoes, like when you're driving towards the storm and you start to go underneath it—there's this feeling of being underneath this monster."

His idea was to film an entire forty-minute feature on storm chasing and tornado science, but when I met him that January, he had another plan as well. "The main thing, if the opportunity presented itself, would be to actually intercept," he said. "We would get the shot of the tornado coming right at you, filming it in IMAX, and then you impact it—that's something that no one has ever done." This seemed the very definition of a stunt, a "pseudo-event," historian Daniel Boorstin's term for an orchestrated occurrence, like sitting on a pole for weeks on end, whose meaning is ambiguous and whose sole reason for existence is that it be reported upon by the media. A tornado, you'll recall, is a cloud, a churning urn of dirt and human funk—not much to look at from the inside. The point was to capture the approaching shot and then its impact with the TIV, and then maybe some of the crazy, mixed-up interior jostling.

The ambiguity that would sustain the "intercept sequence" as a pseudo-event involved sensationalist drama woven into a fabric of scientific high purpose. There was, first, an absolute, sensationalist "first of a kind" hook, the one note guaranteed to draw a crowd. Watch me, O Reader, as I tear in half—*and then eat*—an entire phone book. Then, too, there was a healthy dose of voyeurism—the "eyewitness" appeal shared by everything from traffic accidents to snuff films. Sean's ideal footage, his money shot, was suffused with a bracing whiff of mortality that made it, potentially, both traffic accident *and* snuff film, would satisfy the implied contract with the viewer that had become, in our era and in almost every medium, the dominant dramaturgical mode. It said, *This shit is real.* It was a tornado. It was tornado pornography. It was torn porn.

Against all of this there was a countervailing scientific approach, a deliberate methodology that suggested Sean wasn't entirely crazy. He wasn't, for starters, going to drive the TIV into a violent tornado, as so many people on the chaser grapevine had suggested. Ideally, he would find the appropriate tornado—one that looked impressive but that did not have wind speeds in excess of 120 miles per hour. He would then position the TIV in its path. Finally, he would drive the TIV into a ditch to lower its profile, anchor it to the ground, and film whatever happened next.

His strategy, he explained, depended upon the goodwill and resources of Josh Wurman's Center for Severe Weather Research. On a typical storm, the center's two DOW radar trucks would set up a base line—here Sean took out a piece of paper—the radar dishes making a sweeping, three-dimensional stereo image of the storm, in real time, and able to read wind speeds, direction, and changes in intensity. These details would be reported to Sean on a two-way radio, as the TIV maneuvered the hatchwork of dirt roads on its approach.

Because of the height of the radar and because of ground clutter, the DOWs could not accurately read wind speeds at the lowest levels of a tornado. Wind speeds near the ground are ten to fifteen miles per hour faster. So there was some guesswork involved in determining the winds that Sean might actually face. But if the estimated wind speeds were 120 mph or less, and if the tornado was not intensifying, then Sean might decide to deploy the TIV—that is, to drive it into a ditch and start filming. Bad things could still happen. The worst scenario, he explained, would be if the tornado suddenly intensified, then hit the TIV broadside at the tornado's southwest quadrant, where the twister's own momentum across the terrain combined with its rotational speed to form winds of higher intensity.

"At that point," he said, "it would pick us up and probably toss us to the side. The vehicle weighs thirteen or fourteen thousand pounds, so it would take a real violent tornado to really pick us up." He tapped his pen on the paper. "That's what we're betting on."

The money for all this came from a boutique company that emerged out of his father's military documentary business. In 1997 Sean produced a video entitled *The Art of Camouflage,* which tapped into yet another unrecognized fringe market: the American mercenary dreamscape of gun-toting sharpshooters. A sequel, *The Art of Camouflage II,* was a big hit, and these successes prompted Sean to design a line of camouflage guerrilla wear that would be better—cooler—than anything the manly hunters of the world could make on their own and that they could purchase online through his Internet company, Bushrag.com. Such was the state of the world that despite the near wasteland of the dot-com marketplace, Bushrag.com flourished, thanks to a deep and seemingly bottomless vein of hunters, paintball enthusiasts, right-wing, antigovernment survivalists, and—who knows—perhaps a whole division of disillusioned war veterans who wished to remain forever hidden from view. The camouflage garments Sean designed were ghillie suits, jacket-and-pants combinations onto which long skeins of jute and burlap had been sewn in a piled mass of dreadlock "vegetation," so that the wearer looked like a shaggy creature emerging from a swamp. Sean came up with a catchy tag, "Be the Bush," which, indeed, accurately described the transformation when one climbed into a ghillie suit. They were a tremendous hit. Sean turned over the daily affairs of the company to a business partner and gave himself the job of designing new product lines—rifle covers, hunting blinds, sniper's veils—which left most of the year to build the TIV, and most of the spring, from May to the end of June, to chase and film tornadoes.

IN THE COMPETING world of ideas, voluntarily getting yourself run over by a tornado was a notion, you might assume, that could be claimed entirely for oneself—but in assuming this, you would be wrong. For in the spring of 2004, a new figure emerged from Mooresville, North Carolina, a stock car driver named Steve Green, who was nearing the completion of something called the Tornado Attack Vehicle, or TA-1. As its name implied, and in keeping with the ethos of stock car racing, Steve Green was not about to wait passively for a tornado but would aim his modified Baja trophy truck, which his website claimed could withstand winds of 260 miles per hour, and drive it directly "into the eye of a tornado." I'd had a few brief conversations with him over the phone in May 2004. I was hoping to meet the man and his vehicle before I started my own chase season, but the final modifications to the TA-1 had put him behind schedule. "I'm not a tornado chaser," he told me, out of the blue. "I'm a tornado hunter." The number of people in the *Twilight Zone* barrel-over-the-falls competition of tornado penetration, I realized, had doubled.

In Steve Green, the stock-car-racing culture was fully in evidence, perhaps no more vigorously than in his hot pursuit of corporate sponsorship. Here is the very first sentence on the homepage of his website, www.Tornado Attack.com: "Thank you for having the foresight and the vision to consider the following promotional and advertising opportunity." In a world of subtle advertising balderdash, this was as breathtakingly direct as a jump in the Gulf of Maine. The phrase "promotional and advertising opportunity" pretty much said it all about Steve Green and his project. Like other direct and honest statements, it had a weirdly compelling effect: "I shot a man in Reno, just to watch him die"; "Now I'm going to take your money from you." It said, without quibbling or finessing the point, that the entire program, the whole Steve Green enterprise, whatever he might say in the paragraphs to come about "the safe, scientific extraction of important new information," was a marketing ploy for Steve Green, by Steve Green, featuring Steve Green and your corporation driving head-on into a tornado. If you were a marketing or sponsorship opportunity, Steve Green would sit on your rear bumper, fill your rearview mirror, and draft you or your corporate logo until you were left in the dust or plastered all over his website, the way product lines and decals cover nearly every surface of a stock car driver's fireproof jumpsuit, from helmet to shoes—everywhere but the crotch and the eyes.

The initial press release, in April 2004, presented the project as a dazzling scientific mission. "Never before has man successfully entered the eye of a tornado in [*sic*] a scientific mission," the announcement said. Green, or his publicist, offered this observation: "If we can ever go beyond the barriers and discover the secrets at the eye of a tornado, we may begin to understand and predict their devastating and awesome behavior." The press release announced the participation of Joshua Wurman, whom I called to ask about a few things that puzzled me about Steve Green. Even though he is called a scientific adviser and is quoted in Green's press material, Wurman disavowed any relationship with Green. "He approached us first," Wurman said, "and he made a lot of promises about funding." According to Wurman, Green told him that millions of dollars of corporate sponsorship would be made available to his fledgling program. Wurman, though he remained dubious, kept the dialogue open, until it became clear that Green, in Wurman's words, "wasn't willing to be a team player." In scientific missions that involve dangerous storms and many different people, there has to be a framework of command and control, he explained. "It was the Apollo mission, *not* Neil Armstrong's mission," Wurman said. "If Mission Control instructed Neil Armstrong not to do something, Neil Armstrong followed that command." This didn't sit well with Green, who wasn't the sort of guy to be constrained by anybody, so Wurman broke off the relationship. Green, however, continued to cite Wurman as a consulting meteorologist. Wurman, for his part, was obliged to post a disclaimer on the website of his Center for Severe Weather Research. It may have been a little embarrassing for a serious scientist like Wurman to publicly distance himself from a man who seemed so transparently Barnum-esque. Some of the goals of Green's "Expedition into the Eye," for instance, seemed a little confused. "To record images of the internal phenomena of tornado activities" struck me as odd. What "internal phenomena," what "activities," would one hope to *see* in a whirling mass of mud? "Tornadoes," Joshua Wurman said, gently but firmly, "are clouds. I think everyone knows what the inside of a cloud looks like."

But if you could just push beyond that troublesome point, Steve Green wanted to take you on a coordinated assault that also involved rockets launched into and around "the circumference of the eye of the tornado," and a special "point of view" rocket to provide "a unique aerial view of the tornado's turbulent activities, including the eye." There was an almost fetishistic fixation upon one element of a tornado—the eye, a term that I personally never once heard used by any meteorologist—which seemed straight out of the movie *Twister,* itself an extended tornado penetration fantasy, the analysis of which I will leave to others. Suffice it to say that, like *Twister,* Green's fetish invested a tornado's interior with magical qualities, as if it were some scientific Brigadoon, wherein a tree of knowledge, containing answers to any number of life's difficult questions, hung magnificently suspended in the air. But the focus of actual, bona fide scientific research, Wurman assured me, was not upon the inside of a tornado, but upon its sur-rounding wind fields. In legitimate science, the "near environment" was where all the action was.

On Green's website, under the category "Media Opportunities," were five pages of text. Under "Scientific Study," there was one, which proved to be "Under Construction." "Media Opportunities" introduced six basic ways to spin "The Expedition into the Eye": "The Weather Element," "The Tor-nado Element," "The Pursuit of Knowledge Element," "The Public Safety Element," "The Daredevil Element," and something gamely called "The Integrity Element." This, of course, referred to the advances in science and the benefit to the public good that Green's project would support. That it was clumsy, wrong-headed, and fundamentally unscientific hardly mattered. The science was a necessary gesture, a winking assertion, like a moment of dialogue before the grinding and pumping can begin.

The veneer of "science" over Green's "unique marketing and promo-tional opportunity" was so thin and shabby that one was almost touched by the effort. There was so much souped-up overcompensation at play in his personality—he actually had a "life motto," which came in the form of an acronym, "L.I.F.E.," for "Live It For Everyone"—that I found myself unable to dislike him exactly. He seemed pathetic and emblematic in a way. If Steve Green were a country, he would have invaded Iraq: of this, I was certain. Maybe in a world of staggering duplicity, pathetic and emblematic in its own way, Steve Green's transparencies passed for a kind of stumbling honesty. Like the lies of a person incapable of lying, his facades were almost quaint enough to acquit him. All he wanted to do, after all, was face a beast, do battle, man against nature, and maybe make a little money. What could have been more American?

MAY 14, TWO days after Attica, was an official "down" day for the DOW crew, which meant that their trucks, their generators running, were parked at Norman municipal airport, next to the open bays of a hangar, a few Cess-nas sitting inside in various states of disassembly. Herb Stein was in his Mr. Fix-It mode, working his way down a long list of repairs printed on erasable whiteboard just inside the hangar bay.

I found Sean Casey sitting cross-legged on the tarmac surrounded by tools, his lip bulging with Skoal. Out of the opened lower side panels of the TIV he'd pulled several tool boxes, and from them hammers, wrenches, grinders, drills, extension cords, a blowtorch, a portable arc welder—the entire Mr. Goodwrench ensemble—seemed to spill. First he had turned to an aesthetic problem. Using his blowtorch, he'd cut from a piece of plate steel the handsome image of a tornado with a debris cloud, and this he'd welded onto the front grille. Next he'd addressed himself to the main business of the day, which was to install meteorological instrumentation. Sean held in his left hand an ultrasonic anemometer, to which he was affixing a small metal grate with a kind of black glue that he was squeezing out of a caulking gun. This he would attach to a six-foot metal pole anchored to the back of the TIV. From a "T" at the top of the pole, he would also attach an antenna array—one antenna for communicating with the other DOW personnel, another for sending and receiving meteorological "data packets," and a third for an "asset locating and tracking device" christened by its elbow-swinging inventors the Fugawi, as in "Where the Fugawi?"

Past the shadows of the enormous hangar, in the glaring sunlight outside, the DOW trucks sat parked on the tarmac, their white-cube compartments, muscle-bound radars, and revving 12.5-kilowatt generators in stark contrast to the TIV, with its funny junkyard angles, bulging snout, and generally homemade look. With this riotous visual incongruity as backdrop, as if a clown car had sneaked on to Cape Canaveral, Josh Wurman handed Sean Casey the tools by which a loose, informal relationship would be transformed into something more official. If Wurman represented the aims and methods of a bona fide research operation, Sean had, until now, remained a freelancing camp follower, using the DOW trucks to suit his purposes, providing entertainment to the troops. Unofficially, he and his TIV were good for morale. The TIV's homemade quality, combined with Sean's earnest daily efforts to try to keep it from falling to pieces, made for a very winning combination. Sean had earned the respect of Wurman, who thought of him as a hard worker, which he was. He was well liked among the DOW crew. His ethos of serious play sat well with the younger volunteers. Motel-room parties and after-hours high jinks such as the now famous Affair of the Red Mohawk sealed the deal. No matter how bad things got with the DOWs—

hardware and software failures and trucks breaking down in the middle of nowhere—one could always turn to the TIV for a bit of comic relief. When the TIV wasn't on fire, or stuck in a ditch, or being detained by the local police, when the TIV finally arrived after some spectacular delay, its arrival, it must be said, was like the entry of a team mascot into an arena, an oversized event for attention-starved meteorologists waiting around for the weather to shape up. It was, moreover, just the combination of exaggerated features, of cuddliness with aggressiveness—like a fighting marmot staring boldly into the wind, ready to take on all comers—that made Sean and the TIV the right mascot for the DOW crew. When he arrived, he did so with his head sticking through the hatch, in black goggles, like the intrepid commander of a parade float honoring Murphy's law.

But he was more than a mascot, of course, and he knew it. He brought to the table a tremendous public relations opportunity for Wurman's new research company, as Wurman's appearance in *Forces of Nature* already made clear. Moreover, Sean planned to chronicle an ambitious field research project, a follow-up to the 1995 study entitled "Verification of the Origins of Rotation in Tornadoes Experiment" or VORTEX. The new study, a mammoth two-year effort called VORTEX II, would become the driving narrative of his own full-length IMAX film. Wurman, who was a member of the steering committee for VORTEX II, had an interest in keeping severe local storms research in the public eye. It made sense, in other words, to bring Sean and the TIV into the fold. Therefore, the TIV would be outfitted with meteorological instruments. As an armored vehicle sending valuable near environment data to the DOWs, the TIV would enter the realm of bona fide science.

Part of that transformation was under way in the airport hangar, as Wurman handed Sean a white cylinder about a foot long, a temperature and humidity sensor, that had been express-mailed from Boulder. Josh also pulled from a box a tangled-up length of wire, which he gave to Sean.

"This was the cable that came with what you ordered," Josh said, "but we decided it was too short. But I think this is the part that goes into your data logger. See that? That little circuit board?"

"Yes," Sean said from behind his dark sunglasses, holding his newly acquired temperature and humidity sensor like a fat baton—or a battlefield commission sealed in bubble-wrap.

DOW trucks, their radar in the transport position, and the Tornado Intercept Vehicle (TIV) on May 16, 2004, in York, Nebraska. © Kenneth F. Dewey/The High Plains Regional Climate Center

I followed Sean back to the TIV, which gave me another view of the strange disparity between it and the DOW trucks, a disparity that did not resolve itself as one got closer. Steve Green's Tornado Attack Vehicle, though a bit strange, looked like the product of a crew of professionals—a pit crew capable of turning out a $300,000 musclebound SUV fantasy. There was a precision in every feature, in every weld, in every measured part, that spoke of work done to the close tolerances that made doors and hatches and hoods spring open gladly and close with a satisfyingly solid, metallic *click*—something almost German, which seemed to look at you and laugh. It was a machine that had its shit together. How strange, then, that in the weeks to come, Green in his competent car would appear the crazy one, while Sean Casey, with his rattling behemoth held together with baling wire, this oddity of the road with its faulty taillights and smoking dashboard, would somehow back its way into scientific legitimacy. That the TIV now appeared, along with DOW 2, DOW 3, and the Scout vehicle as a blip on the screen of the Fugawi monitor, that it was considered an "asset" by a scientific project funded by the National Science Foundation, signaled an unanticipated and significant change in Sean's mission since I'd first interviewed him in January.

Back at the TIV, in the bright sunshine, with the DOW generators humming away, Sean sat down once again with his glue gun and his anemometer.

"Maybe I'm a scientist," he said at last.

There it was again. Without the "maybe," the voice one heard was of someone you may have long forgotten—a childhood voice, an undisguised voice capable of great leaps of faith. With the addition of the "maybe," however, you heard an adult mooning around wistfully. It was another modest joke, offered for my benefit, but it was also an admission of the transformation, one that included a new stipulation:

"We had to agree that we wouldn't intercept a tornado," Sean said, "and we had to revise the mission statement on our website to reflect that change."

After a while, Wurman came by to inspect the installation. He didn't like what he saw. The instrument package needed to be higher, he said, to avoid the heat and wind turbulence created by the TIV moving down the road. He asked Sean to adjust the position of the anemometer and then moved on, dialing a number on his cell phone as he walked away.

"Maybe I'm *not* a scientist," Sean said.

Whatever he was, one thing was certain. He drove a curious machine. It made people step forward toward it. It was a bit like the circus coming to town, every time he stopped. And this, too, was something he enjoyed about being on the road. Maybe he was a carny at heart, on tour once again. He joked that perhaps his most important job was to divert attention from the DOW trucks, so that the real scientists could get their work done. Or maybe he was just a guy, approaching forty, who'd found a sly way to give voice to something that had scooted past the daily thicket of tasks he gave himself, jobs that involved steel fabrication and electrical wiring, and figuring out how to not get killed by a tornado. After these more immediate concerns, it was admittedly second- or third-tier stuff that may have occasionally swung around him like a breeze around a wind sock—stuff about who, in fact, he was and why he sat with a caulking gun next to a giant silver tank.

FOUR

Catastrophilia

Only a catastrophe gets our attention. We want them, we need them,
we depend on them. As long as they happen somewhere else.
—DON DELILLO, *WHITE NOISE*

Pray send me some storms.
—MARY MACLANE, 1902

Every map is an overview—or an overthrow, a usurpation of God's point of view, looking downward upon creation. Consider William Clark, bending over a map he is making of the territory west of the Mississippi that he, Meriwether Lewis, and the Corps of Discovery have traversed and named. Their journey, epic in every sense, has led to this map, currently under construction, this instrument, this tool, which changes him and us—as every terra does that becomes cognita. From here on, with the outlines demarcated, so much is foreknown, foregone that even big surprises—of gold and silver, zinc and copper, and the rushes thereto—are contained within a box, a frame, a purview, a map, of conquest and dominion. Places get staked and named: Neversweat, Anaconda, Amalgamated Copper.

Every landscape, by contrast, is an embrace of a different, humbler spatial rhetoric, a looking through, often upward, from the limited, land-borne position of human perspective and human vulnerability. Nearly a hundred years after the journey of Lewis and Clark, a young woman wanders the slag heaps and sulfurous wastes surrounding Butte, Montana. Her name is Mary MacLane and she sees all around her direct evidence of the harsh consequences of Clark's map, of the limitations of "progress." Her diary, which becomes a best-selling book, is written from the point of view of that desolate landscape. It is like a minor note, heard against the resounding back-drop of a major chord. For we have favored one view over the other, the map over the landscape, the major to the minor chord. The map's legacy, the legacy of the Enlightenment, the sense of custodianship of the natural world, a sense of orderliness, of historical linearity, of progress, of culture moving forward in a glorious series of ever-increasing material improve-ments, what the naturalist David Quammen has called the cult of utility, has been our dominant trope. It's not hard to see why. Perhaps, staring up in awe at the stars, for instance, one can say only so much before one starts to shiver and look around for a blanket, or a cave, or a fire.

In 1858, a visitor to Washington, D.C., could have observed on any given day a sizable crowd entering the Smithsonian to view what the institution's annual report called "an object of much interest"—not a fossil skeleton of a Tyrannosaurus, nor an exhibit of North American beetles, but a "large map of the condition of the weather over a considerable portion of the United States."[1] It was a weather map, the first of its kind to be placed on public dis-play. Weather information gathered by citizen scientists, volunteer observers of temperature and pressure and wind direction, from more than 300 reporting stations was sent by telegraph and then displayed on the large map. "Circular disks of different colors . . . were attached to it by pins at each station of observation, and indicated by their color the state of the atmosphere—white signifying clear weather; gray, cloudy; black, rain, etc." It was by far one of the Smithsonian's most popular exhibits.

In a world where geographic distances were still significant barriers between people, the weather map must have seemed a wonder. The rail-roads were up and running, of course, though the transcontinental link was almost a decade away. It still took an entire day by train to get from Wash-ington to New York City, though a system of telegraph cables was linking distant cities along the Eastern Seaboard and extending westward. The first, partially successful attempt at laying an undersea telegraph cable had occurred two years earlier, William Thomson, later Lord Kelvin, himself supervising the great rolls of insulated cable dropping to the bottom of the ocean; but telegraphy was new and underdeveloped. American newspapers received reports from abroad as they arrived on steamships like the *Prince Albert,* which docked at St. Johns, Newfoundland, at five o'clock in the morning, June 5, 1860, delivering, with its cargo, a flurry of news, relayed as soon as it arrived by telegraph to *The New York Times,* whose headlines, for two cents, one could read two days later, on June 7:—Garibaldi entering Palermo; trouble with the Reform Bill; rumors that the French ambassador to Turkey would soon publish a speech "of an alarming nature"; and horse racing results (Umpire, "long distanced by the winner, Thormanby"). Though the *Times* trumpeted this international "News by Telegraph . . . Two Days Later from Europe," the news was actually almost two weeks old.[2]

Not that that was a big secret. The reader of the *Times,* in all likelihood, took into account the two-week lag as one might factor in extra time for a crosstown errand. The lapse was part of a set of assumptions about reality that made the present more of a mystery than it is today. As one stood on Forty-second Street and read that Garibaldi had entered Palermo two weeks ago, it was anybody's guess where Garibaldi was at the moment. What a wonder, then, to have this filter removed. On the Smithsonian map, people watched as the color-coded weather disks, stamped with wind direction arrows, were turned to provide the viewer with what must have been, at the time, an exotic feeling of modernity: the awareness "of weather which . . . friends at a distance are experiencing," the simultaneity of experience across the impossibly great distances of the American continent, of electronic pulses traveling over telegraph, providing "live data," as the Smithsonian's annual report called it—an indication, at the present moment, as one stood in front of that great map and tapped one's umbrella on the floor or whistled quietly through one's teeth, of which way the wind was blowing, right now, in Duluth or Chicago or St. Louis. The phenomenon of "weather citizenship," an awareness of the breath and pulse of the body politic, had been born.

If the history of cartographic reckoning in America, beginning with Clark, for example; continuing with the Smithsonian weather map; and culminating with satellite images of clouds moving eastward across the country—everything leading up to our own era—the slow rendering of a continent by exploration and conquest, if this history resounds like the major chord that it is, the dominant motif, we have also heard the opposing motif sounded by artists like Frederic Edwin Church, the most popular landscape painter of his day, who, in the same year as the Smithsonian weather map exhibit, was displaying in New York City a new painting called *The Heart of the Andes.*

For the last three weeks of its New York exhibition, nearly five hundred people per day had come to see Church's primordial vista, with its almost suffocating tropical density and impossibly rendered detail. *The Heart of the Andes* was a sort of cathedral of the grand biome, an overt homage to the great naturalist Alexander von Humboldt, whose famed South American expedition, lasting from 1799 to 1804, Church had recently retraced. Humboldt, perhaps the most famous scientist of his time, was also the last great scientist to propose that the natural world was driven by a process of universal harmony infusing all things, including a unity of purpose in science and art. This unifying principle would soon be shaken by Charles Darwin and Alfred Russel Wallace, two men who had nevertheless been profoundly influenced by Humboldt. Their nearly simultaneous discovery of the mechanism governing the progress and evolution of species, not divinely orchestrated but the result of intense competition, nature red in tooth and claw, stamen and pistil, would of course pit science against religious doctrine. The evolutionists' work, however, would also help widen the gap for many between science and art, especially as the nineteenth century progressed and art became more like an inadvertent last refuge for those whose faith had been shaken but had not quite given up the ghost. *The Heart of the Andes,* and most of Church's subsequent giant landscapes, had a jaw-dropping grandeur that seemed to echo the imperatives of a powerful and abiding movement of millennialist Christian thought in America. Landscape satisfied an eschatological yearning or expectation about the progress of history: that it was moving forward toward an end of days.

In the millennialist view, the great cosmic struggle between God and the powers of darkness was superimposed onto the American landscape, which was as much a religious as a political experiment and whose end had been revealed in the Book of Revelations. Some millennialists, like the Shakers, the Mormons, and the Jehovah's Witnesses, believed that the end of the world was a prelude to a state separate from the fallen realm and under divine rule. But the most popular form of millennialism, as the historian Ernest Lee Tuveson observes, was "progressive and optimistic," more in accordance with the notion of an achievable utopia, a heaven on earth, in which good was "destined to triumph in the world at large."[3] Herman Melville gave voice to this view in *White Jacket:* "We are the pioneers of the world; the advance-guard, sent on through the wilderness of untried things, to break a new path in the New World that is ours."[4] Terrible tribulation lay ahead, of course, but it would be a crucible from which an American utopia would emerge, with Americans, as the *Presbyterian Quarterly Review* declared, the "engineers of the mighty machinery."

Church sought to overwhelm the viewer with scale. As one entered the exhibition room, the eye fell upon a painting almost always singly displayed, which seemed, by a careful manipulation of available light, to glow as if one were looking through a window. With *The Heart of the Andes,* the illusion was enhanced by a walnut frame, ornately carved but not, as was traditional, gilded, so that it was very dark, more like the surrounding interior, which was just the point. At nearly thirteen feet tall by fourteen feet wide, Church's "frame" was really more of a proscenium, installed on the ground and giving the effect of a very large window casement and sill, complete with curtains and offset with tropical potted plants. It was a vehicle for reverie. Church's agent for the picture, a Scot named John McClure, was not above a few Barnumesque touches. The booklets available for purchase—an old road-show gimmick contributing to revenue—were written in the style of a travelogue, to underscore the expeditionary feeling. Visitors were "requested to bring Opera Glasses," one newspaper notice read. Samuel L. Clemens did just that when the painting made its way to St. Louis, and he truly seemed to enjoy the illusion the glasses gave of casting one's eye over a stunning vista.

The disturbing tremors visible in Church's work made themselves most strongly felt in paintings such as *Twilight of the Wilderness,* a moody piece dominated by an American sky. As the United States pitched headlong toward a civil war, the painting seemed to pose, without answering, a monumental question that began with Jonathan Edwards, Joseph Priestley, Joseph Bellamy, and Samuel Hopkins. It continued unabated throughout the nineteenth century. Melville, returning from one of his sea voyages, commented upon it. This cautionary, speculative note, one filled with eschatological expectation, was fine in a darkened gallery, where one could indulge a retrograde, antinomial impulse that cast a shadow upon the vanity of human pursuits, as had

Thomas Cole's earlier series *The Course of Empire* and John Ruskin's pessimistic essay "The Storm Cloud of the Nineteenth Century." But this impulse could not be sustained as one stepped back into the bedazzling light of nineteenth-century discovery and political expansion.

The cult of awe has Increase Mather as its prototypical figure, a man whose ravenous curiosity about scientific discovery was, nevertheless, yoked to an eschatological yearning. For Mather, and the great trend of millennialist thought that followed him, history, if it progressed, did so with a clear end, a Rapture, an End of Days; in this scheme, nature offered a series of apocalyptic revelations. The cult of utility, by contrast, was a Deist vision, which saw man as nature's steward, governing and marshaling nature indefinitely, and as the dominant cultural view for two hundred years, it has taken us very far. Perhaps too far. As Bill McKibben notes in *The End of Nature,* wilderness, the wild untamed natural world, seems largely to have vanished, to have been driven out by the imperatives of the cult of utility—all the great rivers dammed, the forests harvested like Christmas-tree farms, the so-called "wilderness areas" overflown by commercial aircraft and helicopters.

The dream of absolute knowledge may not have been fulfilled, but the fear of its arrival is consonant with the anxiety of a vanishing wilderness. And while no place on earth may now properly be called wild, there is one thing in nature that we as a culture seem to have reclaimed, and now celebrate as "wild," and that thing is the weather, especially severe weather. Indeed, violent storms give the lie to the Laplacean fantasy of control, revealing the boundlessness of nature, its sheer unpredictability, its daunting scale.

The fact is, we wanted both the map and the landscape. We wanted the major and the minor chord. We wanted to be Oz and to be Dorothy, to awe and to be awed. In the morning, we want the descendant of the Smithsonian weather map, the Weather Channel, to tell us whether it's raining in Cincinnati, and at the close of day we want to bundle up and watch a hurricane swallow part of the Eastern Seaboard on *Storm Stories.* How else explain the proliferation of severe-weather drama? Why do we seem to crave images of houses being lifted off the ground by tornadoes, of seaside resorts being smashed to pieces by the winds and shouldering waves of a hurricane? How else explain the Weather Channel itself? Not just a show, but an entire television network—with nearly 86 million regular viewers, almost one-third of the American public—dedicated to the passing clouds, to a subject that, heretofore, has almost universally signaled the arrival of conversational filler, if not conversation's actual death. How close to Frederic Church was someone like Sean Casey, his IMAX film an updated entry into the jaw-dropping machinery of awe. And we couldn't seem to get enough of it.

All of this is to say that the sublime is as American as apple pie, though it has taken perhaps two hundred years, and a momentary, cautionary pause at the beginning of the third millennium, for us to hear it, to recognize it, and to consider it, again.

The sublime is an "emotional response," as the classics scholar Glenn W. Most defines it, "combining in some way joy, terror, and exaltation, to something that seems so entirely to transcend either our own, or else all human, capabilities, that it overwhelms our normal petty instincts for self-preservation and self-aggrandizement, and instead fills us with a sense of exaltation."[5] As a category of emotional experience, the sublime was a late refinement in human history, attributed to Dionysius Longinus, about whom nothing is known. Even the date of his Treatise on the Sublime—somewhere in the first century C.E.—is based mostly on a guess.[6] The treatise was a slender handbook of the rhetorical arts, intended for young first-century Romans ascending to power and influence. What distinguishes Longinus from other writers in this common genre, according to Most, is Longinus' general assertion, odd for a manual of style, that the sublime cannot be taught, that one is essentially born with the capacity to evoke the sublime, or not. His treatise thus becomes not so much a how-to manual for writers and orators as it is a reader's lament for an era that seemed to have lost its way, to have gotten out of the habit of greatness, and that needed someone, Longinus perhaps, to remind it that greatness once existed, and that it could be found again, mostly in fits and starts, by means of the transformative encounter with sublime writers of the past.

What saved Longinus from the dustbin of history was a liberal adaptation by Nicolas Boileau Desperaux in 1674 that shed the cumbersome rhetorical analysis of the original and framed the entire subject of the sublime in such a way that Longinus' sense of transformative emotional encounter could be applied to phenomena other than literature. From this pivotal moment, the sublime was recast to include, for our purposes, powerful encounters with the natural world. Enter Wordsworth and the whole Romantic movement, followed by the post-Romantic gumbo of Victorian verse, in which awe in the presence of the sublime seemed to have degenerated into a cult of the pretty and agreeable. Then, following the First World War, came the great correction of Modernism, in which the beautiful and the sublime were thrown out with the bathwater, supplanted, it seemed, by a mode of ironic distance and detachment that continues to this day.

Or does it? Isn't our particular historical moment one in which Longinus' message in a bottle finally seems to have washed ashore? And doesn't his treatise, written from the point of view of someone surrounded by the banalities and quotidian material comforts of empire (first-century Greece under Roman rule), seem the very substance of late-phase, imperious American disaffection? Nowhere does Longinus complain about the comforts that the Roman occupation brought to his native Greece, but, as Glenn Most observes, these comforts, like our own, "do not satisfy his deepest yearnings—yearnings for passion, excitement, and just a little danger." The sublime offered Longinus an escape hatch out of a world that he believed had seen the best of times come and go. The sublime was a mode of compensation and consolation, a form of distraction from "real world" matters over which he felt he had little control.

Here was a mode invented in antiquity and disquietingly consonant with our own era; here a hitherto lost, unarticulated mechanism of transcendence, that seemed now to emerge in odd, unexpected ways—with people climbing into their automobiles, for instance, and driving across the Plains for weeks at a time, consuming meals, consuming nonrenewable fossil fuels, killing time, as it were, in pursuit of violent storms. Perhaps by doing so, storm chasers had inadvertently rediscovered the Longinian sublime, adding their own participatory spin by making it a marginal form of hardcore recreation, like rock climbing or big-wave surfing, from the tradition of intrepid exploration. They pursued, by means of direct encounter with oversized natural phenomenon, an initiation into the nameless song, the life-altering battlefield moment of clarity that temporarily transcended the quotidian world, and from which one emerged a changed person.

The Longinian sublime carries a burden. It is not the burden, for instance, of the Lewis and Clark expedition's outward journey across the limitless expanse of wilderness, not the journey itself, not the daily encounters with the unknown, but the burden that emerges after the discovery of the landscape's limit, its *boundedness,* and with it the inescapable "sense of ending." The burden of the explorer is that, by right of discovery, after one has survived to reach the waters of the Pacific, say, one enters forever into the mode of the predicate, the mode of consequences, where everyone and everything is forever and always after the fact. Some adjust better than others; we note ruefully, at times with disbelief, Meriweather Lewis's slow dissolution into promises that he simply cannot keep—promises to compile, edit, and complete his journals, which languish for years; promissory notes made for debts incurred. For one grown used to the present progressive, life in the predicate world hurt.

How strange it must have been for the actual Corps of Discovery to reach the Pacific and feel the peculiar burden of modernity fall upon them like shackles, as light as page flutter. The atmosphere or precondition that allows for the Longinian sublime is suffused with this sense of ending. One feels it in one's bones, as William Clark first sights the waters of the Pacific Ocean, and the end of the continental landmass, in November of 1805. "Ocien [*sic*] in View!" he says, mistaking the mouth of the Columbia for the wide waters of the Pacific. "O, the Joy." The celebration was short-lived, for soon the realization took hold that there was nothing left for these men of action but the long homeward slog—and this, of course, only after sitting out a miserable Pacific Northwest winter, with game scarce, their clothes rotting off their backs. His co-commander and friend Lewis was lost in another bout of melancholia. Can there be any doubt as to why? Everyone was growing testy, irritable; Clark, who rarely complained about anything, soon began griping about the weather. It says something, too, that he kept himself busy that winter with his maps, with drawing and rendering the expedition's progress through a wilderness busy with birdsong and death. The clouds offered no relief, no view beyond themselves, no break from the raw, bone-chilling dampness. The natives living along the Columbia River were unimpressed. To them, Clark's men looked and behaved like beggars; they ate dogs; they talked big but they traveled through hostile territory not as men did—in a war party—but with a woman and her infant son, that is, with what might be better understood as a human shield; as gifts, they offered trinkets, not guns; worse, they were debtors, would soon enough become thieves; they had absolutely no skill with the canoe. Clark spent much of that dismal winter taking solace, it seems, in the realm of the cartographic overview, his maps revealing a mind able—perhaps "determined" is the better word—to place itself, like some proto-satellite fixed upon the western half of North America, as if he were a hundred miles above the perpetual sound of wind and rain, above it all.

For Longinus the only means of escaping the predicament of the predicate is to recast oneself, by means of a plunge into past literature. We have that option, too, and the journals of Lewis and Clark have been handy instruments. There we find ourselves alongside the Corps of Discovery on the westward journey in the present progressive, with everything still possible, the Northwest Passage, the Lost Tribes of Israel, the pot at the end of the rainbow, the Garden of Eden before the Fall. But we also have our automobiles, which allow us our portion of the present progressive—like a boxful of nowhere—hours or days suspended beyond the predicate, driving like Sean Casey with his IMAX camera, like some latter-day Frederic Church, preparing his own large-format celluloid canvas of the American sublime.

This is why the Lewis and Clark Expedition captivates us so: the filtering of all experience through a mediating, consumerist lens has become the fact and frame of our era, the inadvertent consequence of more than three hundred years of technological progress that originally sought to carve out of the wilderness enough comfort and ease to make the lives of Americans like Lewis and Clark a little more bearable. Now, it seemed, we'd come full circle, to hunger for retrograde living—or at least, we want to watch as others sail a replica of Captain Cook's eighteenth-century vessel the *Endeavour*, or don Confederate garb and engage, over the weekend, with the Army of the Potomac, or, in the case of the show *Survivor*, are sent to some island in the South Pacific to live off bugs. Or we want to build a vehicle that can survive a tornado. With our poets and novelists, once we have cornered them at a party, we tend to drop the pretensions of art, with respect to the imagination, to ask of one particular scene after another, "Did that *really* happen?" We save our most fervent applause at the Academy Awards for the nervously nodding older couple, everyone now rising in tears from their seats, *on whose actual lives the movie was based*! As we've become increasingly insulated from the physical world, the weather, the shifting of air masses, the ever changing atmosphere, has become one of the few things that seems solid in an increasingly ephemeral world. The craze for "reality" television programming, and the subgenre of weather-related disaster programming, belies a fascination with the real that would seem little more than a final, inevitable debasement if it weren't also symptomatic of a cultural shift, a yearning for sublime experience.

Maybe it's not the sublime that we're after—but a certain proximity to it. Not our near-death experience, but somebody else's. Catastrophe creates a sudden suspension, a reduction of every sort of rule, or protocol, or system of manners, or system of class distinction, or law. The catastrophe genre, so well illustrated by a book like Sebastian Junger's *The Perfect Storm,* for instance, illuminates a world within a world—a horrific ad hoc clinical trial, an experiment that no law would allow, nor would anyone willingly subject themselves to, whereby all is laid bare to the rude deterministic facts of survival and how that gets managed, heroically or unheroically. Call it the cult of proximity, where, if there is a mystery to be discovered, it is one that travels, spatially, from the map view, that first and widest view possible, down an ever narrowing perspectival plunge that takes us closer than even dreams can go. We get a hint of the trajectory at the book's outset: "How do men act on a sinking ship?" Junger asks. "Do they hold each other? Do they pass around the whiskey? Do they cry?" The narrative that follows is a gripping setup for a final, imagined plunge into the very bodies of the drowning crew members of the *Andrea Gail.* It all happens in a chapter called "The Zero-Moment Point," which contains an epigraph from the book of Revelations: "Behold, a pale horse, and his name who sat on him was Death, and Hell followed with him." Everything has been leading up to this climactic point where the *Andrea Gail* is finally crushed by a rogue wave. Normally a writer would take us to the tipping point, as it were, and then turn away from its gruesome particularities, allowing a few scraps from the wreckage to float to the surface, but Junger extends the climax below the waves, lets the water rise up inside the blackness of the sinking vessel, past the chest, past the neck, and then he pushes it further still, investing the entire second half of his chapter with a detailed forensic drama inside the body of a drowning victim, like some sort of fantastic voyage. "When the first involuntary breath occurs," he writes, "most people are still conscious, which is unfortunate, because the only thing more unpleasant than running out of air is breathing water. At that point the person goes from voluntary to involuntary apnea, and the drowning begins in earnest." *Do go on,* some dark little gremlin inside of me commands, and of course Junger complies. "A spasmodic breath drags water into the mouth and windpipe, and then," Junger writes, "one of two things happen."

Reader, do you want to continue from here? Do you really want to know what those one or two things are for a drowning person? Well, you'll have to read *The Perfect Storm* to find out, because I'm not going to tell you. And when you read *The Perfect Storm,* if you haven't already, you'll be waiting for this moment, because you'll want to know. You'll need to know. You have a stake in this. And when you look up from its pages, as I did, your face a little hot, your palms sweaty, as mine were, in sympathetic somatic response to *laryngospasm* and *ventricular fibrillation* alike, then you'll feel like the narrative trajectory has brought you very close, indeed, "as close as one is going to get," Junger writes, "to the last moments of the *Andrea Gail.*" Some critics took Sebastian Junger to task for taking us right down to the level of oxygen-starved alveoli in the lungs, the "grape-like clusters of membrane on the lung wall," but to me this seems but a logical and ever so slight extension of the cult of proximity's imperative to get as close as possible to the action. And by action, as the epigraph from Revelations suggests, we mean death, the mystery and mini-apocalypse that awaits us all.

Nowhere, of course, does *The Perfect Storm,* or any of a dozen other popular accounts of catastrophe ask why they—and we—are so drawn to this sort of last, desperate moment. Asking that question is like turning the house lights up to expose the ropes and pulleys, the catwalks high above the audience, the backdrops and trap doors of the genre contraption deployed. But an entirely different sort of mystery emerges when one notices these things. The secret goal of all catastrophe writing is this: to bring us as close as possible, by proxy, to the edge of an abyss, and thereby render the world changed, an aftermath, as if to say, by way of conclusion, Yes, the world is tragic, but at least it is not banal. "Ours is indeed an age of extremity," Susan Sontag wrote in an issue of *Commentary,* in October 1965. "For we live under continual threat of two equally fearful, but seemingly opposed destinies: unremitting banality and inconceivable terror."[7] Perhaps now, the terror seems more proximate than the Cold War era threat of nuclear annihilation. But who among us would doubt that the "unremitting banality" that Sontag addressed forty years ago, in the spirit of the conditional, does not seem more than ever a "fearful destiny" that has come to pass?

Perhaps what's needed is to breathe life back into the sublime by recognizing what it is and then supplying a new term for its bastard cousin. In his essay, Most provides a passage from Don DeLillo's *White Noise* (1985), in which a family is watching television. The passage below made me stand up.

> *That night, a Friday, we gathered in front of the set, as was the custom and the rule, with take-out Chinese. There were floods, earthquakes, mud slides, erupting volcanoes. We'd never been so attentive to our duty, our Friday assembly. Heinrich was not sullen, I was not bored. Steffie, brought close to tears by a sitcom husband arguing with his wife, appeared totally absorbed in these documentary clips of calamity and death. . . . We were otherwise silent, watching houses slide into the ocean, whole villages crackle and ignite in a mass of advancing lava. Every disaster made us wish for more, for something bigger, grander, more sweeping.*

What emerges here is a phenomenon without a name. This is not a desire for the sublime, but something closer to a penchant for catastrophe—if catastrophe were a flavor of ice cream. To name it, we need something with a little meat, a little fear, but not too earnest, either, something like a wink to acknowledge a world at every point mediated by irony, a term of art whose signature we recognize in disaster films, or any version thereof—in the blanket coverage of war or weather on CNN or Fox; in the hurricane, in the flood, in the tornado—in the slowing down of traffic on a highway, in the combined and collective sense of anticipation and detachment of DeLillo's characters as they sit on the couch watching television, a scene which, by quick substitution could just as easily take place on a bench seat in a car that is approaching the hissing roadside flares of an accident, a car up-ended in a ditch. See the turn of the head, the complicit gaze, as of someone watching drive-by pornography. Now a tornado is bearing down upon a hamlet in South Dakota named Manchester. In a few moments, Manchester, the tiny town, will no longer exist. Maybe you should care more than you do, but the spectacle of the real does not allow much time for this. The condition's name is catastrophilia, and just now, before the commercial break, another vista of destruction heaves into view.

Catastrophilia is the packaged and commodified version of the Longinian sublime. It is the discovery in the violence of natural phenomena of a marketable product. And it is the marketing and sale of that product, natural disaster, for public consumption. Its signature formal element is the presence of a frame—a television set, a windshield, or side-view window, a camera shutter, a video lens, a picture frame, some form of semipermeable barrier that creates the illusion of involvement yet provides the safety of distance, of detachment—that allows irony to slip in, and direct consequence for the individual to slip out. It is the distance between oneself and the shirt one wants to buy. The frame creates the sense of spectacle, through which one sees but does not participate. One can walk away as one pleases, press down on the accelerator, change the channel, and the entire situation—the destruction of Manchester—evaporates as if it had never existed in the first place.

Frederic Church may have made enough money from his paintings to retire to Olana, his rococo dream mansion in the Hudson River Valley, but he was still a believer. He was sophisticated enough, perhaps, to cast his belief alongside the nagging doubts and anxieties about the course of history—where it hung, in delicate abeyance, in the clouds. In doing so he was dramatizing a belief forged through its negotiation and struggle with doubt. It was an engagement with history. He believed in something. He wasn't a peddler. And that's the basic difference. Catastrophilia is decoupled from any sort of vision. It is an absolute end, a phenomenological cul-de-sac, a sideshow tent, presenting a dead-end tautology, like a dog with five legs, or like a celebrity—famous because it is famous. It offers a distraction from history, rather than an engagement with it.

A closer catastrophilic model exists if we let the odometer advance ever so slightly into the twentieth century, to 1902, in which year was published Mary MacLane's bestselling debut memoir, written when she was nineteen.

Catastrophilia has its queen, its earliest practitioner-paragon, in MacLane, the original title of whose book, *I Await the Devil's Coming,* seemed calculated to deliver a resounding shock to a bourgeois America already steeped in its own, multifarious forms of Christian eschatological yearning. Substitute "Christ" for the "devil" and you get a sense of the sort of popular millennialist tract that was passed around Christian reading groups of the time. *I Await the Devil's Coming* was published under a new title, *The Story of Mary MacLane—By Herself,* and sold 100,000 copies in the month. She became an instant sensation.

Mary MacLane was born in Winnipeg, in 1881; her family moved to Minnesota, and then, after the death of her father, James, in 1889, relocated to Butte. By the time her book was published, MacLane had become a social curiosity, even for Butte, whose fields of silver and copper were first staked by Chinese laborers, whose first mayor was a Jew, a town that she herself describes as promiscuous—bohemian in its mixture, its rough-and-tumble assembly of cultures. There were Finns and Swedes and Germans. There were the Irish of Dublin Gulch. There were French and Italians, the whole frontier farrago living side by side, lowbrow and middlebrow, in neighborhoods called Dog Town, Chicken Flats, Busterville, Butchertown, and Seldom Seen. However various and bohemian, Butte's rough edges were covered with the veneer of gentility typical of provincial outposts, desperate to paper over any sort of "wild" blemish. The MacLanes lived comfortably off an inheritance from her father, who had invested well in the cattle and flatboat industries. Her mother, Margaret, married Henry Klenze, a family friend who was not nearly so lucky or prudent. As Klenze depleted the family fortune, her mother occupied herself in other ways. "This house is comfortably furnished," Mary MacLane says. "My mother spends her life in the adornment of it."[8]

For her part, Mary MacLane developed a profound distaste for anything that smacked of genteel conventionality. She despised hypocrisy, and Christian "charity," and seemed to intuitively understand that the power that made the world turn—that dug the mines and fueled the smelters and blackened the skies over Butte—was not a good one. And so she cultivated gentility's opposite, embraced "badness," and sought out, at least in her imagination, the darker pleasures offered by "the Devil," that cosmic persona non grata, who had regained his claim upon this world, as millennialists of the time would assert, and whom Mary MacLane imagined, in a stunning display of intuition, as a kind of steely-eyed business magnate, perhaps a version of William Rockefeller himself.

It's hard to know what to make of someone who declares herself "a genius," as Mary MacLane does at the outset of her diary, except to marvel at this early form of self-branding. The diary is a performance, a one-woman show, and we the spectators in a theater that MacLane constructs for us— it's something between a burlesque house and a carnival sideshow tent— busily changing masks, changing props, cueing herself on and off stage.

She was a prodigy of sorts, a decadent dandy trapped in the provinces, a young woman of great literary ambitions "buried in an environment at utter variance with my natural instincts"[9]—Butte, Montana—where one might go to "a literary club where they talk theosophy," or to "a Cornish dance where they have pastry and saffron cake and the chief amusement is sending beer-bottles at various heads."[10] Imagine Ezra Pound in a Gibson Girl dress stomping around greater Hailey, Idaho. Mary was a drawing room brawler, a village genius, a striving, ambitious personality who had eighteen photographs of Napoleon Bonaparte in her bedroom. The only rival she acknowledged was Marie Bashkirtseff, who played a kind of Nancy Kerrigan to her Tonya Harding. Bashkirtseff was a painter, a literary prodigy, an accomplished musician, an outspoken feminist, and the author of a famous diary *I Am the Most Interesting Book of All:* a prodigy out of proportion to what seems humanly possible. A Russian aristocrat, she grew up on the French Riviera; her parents owned an entire village near Nice; she spoke five languages; her friends and acquaintances were of the highest social and cultural station—counts and barons, painters and writers. She was an intimate correspondent of Guy de Maupassant; her canvases were shown in the annual salons of Paris. Bashkirtseff's oversized life, her actual accomplishments, her world renown, her flirtations with nobility, her proximity in age, the whole French Rivieran polyglottal prolixity of her talents, might have simply overwhelmed a young woman in Butte had not Bashkirtseff also been conveniently dead. Still, death required that MacLane step over a body:

Where she is deep, I am deeper.

Where she is wonderful in her intensity, I am still more wonderful in
my intensity.

Where she had philosophy, I am a philosopher.

Where she had astonishing vanity and conceit, I have yet more astonishing vanity and conceit.[11]

The project, which demanded MacLane distinguish herself against such a
lofty figure as Bashkirtseff, required desperate measures. What MacLane
did, with no resources, and no experience beyond Butte itself, was to locate
in what was happening to the landscape of Butte a kind of open-pit methodology, an absolute allegiance to the profane, a harrowing form of self-
excavation and disclosure that seemed born of an apocalyptic industrial
sublime. Then, in keeping with the presiding spirit of the Gilded Age, she
sold it for all it was worth.

Her diary becomes a kind of girly-show striptease, full of blasphemies,
lesbian confessions, and a resolute contrarian "badness" straight out of the
pages of the Decadent movement of the 1880s and 1890s. She wants to
marry the devil, whom she beseeches: "Hurt me, burn me," she says, "consume me with hot love." At times she reads like Baudelaire with cambric
handkerchiefs, Nietzsche in a striped moreen petticoat.

It all seems to spring from the desolate landscape itself, a desire for self-
annihilation, a wish to see everything—herself, Butte—in ruins, a wish for
the slate of history to be wiped clean. At these moments, which are frequent,
her revelations seem written with a capital "R," as in the book of the Revelation. Hence, she loves a good storm. Storms are richly desired, for example
the tornadoes and storms at the end of the world. "I wish," she says, "for a
long pageant of bad things to come and whirl and rage through this strange
leaden life of mine."[12] She finds in the landscape the widening spell of the
sublime.

Imagine the year 1902, with Mary MacLane sending her manuscript to her
publisher. Now she is taking one of her many walks outdoors, to get away
from the soot and smoke of the smelters of Butte. She walks through sulfurous slag and waste until she arrives at the "sand and barrenness," the bro-

ken hills that become a motif of her diary, a sweeping wasteland, a metaphor for her own emptiness. In twenty years a young poet from Missouri, with the help of Ezra Pound, will compose a long poem that will change the course of literary history. T. S. Eliot's *The Waste Land* will use the image of a desolate waste that might as well be the rim overlooking the Berkley pit. The seven smokestacks of the Neversweat mine are pumping out their poison. There is arsenic in the ground water of Butte. Eliot's is a metaphorical landscape and he addresses the spiritual bankruptcy of an era, but Mary MacLane, in her long morning walks, needs no rhetorical trope, no fancy metaphorical figure. Hers is a wasteland in earnest, like an ant on the back of the Beast itself. Her isolation and loneliness and pointlessness are a predicament she turns into a virtue. She turns the wasteland of her life, the "sand and barrenness" of Butte, into an occasion for apocalyptic, visionary experience. She is primed for the sublime, but she lapses into the perfervid.

"There were pictures in the red sunset sky to-day," the diary entry for March 20, 1901, begins. "I looked at them and was racked with passions of desire." Soon come the "raging elements"; the language is a kind of self-intoxicant. Breathing it in, she offers for display a catastrophilic delirium, in which the stylistic wheels, such as they are, seem to fall off the cart:

A lurid light came from a ghastly moon between clouds. The entire scene was desolately savage and forlorn, but attractive. As I listened in fancy to that shrieking, wailing wind, and saw green branches jerked and twisted asunder in the storm, my barren, defrauded heart leaped and exulted. If I could live in the midst of this and be beaten and shaken roughly, would not that deep sense forget the ache? Kind Devil, pray send me some storms.[13]

The sublime, as Longinus reminds us, cannot be purposefully deployed at a time and place of one's choosing. And yet at every point in which something like the sublime seems to emerge in her diary, we also understand that it is Mary MacLane who is driving the dark clouds forward, heaving the lightning bolts, revving up the whole catastrophilic machine in garish green and orange lighting.

Hers is an attempt to orchestrate the sublime experience for an audience she desperately needs, in order for the escape from Butte to succeed, but for which MacLane has an almost bitter contempt. If she draws her audience rather cruelly—grotesquely—as gap-mouthed animals on "hind-legs" holding opera glasses, she does so because she intuits—again with uncanny precision—that the whole shocking, sensationalist performance is truly beneath her. This doesn't prevent her from getting up on the bally stage and tooting her provocative horn. "I wish to let you know that there is in existence a genius—an unhappy genius, a genius starving in Montana in the barrenness—but still a genius," she says near the end of the diary, in a passage that fairly shouts of the carnival barker: "I am a creature the like of which you have never before happened upon. You have never suspected that there is such a person. I know that there is not such another. As I said in the beginning, the world contains not my parallel."[14] She is caught up, like an advertising "creative type," who knows her spiel is craven but who knows, as well, that the devil's bargain of commerce offers its compensations.

At the end of the March 20 reverie, MacLane smuggles in among the rhapsodic passages something nearer to the heart of her enterprise:

> *I fancied I saw myself and Fame with me. Fame is very fine. The sun and moon and stars may go dark in the Heavens. Bitter rain may fall out of the clouds. But never mind. Fame has a sun and moon and gently brilliant stars of her own, and these, shining once, shine always. The green river may run dry in the land. But Fame has a green river that never runs dry. One may wander over the face of the earth. But Fame is herself a refuge. One may be a target for stones and mud. Yes—but Fame stands near with her arm laid across one's shoulders—as no arm can be laid across one's shoulders. Fame would fill several empty places. Fame would continue to fill them for some years.*[15]

A more keenly felt, more astutely observed, and, strangely, a more moving ode to the phenomenon of fame and celebrity has perhaps never been written. For a brief time, MacLane got her wish. She moved to Greenwich Village and lived the high bohemian life. She was a woman of note, a woman of the moment—making the scene and being seen in all the best places. Nobody before her used natural imagery, especially storm imagery, as she had in the service of catastrophilic sensationalism. One thinks of the fame that MacLane sought so desperately, and then one thinks of her tempestuous diary—so strange it is, so fraught with catastrophic winds and apocalyptic storms. MacLane discovered that she could use the storms of an American landscape to become famous, and in so doing she tapped a market for weather disaster that others would rediscover. In years to come, however, it would be the weather itself that achieved an even stranger sort of celebrity.

FIVE

Paparazzi del Cielo

It is the Atmosphere which adorns with azure vault the planet in which we move, and makes us an abode in the midst of which we act as if we were the sole tenants of the infinite—the masters of the universe.
—CAMILLE FLAMMARION, *L'ATMOSPHERE: METEOROLGIE POPULAIRE*, 1888

C all me the Extreme," Matt said, hobbling over on his crutches to breakfast one morning at a restaurant in York, or Grand Island, or Beatrice, or Bellevue. I'd lost track of where Matt had first said it, though I was certain it was in one of those big, rectangular-ish states in the middle of the country.[1] It was a call-back joke from the night before, a spoof of a commercial for the Weather Channel that was airing, every five minutes it seemed, on the Weather Channel which, by virtue of a cooperative agreement with 20th Century Fox, was featuring clips from the movie *The Day after Tomorrow*—a tidal wave engulfing the Statue of Liberty, a cluster of tornadoes hoovering up South Central Los Angeles—little apocalyptic snippets with a basso profundo voice-over that said: "Get . . . ready . . . to experience . . . the . . . extreme." It was all a part of something called "Extreme Weather Week," the Weather Channel's bid to capitalize on the stormy month of May by selecting highlights of its vast repertoire of "Storm Stories"— docu-dramas featuring real people trapped by raging floodwaters and hauled by helicopter from the tops of their pickup trucks. It would be a five-day catastrophic bacchanal of extreme weather. "Extreme Week," of course, was but an amplification, a turning of the dial a notch or two above the channel's already heightened state of disaster dramaturgy, a frothing foul-weather frenzy that the station had been whipping up since March.

"Okay, Mr. The Extreme," I said. "What are you having for breakfast?"

"The Extreme," you'll recall, was also the nickname of Dr. William Harding, the character played by Bill Paxton in the movie *Twister*, who had earned that appellation in the heady, reckless days of his youth, before becoming a responsible tornado scientist saddled with the rigors of National Science Foundation grant applications and the thwarting of dastardly teams of tornado scientist–profiteers who sought to line their pockets with the knowledge gained from within the heart of nature's most violent storm. Matt's *Twister* allusion, if he meant to make it, was one that many viewers of the Weather Channel would savor, even though *Twister* was currently being supplanted by *The Day after Tomorrow* in an apocalyptic media storm. The culture had been so taken by extremes—extreme makeovers, extreme dating, Glen Campbell's arrest in Arizona for "extreme drunk driving"—that an apogee of sorts had been reached, an extreme extremity, which had now come full circle and had domesticated itself, like a comet in the backyard, hanging clothes upon the line.

Or ironing. Matt had clipped out a story from *The New York Times* about the new "sport" of extreme ironing, which, according to its website, combined "the thrills of an extreme outdoor activity," like mountain climbing or kayaking, "with the satisfaction of a well-pressed shirt." It was a brilliant parody that seemed to have spun wildly out of control, so that there were now, allegedly, 1,500 people worldwide who, in a spectacular turn of phrase, called themselves "ironists," competing each year at the Extreme Ironing World Championship, where they ran an obstacle course while pressing shirts and linens. "Hot Pants," the pseudonym of a recent gold medalist from Germany, won a trip to Hawaii. Said an admiring American contestant, "She really took care on her collars and cuffs."[2]

Though I didn't yet realize it that morning in Nebraska (or wherever), as I wondered what Matt would order for breakfast, we were on the cusp of a two-week storm-chasing campaign that would take us through Kansas, parts of Iowa, and into Nebraska to within twenty miles of the town of Yankton, South Dakota. Among all the many things that this trip would come to represent for me, it was, in the first, the last, the most direct, and the most keenly felt instance, a physical exercise in *extreme sitting*. The prairies are a big place, bigger than most people imagine, with oceanic distances separating people and things, and one crosses these distances, hour upon hour, mile stacked upon mile, it almost goes without saying, *while sitting down.*

It was a given that Matt, my guide and mentor, was a virtuoso at this sort of thing, but the term doesn't begin to capture the long-haul sitting we did that May. But "we" is wrong, of course. "We" might pull over to fuel up, or "we" might stop to scan the landscape, but I, because I had full use of my legs, was the one who would usually hop out and pump the gas or stand next to the van for a stretch. For Matt, getting out of the van was a fairly involved procedure that required hefting his prosthetic left leg out the driver's door, opening the sliding side door, pulling out his crutches, and then hobbling to wherever he needed to go. More often than not, Matt opted to stay inside the van, where he would sit for hours without the least sign of discomfort. Among all the regular distractions of a chase—watching the skies, deciphering forecast information, scanning the radio dial for any respite from country-rock—this patience of Matt's was the sort of thing that might go by without notice, without record, which is why I want to mention, among his many other laudable traits, that when it came to sitting, Matt had endurance. He could have outsat Rodin's Thinker, Whistler's mother, the Buddha. He was the Iron Man of extreme sitting.

Extreme sitting, it turns out, has its own set of hazards, most of which fall into the category of the unforeseen, because, simply put, so few people sit so extremely. Chasers share with airline pilots, truck drivers, old people, and anyone like Matt with reduced mobility, a set of ailments that might make one think twice about joining the fray: myalgia or stiffness in the joints, which I soon felt in my right knee; Jim Leonard, one of the most successful storm chasers in the country, had neck trouble from years of craning his head to look at the sky. Carpal tunnel syndrome, from gripping the steering wheel. Rotator cuff problems and tennis elbow. And—I might as well say it—hemorrhoids, jock itch, constipation, and athlete's foot. Aside from more peripheral problems such as sunburn, dry skin, sleep disorders, depression, and food poisoning, the most life-threatening consequence of extreme sitting—besides traffic accidents—was something called deep vein thrombosis, the slow blockage of a vein, usually in the leg, by an embolism—a blood clot—that can kill a person instantly. The war correspondent David Bloom died, at 39, in just this way, while covering Operation Iraqi Freedom.

That morning Matt was hungry, which was something that he doesn't always feel before the anti-inflammatories and the analgesics kick in. Because he had suffered a deep vein thrombosis in his right leg—the good one—he routinely injected himself with an anticoagulant before strapping on his prosthetic. After so many operations, so many visits to the hospital, he was his own field medic. He had an arsenal of analgesics and a first aid kit so extensive that he could perform minor surgery on himself if he had to. Sometimes I'd leave our motel room for coffee, then return to find him still in bed, listlessly lampooning the Weather Channel. This was like shooting fish in a barrel—he'd be the first to say so—but the Weather Channel, for all its faults and cheesiness, gave Matt something to work with, first thing. Perhaps ire was an analgesic, or a fuel. Soon enough, he'd begin his daily patter, cracking wise, donning the mental storm-chasing armature of MOPE, becoming a self-described "nattering nabob of negativity," watching a show about World War II on the History Channel. "Things seemed clearer than they seem now," he'd say, clearly nostalgic for an era that had come and gone long before he had arrived on the scene. "I even miss the Cold War." Once, he asked me about my own morning routine—whether it involved television. I told him no. Then he said, by way of apology, "Mornings are rough. It takes a while for the medicine to work." On a bad morning, he had no appetite, but he knew he had to eat something. So he'd order something truly extreme—a big cinnamon bun, the kind with enough confectionary glaze to choke a horse. It was not so much a meal as it was self-medication: putting something in his stomach that would buffer the caffeine and at the same time raise his blood sugar enough to bust through the lethargy that sometimes beset him. Matt didn't often go for a regular breakfast, say, of scrambled eggs and toast ("because of the chance of food poisoning," a real concern considering all the greasy spoons where most chasers ate), but today he made an exception and ordered eggs and toast. He surveyed the restaurant, which was filled with long-haul truckers smoking cigarettes and flirting with the waitresses. He spotted a few tables filled with tornado tourists wearing identical jackets with the name of the tour group printed on the front. The waitress brought Matt a large glass of orange juice, which he contemplated for a moment.

"Okay, do you want me to be an extreme chaser geek for five seconds?"

"Sure."

"All right," he said. "This glass, for instance," which he now raised from the table and then replaced with the care one might reserve for a museum artifact, "this glass," he said, "is *wedge-shaped*." He leaned hard into the last phrase and eyed me, meaningfully. Our waitress passed by with coffee for another table. Matt continued: "I've determined that it looks like *Kellerville, June 8, 1995*." He then placed salt and pepper shakers around the glass. "I was right here," he said, moving a spoon quickly into position, "driving Probe 2." What followed was an impromptu monograph on the Kellerville, Texas, tornado, an F-4 pavement peeler that Matt intercepted while driving a VORTEX probe for the National Severe Storms Laboratory. They'd arrived late, after tornadogenesis, but the P-3 aircraft flying above saw the whole thing: a tornado that stretched nearly thirty miles from McLean to Mobeetie, Texas, that was nearly a mile and a half wide, and that was, beyond a doubt, superbly, sublimely *wedge-shaped. Wedge-,* as opposed to *wire-,* or *rope-,* or *needle-shaped; bowl-,* or *bulb-,* or *cone-shaped; segmented, truncated, sheathed,* or *flared* or *stove-pipe-shaped; concave, convex, loop-, ring-,* or *knot-shaped.*

If we had been somehow magically lifted like a sounding balloon above this diner, above Grand Island, or Columbus, or Omaha, upward through the inverted cap, the pressure dropping as we rose, to 500, then 400 millibars, if we could have taken in the whole picture beneath us, the big, mostly Republican, mostly beef-eating picture, we would have seen many whom Matt would describe as afflicted with Severe Storm Syndrome drinking their first cup of coffee in diners and truckstops across the region that morning. With his storm-geek impersonation, Matt was pointing to an aspect of chaser culture that he did not want me to miss. It was a unique way of viewing the world, a way of sitting down to breakfast and seeing the *Coriolis effect* in the swirl of coffee cream. A way of busily, purposefully, cutting a *serious RFD notch* into a stack of pancakes, a way of spotting a *gust front* in the flow of syrup over a plate, and divining, in the contours of a glass of orange juice, a *tornado* from nearly a decade in the past.

Matt had chosen to enter this world when he'd moved from Ohio to Norman in 1986, for no good reason other than to get closer to big weather. He was part of a spectrum of contemporary storm chasers that included, as its earliest practitioners, Roger Jensen, who began chasing storms in his father's

DeSoto near Fargo, South Dakota, in 1953, and David Hoadley, who began photographing storm damage in Bismarck, North Dakota, in 1956. Jensen, who died in 2001, was a monkish figure, who lived with his parents all his life, sold vegetables, and "grew ornamental flowers and cacti," and who worked many years in a turkey processing plant.[3] His was a mind focused on other things, primarily storms and storm photography. He pursued his hobby as an amateur in the first sense of the word—a lover—who lived a quiet, almost secluded life, occasionally publishing his photographs in the *Bulletin of the American Meteorological Society,* in *Weatherwise* magazine, in the winsomely titled book *Clouds of the World.* In the early 1980s, Jensen was befriended by Hoadley, who by then had begun publishing a newsletter called *Storm Track,* now widely regarded as the official organ of the storm chasing world.

Hoadley, who has been described as the "mild-mannered . . . gentleman of chasing," with the "uncanny ability to describe his emotions in nature like no one else,"[4] is a cross between elder statesman and apostle. At the National Storm Chaser Convention in Denver, these qualities were in evidence as he spoke about the early days of storm chasing—before the Interstate Highway System, before the advent of computers, before anyone had given much thought to getting into a car and driving after a storm. He'd taped to the conference walls old surface maps that were yellowed with age. They looked like ordinary maps of the United States, but instead of cities and towns, they were arrowed with wind barbs, indicating the speed and direction of surface winds, and with numbers corresponding to barometric pressure, tempera-ture, dewpoint, relative humidity, and other information. With these surface observations, Hoadley would have sharpened his pencil and begun the slow process of "hand analysis," making connections and establishing patterns and gradients of pressure and of flow that began to reveal what the weather was doing—and what it was going to do. Hand analysis was an "old school" forecast method that had for a time fallen out of favor in the computer age, but it seemed to be making a comeback, as meteorologists and chasers alike began to recognize the limitations of computers and the hidden value of sharpening a Number 2 pencil and connecting the dots. Indeed, on a recent tour of the operations room at the Storm Prediction Center, I noticed that each forecaster brought his own little box of colored pencils, which sat modestly at each work station like a school lunch pail. As Stephen Corfidi, surrounded by some of the most sophisticated meteorological hardware in the world, sharpened his little blue and red pencils and patiently traced a hand analysis, I sat and watched him for half an hour, transfixed. It helped him, he said, understand the big picture. Others agree. "The process has a curious way of forcing us to think about things we are seeing on the map that we wouldn't otherwise notice," writes Tim Vasquez, author of the *Storm Chasing Handbook,* a comprehensive guide sprinkled with gentle, Zen-like admonitions for chasers to slow down and pay attention to what they were doing. Hand analysis was one such method of slowing down:

> As you trace an isobar past Amarillo, you suddenly notice that the dew-points are lower than you thought. Aha—that dryline is on the move. Your hand brings an isobar past Liberal, and you realize that you're being forced to think about why the wind barb indicates such a strong easterly wind. Are the dynamics aloft indeed stronger than you had thought?

From the opening epigraph—"The journey is the reward," a Taoist proverb—to the quotes from Robert Pirsig's 1970s blockbuster, *Zen and the Art of Motorcycle Maintenance,* to the sidebars from *The Tao of Photography,* to his argument favoring old school methods like hand analysis, and with other gentle nudges, Vasquez takes on weather wonks and yahoos alike. Both seem to have lost the way. "The classical chaser" (the weather wonk), the storm geek is besotted by meteorology. He sees a chase primarily as a complex puzzle with a tornado at the end that "fascinates, but fails to touch him." He has gone too far in one direction. At the other extreme is what Vasquez politely calls "the romantic storm chaser" (the yahoo), the seeker of sublime encounter, descendent of Mary MacLane, Wordsworth, and William Blake, who can't be bothered with maps and data. Roger Edwards, a mesoscale and outlook forecaster at the SPC and an outspoken critic of chaserdom, had applied the term "yahoos" to describe irresponsible, thrill-seeking storm chasers. In an essay entitled "The Reality of Storm Chase Yahoos," Edwards, who seldom minces words, defined a yahoo as a "chronically inconsiderate bonehead, the normally sane person who often loses his ability to think clearly and act safely in the heat of the moment—under pressure to catch up and get that intense footage—or the vacuum-brain who doesn't have that ability at all." Edwards cited yahoos who "run others off the road, set up tripods in traffic lanes, drive 90 mph on a wet two-lane, [and] roar across private property." Also yahoos were "media crews, justifying all sorts of dangerous actions on the roadways to get the most extreme possible close-up footage of neighborhoods being shredded apart, all in the name of 'serving the viewing public.'"

According to Vasquez, each chaser type needs to be brought closer to the other, so that the romantic chaser, perhaps basking on the hood of his car, naked, his nostrils flaring at the rich snuff borne on a southeasterly wind, might suddenly somehow contemplate all of this "in the context of the forecast situation," whatever the hell that might be. Or maybe the storm geek— always abreast of the forecast situation, of course—might avail himself suddenly of the romantic perspective, so that a widening cloud base might convey "a sense of timelessness, this same scene conceivably unfolding on a Wednesday a billion years ago, man's presence just a speck within the Holocene sliver in which we live."

I liked Tim Vasquez, and I liked his book. I'd met him at the National Storm Chaser Convention in Denver. He seemed a little earnest, like someone on a mission, someone who needed to spend a good, solid weekend, perhaps an entire holiday, with the Marx Brothers. Why? Because the Marx Brothers were perhaps the best, strongest, and most readily available antidote to a serious problem that Vasquez seemed to overlook. It wasn't that his ideas made too much sense, but that his idea to merge the romantic with the classical chaser mentality seemed to be occurring in a time warp, a period of suspended animation, as if nothing had happened in the world since the publication of *Zen and the Art of Motorcycle Maintenance.* Indeed, to take Vasquez's argument seriously would be to apply a classical sensibility to the entire phenomenon of storm chasing as a human pursuit, and thereby observe it against the backdrop of a historical moment in which a cultural, political, and economic mind-set seemed to have overrun the country like a disease. This was our unwillingness to face the fact of American dependence upon Middle Eastern oil and the consequences thereof—horrific in the short-term entanglement that was Iraq, catastrophic as global warming emerged as an established scientific fact, an ongoing process that couldn't be stopped. Against this backdrop, storm chasing itself, for all its incredible complexity, seemed an extravagant, late-phase indulgence, a way of taking up the violin while Rome burned. There was just something inescapably untenable about it all.

Tim Vasquez and David Hoadley tried to urge their fellow chasers to slow down, the way the National Cattlemen's Beef Association might urge Americans, the most cholesterol-choked people on earth, to balance their diet with beef. At the Denver conference, Hoadley filled his lecture with lots of his signature funny cartoons, which he displayed on an overhead projector, gently spoofing various chaser attitudes and predicaments. He told an amusing anecdote about driving into a ditch on a muddy road in the middle of nowhere, and deciding to take a photograph of the storm he was chasing, just to kill some time before a farmer came to rescue him. This photograph of a cumulonimbus cloud, taken over forty years earlier, a throwaway shot at the end of a busted day, would soon be reproduced by the millions in a new issue of weather-related stamps called "Cloudscapes," to be released by the United States Postal Service. His address was a kind of extended yet entertaining public service announcement, which got a standing ovation. I rose with the rest, genuinely impressed, but I wondered too, what we were rising to applaud.

A taxonomy of storm chasers would begin with these two figures, Hoadley and Jensen, as epitomes of one type of amateur—the old school, pre-*Twister* veteran chaser. Hoadley and Jensen were revered more or less in direct proportion to how little their view of the world seemed to hold sway. Their enthusiasm predated a viable market for catastrophilia. Hoadley was the unhurried gentleman, Jensen, the reclusive monk, summing up the whole point of the enterprise, explaining in his best North Dakotan why he chased storms: "Gosh," he said, "it's for the awe at what you are seeing." He and Jensen were two Dakota visionaries, each in his way quietly engaged in the pursuit of sublime experience. They represented the better and perhaps bygone end of the spectrum of storm chasers. On its other end stood the equally emblematic figures of the earliest and most successful practitioners of severe weather marketing.

In the realm of commercial chasing, Warren Faidley had for many years made himself a presence that was hard to miss. A native of Tucson, he had been traveling around the country since 1987 taking photographs of severe weather—stunning shots of desert lightning, hurricanes, tornadoes, and cloudscapes—and had, over the years, compiled "the world's largest stock photography agency dedicated to the weather," according to his website, "The Storm Chaser Official World Home Page." Faidley seemed to have understood sooner than most that a library of weather images, especially images of severe weather, was something the world couldn't do without. When an advertising agency wanted to conjure the idea of safety amid danger—for an automobile tire designed to efficiently sluice away troubled waters, for instance, Faidley's company, Weatherstock, could provide the menacing storm imagery. When someone wanted a lightning bolt in the background to lend a little excitement to a powdered dietary supplement, Faidley's company had thousands of lightning bolt images to choose from.

The business had begun twenty-six years earlier, with a lucky shot, a single chance encounter with a lightning bolt in 1988 that struck a light pole near a group of fuel storage tanks. At the time, Faidley was flat broke. For weeks, he had been living on ramen noodles; he was behind on his rent, and was contemplating selling his photographic equipment for cash. He had rolls of film in his refrigerator but no money to develop them.

When a massive, four-pronged lightning bolt descended from the sky, one branch of it landed behind him, knocking him to the ground. Another branch struck directly in front of him, four hundred feet away. This image would change his life, because it turned out to be one of the closest photographs ever taken of lightning. Faidley sold the image to *Life* magazine, which described him as a "storm chaser." A year later, he made the phrase a registered service mark for his stock photography company. He compiled a catalogue and parlayed his lucky break into a full-time career. (He has billed himself as "the only accredited journalist and professional photographer in the world who pursues all forms of severe weather and natural disasters as a full-time, year-round profession.") He captures images of tornadoes in the spring, shoots lightning and wildfires in the summer, tracks hurricanes in late summer and fall, and builds the business in the off season.[5] Chances are you have seen a Weatherstock image as you thumbed through a magazine, or a textbook, or a calendar, or peeked at a postcard, or watched an episode of *Buffy the Vampire Slayer.* Brief video clips from Weatherstock have appeared in television commercials, documentaries, music videos, and motion pictures. By any measure, Faidley's story has been one of genuine success. In the mid-1990s, his image of a tornado appeared on the movie poster for *Twister* and on all subsequent product packaging—videos, DVDs, and movie soundtrack CDs; Faidley, who by then had also registered the name "Cyclone Cowboy," was the subject of a 1996 Weather Channel book, *Storm Chaser in Pusuit of Untamed Skies,* the immense popularity of which was assisted, in a moment of corporate synergy, by the Weather Channel documentary about his life, helpfully entitled *Storm Chaser Warren Faidley: In Pursuit of Untamed Skies.* Faidley soon appeared on television and cable shows on every major network and was touring the public lecture circuit giving talks on storm safety while selling his books and videos. The flow of weather had become a revenue stream, an unending harvest of the skies. It had not come, however, without a price.

Some people—mostly storm chasers who had been in the game at least as long as Faidley—had spoken to me about the Cyclone Cowboy with more than a hint of derision. To these few, Faidley represented the entrance of crass commercialization into chaserdom. As they saw it, he, more than anyone else, had pushed his own photogenic face into the weather frame. He represented an upstart invasion of self-promotion, self-marketing, what in some circles is called self-branding, into a realm meant for lovers of weather for its own sake, techno-geeks who relished the storm-chasing cocktail of cloud physics and a straight shot from the adrenal glands. Some thought that, as a great popularizer of severe weather, Faidley had helped clog the highways of Tornado Alley with hordes of the great unwashed, the way a favorable review in *The New York Times* can wreck a perfectly good little bistro.

Then again, to many chasers, Faidley was an exasperation because, on a number of occasions over the years, he had exemplified the triumph of the lucky hunch over experience, knowledge, and skill. Faidley's chase car, a black SUV that he christened the Shadow Chaser, had often been spotted heading 180 degrees away from the direction most chasers had decided to go; this helped earn him the nickname Wrong Way Faidley. But Faidley seemed to resemble the lucky dilettante at a poker game: his hunches often proved correct—and he would walk away with the best shot of the day.

A few outspoken critics emerged with trenchant analyses of the Faidley phenomenon. One was Roger Edwards, whose postings on Internet discussion groups at times resembled the withering jeremiads of the Puritan fathers, with Faidley singled out as an aspect of the general decline of civilization. Another outspoken critic was Matt Biddle, whose own website, www.moderaterisk.com, was more known for pointing out Faidley's inaccuracies and for its commitment to popping the Warren Faidley self-promotional bubble, without ever mentioning Faidley by name. But when Biddle began to impugn Faidley's integrity as a photojournalist, implying that Faidley may have doctored some of his tornado images, Faidley was swift to respond with a cease-and-desist order from his lawyers. Biddle, who was a graduate student and whose website operated under the auspices of the University of Oklahoma, decided to remove the offending material rather than be pestered by Faidley's lawyer. Thereafter, with a nod to the tribulations suffered by a certain Minneapolis-based R & B celebrity, the Moderate Risk website began referring to its principal author as "The Chaser Formerly Known as Matt."

A certain amount of grumbling in the world of storm chasers might have been the inevitable result of Faidley's rapid rise to celebrity, part of his cost of doing business. But a more disturbing strain of anti-Faidleyism began to emerge after the Affair of the Allegedly Retouched Tornadoes. Hackers, according to Faidley, broke into his website, infecting it with viruses and worms, and they bombarded him with spam. Someone began manipulating his search engine ranking. One chaser purchased the domain name "warrenfaidley.com" and tried to extort Faidley to relinquish his registered service mark "Storm Chaser." Faidley even reported receiving death threats. This was, as he put it, the "dark side" of the chaser world striking out wildly, recklessly. In response, the "Legal Notices" link on his website expanded until it fairly bristled with preemptory warnings against copyright violation, computer sabotage, and slander, including helpful links directing would-be Internet assailants to judgments in his favor, and a promise from his lawyers to "vigorously pursue . . . the hosts, owners, and/or moderators of any Internet discussion group who allow[ed] a pattern of continued abuse" of Faidley.[6]

Against this backdrop of legal admonishment, preemptive litigation, and bad blood, I drove north one fall morning under a low sky and fog to Springfield, Massachusetts, to hear Warren Faidley speak on storm chasing.

The venue that night was the Springfield Public Forum, the oldest ongoing free public lecture series in America. It began in 1935 and, in the year of my visit, featured an impressive list of speakers that included David Gergen, the television political pundit and former White House adviser; Walter Isaacson, former CNN chief and current *Time* magazine editor; and Joseph Nocera, a business writer for *Fortune* magazine. Faidley's presence in the series might seem to reflect a momentary lapse in curatorial focus, but it had always been the practice to toss lighter fare into the high-profile mix, to feature world travelers and adventurers, for instance, like Jim Whittaker, the first American to climb Mount Everest, or great literary populists like Isaac Asimov, just as the nineteenth-century lyceum and Chautauqua lecture circuit had sprinkled the array of celebrity orators, such as Thomas A. Edison and Ulysses S. Grant, with a few magicians, illusionists, and vaudevillians like Clarence Nash, who could impersonate a duck reciting "Mary Had a Little Lamb."

I parked a few blocks from the Springfield Municipal Group, a pair of identical Greek Revival buildings separated by an immense campanile. The complex was constructed in 1912, according to a city brochure, with the aid of "nearly 2000 Italian artisans and their families," who clearly knew a thing or two about building campaniles. The interior of Symphony Hall mirrored the ambitions of its builders. It was a tremendously large public performance space: a first balcony that wrapped around the entire space in a fat U, and a third, uppermost tier that seemed, from the orchestra section, like a glimpse into the echoing galleries of Carlsbad. The place could seat 2,611 people. As I craned my neck, admiring the hall's faded glory, the smallest fraction of that capacity had taken seats in the auditorium's main section—gray-haired retirees and their grandchildren, parents—mostly fathers—with children in tow, everyone murmuring softly. Then, two women—attractive, conservatively dressed, tightly wound, and looking as if they'd just arrived from a Junior League fund-raiser—walked swiftly across the stage. From behind a podium nearly obscured by a spray of flowers, and after a few introductory comments, Jackie Keady, a member of the speaker selection committee, began to recite into the microphone the story line about Warren Faidley that Warren Faidley, or his website, or his autobiography, had provided the world:

Born in Kansas. Raised in Tucson. Rode a bicycle into a dust devil when he was a little boy. Always wanted to be a Navy fighter pilot. Studied journalism at the University of Arizona. Worked for the Tucson papers. Quickly got bored and started taking photographs of lightning storms. Got a lucky break with *Life*. Now a world-famous photojournalist. "Warren's entire life has been shaped by bad weather," Jackie Keady intoned, to a slow appreciative rumble of laughter from the audience. As is so often the case with autobiography, Warren Faidley's "life," given to us in necessarily truncated form, was filled with "story elements" that fit together a little too perfectly.

Many facts seemed revved up to the highest possible state of excitation. Faidley was, for instance, a "bestselling author" if one meant "bestseller" in a more limited sense than the phrase normally conveys among specialized titles.[7] He had been known to advertise himself as an early consultant to the movie *Twister*,[8] which, like many parts of Faidley's biography, required qualification.

His life in print came across as a kind of caffeinated cartoon. I had read *Storm Chaser* before coming to Springfield. It was a picture book, written in comic-book boilerplate, with Faidley casting himself as action-hero adventurer, battling it out *mano a mano* with the forces of nature: "I made a dash for the car as a rogue bolt of lightning whizzed overhead," for example. In these action-packed scenes, one is liable to find a good deal of cursing: "I swung open the door, cursed, dropped a roll of film on the ground, cursed again." And we are privy to any number of the hero's innermost thoughts, occurring while Faidley is diving into his car or fleeing for his life while the storm rages around him. "I watched the reflection in the car's windshield," he says. "The ensuing thunderclap was the storm's way of laughing at me."

In time, it would become clear that the single most important feature of Faidley's life was his failure to achieve his boyhood dream of becoming a Navy fighter pilot. (His eyesight wasn't good enough.) All that followed— the chasing, like so many sorties over enemy territory; the close brushes with disaster, like actual dogfights with the sky; the peripatetic life; the name of his SUV, the "Shadow Chaser," which might have been emblazoned on the fuselage of a jump jet—all of it, right down to Jackie Keady's rapidfire account of his accomplishments—seemed to be compensation for that early disappointment. It was something deeper than mere dorkiness that compelled Faidley in *Storm Chaser* to cast himself as a pilot manqué. In one

spread, he stands tall, wearing something very much like fighter pilot garb—
a bomber jacket and khakis—while staring off into the sunset, his hand rest-
ing on the Shadow Chaser, while on the opposite page, he sits inside his
trusty vehicle, on his head a communications headset, map in his hand,
every inch a pilot running through his preflight checklist.

There was something a little sad about all this, a feeling that was not dimin-
ished by Faidley's appearance in a concert hall filled with children and grand-
parents. The Weather Channel, he would tell me later, wanted nothing to do
with him. He had been driven to self-publish a book about storm survival that
was not only derivative of the wildly successful "Worst-Case Scenario" books
but had the unfortunate quality of seeming to play to public fears about
terrorism after 9/11. The back jacket of *How to Survive Any Storm: Severe
Weather Handbook* made the illogical link between severe weather and the
threat of terrorism. "During these times of domestic threats—we must not
forget that weather-related hazards poise [*sic*] ever-increasing dangers."

With her introduction finished, Jackie Keady called Warren Faidley out
onto the stage. The audience broke into applause, but the stage remained
empty. Instead, a video-projected image—huge, perhaps fifteen or sixteen
feet tall—of a Voice of America story about Faidley began to play. A powerful tornado approached the camera frame as the narrator, a VOA reporter
named Ted Landfere, spoke of "nature's most ferocious . . . whirlwinds, sometimes reaching four hundred kilometers an hour, [that] sweep across the
High Plains of the United States every spring, many times leaving death and
destruction in their paths." There followed a series of images of Warren Faidley talking into the camera, intercut with images of tornadoes and storms.
As projected onto the auditorium screen, Faidley's head—his handsome,
boyish face, his stiff jaw, his thin lips, his perfectly combed hair, the perfection of the visage, wrinkle-free, untouched by time.

What struck me most forcefully was the powerful effect lurking beneath
the whole puffed-up Voice of America presentation. It was all very much like
the scene from *The Wizard of Oz* where Dorothy and her companions are
brought in terror before the Wizard in his great hall. Indeed, the whole mise-
en-scène in the Springfield auditorium reminded me of that famous scene.
The great hall was, for starters, similarly overscale, perhaps even grandiose,
like the one in which Dorothy and her companions cower. The disembodied

voice echoing up to the rafters, and Faidley's large head facing us, were of a piece with the booming voice of Oz, punctuated by pyrotechnics.

Of course, Faidley's image got no similarly emphatic rhetorical embellishments. Instead, we had the calm Apollonian surround—the appealing surfaces of Faidley's Adonis-like face, the perfect hair, the eyebrows that seemed almost penciled in, the tranquility of computer screens aglow behind him offering the reassuring "newsroom" background, all of which, when juxtaposed with shots of howling tornadoes approaching the viewer or lightning bolts flashing across the screen, reinforced a different, more subdued visual rhetoric than that presented to the viewers of Oz. Faidley was not the tornado or the lightning bolt in the way that Oz was the fireballs erupting around him. With Faidley, the stakes were lower: he was not a demigod but a calm-voiced Kansan Virgil—*born in Topeka!*—our guide into the whirlwind. Oz asks more of Dorothy and her friends, and of us. Oz is godlike in his house—the vaulted, cathedrallike ceilings, the long, echoing corridors; in his isolation—it takes a lot to get an appointment; in his demeanor—fireballs, etc; and when Toto pulls back the curtain, exposing the chicanery, Oz falls from a higher place. If Faidley, by contrast, was not a god but a guide, this opening salvo of his, this overture of images, nevertheless established something important. Though we may live in a more skeptical age, in which we are all learning to see around the corners of everything, pulling the curtain to uncover the latest marketing or political ploy, and though we may smile at the Cowardly Lion blubbering before Oz, the Tin Man toppling over himself with fear, the Scarecrow, his legs suddenly splayed, Faidley was exploiting an enduring human weakness straight out of the Oz playbook: we tend not to question the authority of a large talking head.

The big buildup seemed an attempt to counteract the long slide show that followed of hurricanes, lightning bolts, tornadoes, hail, hailstones. I slumped into my chair. Stories about hailstones are like other people's dreams: something important always gets lost in translation. But I sat up when Faidley began talking about the current state of storm chasing. By way of providing a taxonomy of the realm, Faidley made the basic distinction between hobbyists and scientists, the heirs of Jensen and Hoadley, on the one hand, and the followers of pioneering scientists like Neil B. Ward and Ted Fujita, on the other. Then he mentioned a third, underappreciated group—the storm spotters of the world, the community volunteers who are generally dispatched by local emergency management personnel to report upon the weather. To Faidley, this home guard of volunteers, operating their own vehicles on their own time, were "probably the number one group of chasers overlooked. They never get any credit for what they do, [yet] of all the chasers, they probably are the most beneficial."

Finally, he addressed a fourth group, "thrill seekers," "chasers who were mostly inspired by the movie *Twister.* . . . They go out just for the pure thrill of it. They have no idea about the weather. They don't carry cell phones with them. They don't have radios to report back what they're seeing. Their only mission is to see how close they can get to a storm, and somehow end up on the five o'clock news."

Most chasers were "post-*Twister*," and they included a large number of commercial chasers, who sold video footage or still shots to the media; who consulted for film, for television, or for news programs; or who worked as storm tour guides on the Plains. As the number of commercial chasers increased, so did competition for the "money shot." After the race to capture a good shot came a second race to the news agencies that would actually buy the footage. Chasers with thousands of dollars to spare purchased equipment that allowed them to compress and beam their video captures directly to television stations. Few had that kind of scratch, however, so instead they highballed their way to the nearest Internet port. Tornado tour guides were also pressed by the competition to get on the right storm and fulfill their pledge to bring clients close to a tornado. This, too, tempted some to rush around the countryside at breakneck pace.

Somewhere in between the amateur enthusiasts and the tornado tours were the severe weather chase teams, another growing phenomenon, in which weather freaks who didn't want to pay for guide services pooled their resources and traveled together across the Plains, usually in vans, in search of big weather. I met one of these chase clubs in a gas station in Beatrice, Nebraska, one afternoon, where I and perhaps a hundred other chasers were waiting around for the weather to shape up. A black Hummer H2 came to a stop in front of the pumps, followed by three other white rental cars, all of which, with the addition of magnetically mounted radio antennas and liberal amounts of duct tape, had become modified chase vehicles. The

Hummer meant business. It was bristling with pseudo-official effects—yellow emergency road flashers mounted on the hood and on each side door a yellow decal in the shape of a sheriff's badge bearing the words "Severe WX Response." Out of the Hummer, Phil Henry emerged, a close-cropped silver-haired sixty-year-old inventor, entrepreneur, and race-car-driving alpha geek. There was no stopping to chat with Phil Henry; he strode into the convenience store and then strode back into his Hummer. He had information about a developing storm and was in a hurry. He handed me a business card and pulled away from the pump to let the other cars fill up. I stood there like a yokel watching in disbelief as the Severe WX Response team fueled up. Watching along with me was a team member, a round, big-haired woman in her seventies named Carolynn Kindelon, of Kailua, Hawaii. She handed me her business card ("Carolynn K's Hawaiian Style Olde English Toffee"); then she, too, was on her way.

All of these chaser types, including, perhaps, those responsible for making Hawaiian Style Olde English Toffee, were casting a shadow over all of chaser-dom, it seemed. "In the central part of the United States," Warren Faidley told his audience in Springfield, "you may have hundreds of people out during a severe weather event, clogging up the roads and upsetting law enforcement." Local officials, police, and even a few state legislators were now discussing ways to prohibit or at least regulate the practice of storm chasing.

Warren Faidley, who perhaps more than any other individual chaser was responsible for bringing storm chasing to this point, was now distancing himself from the whole mess. Faidley, who had gone to an awful lot of trouble to register the phrase "Storm Chaser" as a proprietary service mark for his stock-photography business, was now, in fact, chary of using the term. "Now when I go out," he told his listeners, "I don't even call myself a chaser. I like to lean toward 'photojournalist,' because storm chasers are starting to get a bad reputation."

"Pretty soon," he said, "it's going to be like a Mad Max movie."

MATT BIDDLE, TOO, had helped contribute to the creation of "the beast" that storm chasing had become. I didn't count helping the movie *Twister* get made: had Matt declined to guide the B Unit film crew to photograph storms, some other chaser would have stepped in. Mostly Matt had remained an underground figure, a highly respected contributor to Internet discussion groups, whose observations and opinions influenced many chasers. But he had lived the life of a commercial chaser. His El Camino had borne the decals of his company, Moderate Risk, and its sponsors. He was one of many whose business cards, now curled and yellowed with age on a bulletin board at the *Twister* Museum in Wakita, had become a kind of exhibit, a memento of a time that had clearly come and gone.

MAY 15, 2004, the day Matt and I departed on the Kansas/Nebraska campaign, was perfect for a picnic—brilliant sunshine, a calm breeze, a rural Oklahoma farm surrounded by fields of ripening winter wheat, a day perfect for softball, horseshoes, and barbecue, a day that fairly called out for Frisbees and sunscreen, with the sound of kids horsing around by the water. What one found, however, at Mark "Rocky" Rascovich's annual chaser picnic was a bit strange. Matt had agreed to stop by on our way out of town. Cars lined the dirt road leading to a rambling ranch house, but not a soul could be seen or heard, anywhere. It was two in the afternoon. The shades were drawn. As Matt and I walked through the front door, a darkened living room erupted in applause. About thirty people were crammed into the space, sitting on the carpeted floor, on couches, or standing shoulder to shoulder watching the end of a chaser highlights video on a big-screen television.

This was a chaser picnic at full throttle. Somebody from New York State slipped in a highlights DVD that included a nicely produced "Salute to the Ridge May 1–12," an amusing video sketch of all the tourist traps the chasers had visited while waiting out the ridge of high pressure. Set to the tune of "I Can See Clearly Now the Rain Is Gone," it showed them idling away their hard-won vacation time, languishing in their cars, nearly blind with boredom. The World's Largest Ball of Twine got a big laugh. Then came the payoff—May 12 chase footage of the tornadoes near Attica, Kansas, a gripping sequence that showed several tornadoes at close range, intercut with moments of bracing cinematic vérité—an unflattering profile of a chaser driving his car, undisguised fear flashing across his face just long enough for everyone in the room to see it, in all its candor, and to recognize one of those moments when self-preservation trumps any narrative pretense, a moment of the sort one hears on black box recordings recovered from airplane crashes—dead air and the sound of people being jostled around, trying to save themselves. In the video, there came a sudden moment of recovery, when the chaser turned to the camera and said, "I'm scared shitless, but I'm having fun." This, also, got a big, appreciative laugh.

In the kitchen I met Rocky, a tall, lanky man who worked as a DJ for a local Christian radio station, and his wife, a gracious hostess who kept piling food onto my plate. Rocky had been concerned about having a chaser picnic on the very Saturday when the weather seemed ready to break. The high-pressure ridge was eroding and storm-hungry chasers were using the day to position themselves in eastern Nebraska, near Hastings or Grand Island. Would anybody come? Then, too, there was the question of alcohol. Rocky had asked that everyone abstain. This also threatened to thin the crowd. But the picnic seemed to be hopping in any case. I met Stuart Robinson, an affable man from Leicester, England, just one of a seemingly endless stream of Brits taking advantage of a cheap dollar to tour the Plains in search of big weather. Indeed, nearly every tour group I encountered that month had at least a couple of English weather freaks on board, smiling happily. This was the country that invented trainspotting, after all, a hobby that offered a nearly seamless transition into "weatherspotting," which had the advantage of sleepovers in budget hotels and the chance to partake of the grand buffet they'd heard so much about. And so the British idled away the hours in strip malls waiting for the weather to shape up. They smiled at the "skyrocketing" prices of gasoline and viewed the waste land along the Interstate highway system as if it were a curiosity, a kind of ruin, yet to be so labeled—and if the grand experiment that was America led finally to another dinner at Applebees, that was really none of their concern. There was, in short, nothing about chasing that they didn't seem to love, and so each spring they came in droves.

At the picnic I also met Gene Rhoden, who was, in Matt's opinion, one of the top five chasers in the country. Rhoden had a unique eye for storms, a way of seeing and understanding complex, fluid situations that was akin to the way certain great basketball players are said to have a "vision" for the game, a knack that brings out the best in other players. It was a quality that came out in his photographs as well—an ability to find the shot that other chasers overlooked because of their obsession with "capturing the tornado," the tornado a kind of fixed idea, a category killer blotting out other forms of the sublime. But Rhoden's broader taste and his eye for storm structure helped make him a rare exception in this world: someone who, like Faidley, made his living chasing and photographing storms.

In the foyer I saw Shane Adams, a frequent contributor to the Internet discussion group WX-Chase. In T-shirt and jeans, with long blond hair, Shane looked like a buff roadie for Metallica. Later he would tell me that he'd grown up in Healdton, a town in southwest Oklahoma, dreaming of being a rock star. Shane and his best friend at the time, Brett Bivens, spent their years at Healdton High School listening to Mötley Crüe, Quiet Riot, Dokken, "all the mainstream hair bands." They adopted the hair of their heroes—"sort of a bilevel look, spiky at the top and long in the back. They call it a mullet these days"—and they cultivated hard-drinking, bad-boy habits. In a conservative rural town where "everybody else had cowboy hats and wore Wranglers," Shane and Brett were instant outcasts, playing ear-splitting music in garages, hoping to make it big somewhere else, to "make something of ourselves." But the band never got out of the garage. After Shane graduated from high school in 1990, he entered what he admitted was "probably the lowest point in my life." Living with his parents, working menial jobs, he remained an outsider, writing poems and songs. "We'd sit and write, just me and [Brett] and an acoustic guitar. That was what our life was built around."

Then Shane moved to Norman, Oklahoma, where he lived with a group of guys—freebooters, party animals, and assorted employees of a popular hangout called Mr. Bill's in full-on bachelor squalor, with piles of dishes in the sink, spontaneous parties that never really began or ended, and no heat in the winter. "We'd all sit around the TV watching hockey, wrapped up in blankets, wearing beanies, and seeing our breath freeze in the air." This they called the Heinous House. Shane was then twenty-four, working as a day laborer for cash, trimming trees, doing landscape work, and rehearsing in a garage with a band named Imagika. And then, on June 6, 1996, his life changed forever.

He and a friend named Greg Clark decided to quit a landscaping job early and chase after a storm south of Norman. By chance, Shane caught on videotape a funnel cloud forming to the west. "God, or whatever, smiled on me and gave me my dream right there in about twenty seconds," he said. It was pure unadulterated dumb luck, and it had happened so fast, the tornado forming and dissolving so quickly, that they weren't even sure they'd spotted anything at all. This minor problem didn't stop Greg from pitching the tape to a local television station, which then played the clip on the evening news, crediting Greg Clark and Shane Adams as the photographers. There was a big celebration that night at Mr. Bill's with toasts and shouts of joy, and at least one public oath, delivered by Shane, who gathered everyone together and raised his glass in the air. "From this moment on," he declared to the quieted crowd, "my life is dedicated to the video documentation and pursuit of tornadoes." Somebody shouted, "Hell yeah!"; then Shane and Greg toasted each other, and that was that. A yahoo was born.

"I was definitely a yahoo," Shane told me. "I didn't know what the hell I was doing." But a passion was born, too, a desire to *get it right.* He sent his video to the National Weather Service Office in Norman for evaluation, and began doing something he'd rarely ever done in the days of the hair bands: he started hanging out at the library, reading books on meteorology. In February the National Weather Service returned his video with a note that said, in part, "Based on your video we are adding another tornado to the official 1996 count."

I like to imagine Shane, who was then living in an apartment and working as a dishwasher in a sports bar, who was, by his own account, more or less adrift, sitting in the lean light of an Oklahoma winter afternoon, holding an official piece of correspondence written by a scientist and informing Shane Adams that his effort had made a small but important contribution to the climatological record. For the first time in his life, Shane had linked himself to something that transcended the impossible disadvantages of having grown up in Healdton, Oklahoma. For a moment, Shane Adams, self-described yahoo, was as much a part of the tradition of the citizen-scientist, say, as any of the 2,000 volunteer weather reporters, mostly farmers, who sent John Finley detailed storm information in the 1890s. I wondered what John Finley would have thought of the word "yahoo" as it was applied by the cantankerous Roger Edwards.

Shane's old high school friend, Brett, was also living in Norman, working as a bartender at a Mexican restaurant called the Border Crossing. Brett told Shane about a well-known chaser, a regular customer, who'd worked on the movie *Twister*. That customer was Matt Biddle, and soon Shane was hanging out with him, talking about chasing, learning as much as he could. "I was so taken with tornadoes," he remembered, "that there was no room for anything else."

He'd entered a tribal realm. If chaserdom had a totem animal, that animal would be, without question, and appropriately enough for chaser dudes everywhere, the wolf, the intelligent hunter. I learned this almost by accident one afternoon in the library of Columbia University, where I came upon an admirable monograph written by a man named Daniel E. Gershenson and published in the *Journal of Indo-European Studies*. "Apollo the Wolf-god" is the sort of dense, wide-ranging scholarly article that never sees the light of nonacademic day and that requires the reader to plow through numismatic argument, citations and counterinstances that make one's head spin, and set pieces on mole crickets, weevils, hamsters, and a kind of rye fungus that, when dampened by spring rains, produces lysergic acid, a natural form of LSD. But there were moments that made me sit up straight and want to shout "Eureka!" before slipping back quietly into an Indo-European studies–induced coma.[9] It was not the sort of thing one associated with a chaser dude like Shane Adams, in any case, but it explained him, and much of chaserdom, to a remarkable degree and connected the whole chaser phenomenon to a complex and now largely lost set of mythic associations of ancient provenance.

The word "wolf," for instance, is deeply connected by a complex of etymological associations to the very thing that chasers chase: the wind that howls, as we say, evoking a metaphoric, if fossilized wolf. In German, *wolf* was another way of naming the wind. (The name "Wolf Blitzer" thus turns out to be more than a little windy.)[10] The wolf is the storybook creature that huffs and puffs and blows down houses; the tale of the Three Little Pigs takes the wind-wolf association, a figurative comparison that seems natural enough, and makes it literal in a way that has little, if anything, to do with the actual attributes of *Canis lupus*. When compared with the wolf of *Little Red Riding Hood*, for instance, and of many other tales in which the wolf enjoys wolf-like attributes (cunning intelligence marshalling a fierce appetite, and the teeth to back it up) the literal wolf-wind of the Three Little Pigs seems, indeed, a bit strange and unresolved.

Gershenson explains that the wolf had long been linked to a potent god, Apollo, whom we know as the deity of sun and light and reason. But, he claims, Apollo's identification with the sun came relatively late; the earliest record is a fragment from a play by Euripides. Prior to this, the Greeks knew the god by a variety of epithets including one that was central to chaserdom: Apollo Lykeios, "Apollo, the Wolf-God," son of Zeus, the thunderbolt-flinging lord of the heavens whose lusty preoccupations required that he delegate a substantial portion of his meteorological authority. To others he delegates the rosey-fingered dawn of Homer, while Apollo Lykeios, among other things, brings the fructifying winds of spring. The temple of Apollo Lykeios at Argos was the site of an oracular cult similar in stature and influence to the cult of the Temple at Delphi.[11] The temple at Argos was built to honor the victory of a wolf, Apollo's proxy, over an ox, stand-in for Poseidon, near a sinkhole through which a great wind blew. The wind, of course, was "part of the realm of the beyond, the unseen area beyond the visible surface of the land, sea, and sky, properly identified . . . as chaos, the hidden world of things that are not manifest."[12] As an oracular cult, then, the followers of Apollo Lykeios were particularly invested in the wolf-wind "as messenger from outside, from the chaotic world, to the world of order."[13] It was impossible not to notice the parallels between the ancient followers of Apollo Lykeios and contemporary storm chasers, who were also heavily invested in oracular business, in making sense of things that were not manifest—surface lows and triple points, invisible boundaries of air and pressure, speed and direction—in bringing the chaotic world of wind and weather into the Apollonian realms of sense.

Gershenson contends, further, that Apollo the Wolf-God, the "well-known and widely-attested weather deity," had his own season of festivals in antiquity—"the Lykios," which corresponded to the months from March to May, the very season of greatest interest to storm chasers; during that part of the year, the wind-wolf, the great loping chaser of fleecy, sheeplike clouds, was propitiated. And Apollo the Wolf-God was the patron of a particular group of social outcasts or "youth confraternities"—*Jungmannschaften,* as

nineteenth-century German anthropologists called them—bands of "spir-
ited young men and women," a league of outriders, "estranged to some
extent from the entire community," isolated and self-isolating lone wolves.
Suddenly, the parallels to chaserdom's alternative community of weather
wonks—the cultish bands of loners roaming the American Plains, wolfishly
gobbling up gallons of fuel, Mountain Dew, and Doritos across the American landscape for hundreds of miles at a sitting—began to swim into focus.

Generalizations are, of necessity, unfair, error-ridden conceits. But how
much of a mistake would it be, I wondered, to say that the Shane Adamses
of the world—the young and restless initiates of the cult of the wolf-wind,
the chaser-dude devotees of all things meteorological—how wrong would it
be to say they fit the *Jungmannschaften* paradigm fairly well? One difficulty
with such a view, it seemed, was that most of the chasers I met were not, in
fact, particularly young. But young is as young does. Age, among chasers,
merely provided the means—the job, the career, the disposable income—by
which one clung to youth, as any man or woman past forty will readily tes-
tify. SUVs with tens of thousands of dollars' worth of meteorological toys
attached spoke to this fact as well. A second difficulty would be in character-
izing chasers as outcasts or outlaws, when in fact the chaser world, at least as
manifest in the two main Internet forums, Storm Track and WX-Chase, was
at great pains to inculcate responsible behavior, to chastise reckless driving,
even bad manners, and to demonstrate, by their words and actions, a spirit
of public service. Chasers, in this view, were a traveling "home guard," spotting
tornadoes and reporting them to the authorities. They provided "ground-
truthing" to Weather Service field officers, confirming, with firsthand observation, what radar could only suspect. They saved lives. A few participated
in the useful, unglamorous business of poststorm damage surveys. Nevertheless, the tone of these responsible, "safety first" chasers seemed only to
underscore a real problem, the way a sermon no matter how filled with the
Holy Ghost, can point beyond the walls of propriety to the devil's play-
ground, where a whole lot of sinning is going on. "Types always come to us
from some fast truth somewhere," the novelist Richard Ford has said, and
even if I was a little chary of casting chasers as a type—reader, I can already
hear the clatter of keyboards as chasers post angry diatribes against my
effort—most were as self-aware as my guide, Matt, as ready to admit and

perhaps relish the chaser absurdities, some of which he seemed to hold on to, for old time's sake.

I noticed, for instance, that Matt had customized our van by taping the Moderate Risk logo onto the back. He'd also placed near the door handle a small rectangle of weatherproof tape, on which he'd printed his last name as if on the side of a race car or, better yet, the fuselage of a jet fighter. Later, he would put a "name plate" for me on the passenger door. It was a little flourish of absolute geekiness, used ironically, or semi-ironically, but harking back, perhaps, to a time in the not-too-distant past when chasers less prone to irony might actually have fancied this sort of gesture. Shane Adams certainly remembered those days of earnestness. "When I walked into a room," he told me, "I wanted people to know I was a storm chaser." On the dashboard of the van, just above the steering wheel, Matt had left his driving gloves, black, fingerless, and well-worn; they, too, seemed possessed of the quality of the semi-ironic. They had a functional value, I was certain, for if Matt was anything he was practical and efficient, a quintessential "emergency management" type, seeing all contingencies before they happened. Maybe the gloves helped him grip the steering wheel. Maybe they were for padding. But I was certain that they functioned in other ways as well. They were, more or less, dorky-looking, and wearing them was like showing up for a friendly volleyball game in knee and elbow pads, ready to rumble. Sean Casey had smiled when he saw Matt put on those driving gloves. Perhaps to Sean they were "uncool"; that is, they were accoutrements that suggested an earnestness in excess of the occasion. Maybe the gloves were part of an ensemble formed back in his first days of chasing, back when Matt may have needed some outward sign to show himself and the world that he wasn't just some schmo driving an El Camino around the countryside. He was *chasing*. And now, while he no longer needed a sign, he liked wearing those gloves anyway, perhaps out of habit, out of superstition, out of a kind of semi-ironic, backward-looking glance at the "Chaser Formerly Known as Matt."

Indeed, Matt's life had changed. He was older now. He had a child. It was not particularly easy for him to go running off for weeks with a writer like me. Chaser culture had grown, gotten out of hand. "There was a time," Matt would say, "when I might occasionally—accidentally—run into another chaser out in the field. I might see Bobby Prentice, for example, and we'd stop and get out of our cars and laugh about how amazing it was to find each other in the middle of nowhere." Now you couldn't go anywhere, really, without finding another chaser. I had come, of course, to see the carnival that storm chasing on the American Plains had become. But Matt, playing Virgil to my gawk-eyed Dante, guiding me through the second circle that was Tornado Alley in the springtime, had come, it seemed, to say good-bye.

Big weather, like the proverbial watched pot, comes to a boil slowly. The more attention you focus upon it, the more it dallies; storm chasing thus comes to seem a test of patience, a game of waiting. The serious chaser is, therefore, more likely than other inhabitants of the American republic to be found by the side of the road, in parking lots, in gas stations, in libraries, motel lobbies, and franchise restaurants, engaged in serious—one might even say extreme—waiting. Extreme waiting is not to be confused with *loitering,* just as televised live footage of a town being wiped off the face of the earth by a tornado or hurricane, for instance, is not to be confused with catastrophilic profiteering: in the former case, it is argued, a service is being provided to the public. Most of the seasoned chasers I met were infused with a sense of public service, carrying with them the phone numbers of the National Weather Service forecast offices. When local residents approached them for weather information, they provided it with Boy Scout courtesy. Others volunteered or were hired by scientific research teams, like Josh Wurman's volunteers, or Herb Stein, who received a modest stipend for his work each spring with the DOWs. There was also an economic argument to be made: extreme waiting led to impulse buying of snack foods, for example, and chasers' consumption of food, lodging, and fuel helped local businesses and boosted the tax base of towns, cities, and states. Waiting was loitering with a purpose, so it was more or less tolerated by the general population.

One morning in the lobby of a Day's Inn just outside Omaha, I spent some time absorbing the ambiance of the weather wonk chaser-scientists working with Josh Wurman. A group of about a half-dozen meteorology students, volunteers from Penn State and OU who were spending part of their summer with Joshua Wurman's Doppler on Wheels program, leaned over a laptop computer looking at weather information.

"Bam!" said Chris Shabbot, a musclebound guy with close-cropped red hair. "The cap is not as bad as it might be. We just need to heat temps a little over thirty [centigrade] at the surface. We're looking at low seventy dew points coming this way." The cap Chris referred to was the inversion of relatively warm air over a slightly cooler, moist air mass. Above that, you wanted increasingly cool air aloft, which wasn't quite happening yet, and some form of heating at the surface or cooling above. The Storm Prediction Center had lowered the storm risk. The problem was that a high cloud cover threatened to inhibit solar heating during the day. Heating from the sun was one of two primary ways that the atmosphere became unstable. The other was "top cooling," cool air moving in from a front, say, enveloping a zone of warmer air. But this wasn't in the cards, either.

"If only we could throw some ice aloft," Wurman joked. On the bright side was the convective available potential energy (CAPE), sometimes called juice, the amount of moisture available in the atmosphere to feed severe storms. This morning the CAPE was off the charts, topping 6,000 joules per kilogram. If somehow the cap could be broken, the storms would be fearsome. "Crazy shit happens when the CAPE is that high. There are going to be tornadoes today," Matt said. "I'd bet big money on that."

Josh Wurman was pacing, talking on the cell phone all morning, trying to renew the license on some critical computer software. Miana and Jena, two meteorological undergraduates, were sitting in the Scout car, singing to the sixties girl group, the Shirelles—"Momma said, there'll be days like this, there'll be days like this, Momma said." Curtis Alexander, one of three lead forecasters working for the DOWs, entered the lobby. He had the 18Z sounding, a profile of atmospheric temperature, humidity, wind direction, and other data taken from balloons launched at Weather Service forecast offices across the country. Curtis had a big smile on his face.

"Howie's declared the day down," he said.

Howard Bluestein had developed such a reputation, over the last few years, as a stay-at-home chaser-scientist, according to the grad student grapevine, that some had privately begged not to be assigned to his crew, knowing that too many marginal spring days like this would pile up, days when despite the obvious problems of cloud cover and storm initiation, despite what Bluestein had to say about the matter, "crazy shit could still happen." A

CAPE of 6,000 joules might somehow magically compel storms to form—beautiful, riotous, off-the-chart storms, with tornadoes corkscrewing earthward in rapid succession. Things like that happened even to the best scientific teams. They were what made the game interesting. But Curtis's broad smile suggested that there was something else that made the game interesting as well. Perhaps it was the satisfaction of knowing that the simple, steadfast behavior of being fully deployed, fully operational in the field, no matter what, even on a marginal day like today, often made a difference in the long haul between an average year and a spectacular one.

Across the lobby, meteorology students from a school called the California University of Pennsylvania at Pittsburgh, or CUPP, who had been following the DOW trucks for a number of days, lay on the floor, catching up on a little sleep. One of them, a pretty young student of broadcast meteorology, got up, studied herself in a mirror, and gave her own assessment of the current conditions. "My face," she said, "is extremely dry. Is there a place to get moisturizer?"

After breakfast, Matt and I walked across the motel parking lot to observe more waiting in earnest. The DOW trucks were stationed at one end of the lot. With their radar dishes in the stowed position, pointing straight up, they looked like extravagant cocktails, supersize martinis bolted to the back of a pair of two-ton trucks. More than anything, they were big enough and odd enough looking, at first glance, to seem like part of a traveling carnival—a cup-and-saucer ride—that had blown the Interstate exit and gone astray here, in York, or Grand Island, or Beatrice, or Bellevue. And in fact, although they filled a specific scientific purpose—to render with extraordinary clarity the wind fields that surrounded tornadoes—they also fulfilled a secondary function that placed them at the leading edge of an unofficial carnival of shutterbugs and curiosity seekers for, as soon as the DOW trucks came to a stop anywhere, people approached with cameras and questions—local reporters and TV crews; local residents; passing storm chasers.

The generators of the DOW trucks were humming and Josh Wurman was talking on his cell phone, ordering a piece of equipment, and Herb Stein was busy repairing something. In the cab of DOW 3 sat two other "mission critical" crew members, Curtis Alexander and David Dowell, both of whom performed several roles for the DOW team, none more important, however, than what they were doing now, which was forecasting the day's weather. They wore the uniform of the full-on storm-geek chaser-scientist—shorts, T-shirt, white socks and sneakers, wire-rim glasses, close-cropped hair. They spoke in the cryptic *meteorologia* of the trade, while some of the undergrad students poked their heads through the truck's side windows, or, taking the back route through the radar cabin, stuck their heads between the two men like a kid brother poking up from the backseat on a cross-country drive. I stood on the running board and listened to their discussion. It took a few minutes of eavesdropping before I came to understand, in the most rudimentary way, that they were at loggerheads about the day's target area. But "at loggerheads" is probably too strong a phrase; this was like a disputation among Vatican cardinals, or between a pair of angels, each aware of the other's merits, each softly pushing his case forward, wishing nothing more than that together they both arrive at the truth. David was the darker, thinner, quieter and more intense of the two. He'd completed a postdoc at the National Center for Atmospheric Research at Boulder, Colorado (NCAR), and now had a full-time position at the Cooperative Institute for Mesoscale Meteorological Studies at OU in Norman, Oklahoma (CIMMS). He had the severe-local-storms and research bona fides, in other words. He also had something extra on the side: serious chaser chops, ten years of practical field experience intercepting storms. It wasn't necessarily the kind of thing one put on one's professional résumé, of course, where published scientific papers were the coin of the realm, but to someone hiring a staff of field researchers, someone like Joshua Wurman, who would spend a minimum of $1,000 every day in the field, scientific credentials meant very little if his transmitters and magnetrons and parabolic beams and amplidynes and custom-built data-acquisition PCs were in the wrong county when a tornadic storm blew by. Despite the wire-rim glasses and the ultracalm demeanor, there was a Daniel Boone–ish orienteering skill at targeting storms that may have been one of David Dowell's strongest, if unacknowledged, assets.

Dowell was assisted by two other men—Bob Conzemius, who often served as the DOWs' nowcaster back in Norman, and Curtis Alexander, a graduate student at OU's School of Meteorology. Conzemius was a powerful contender in any argument about the day's forecast, even as a disembodied voice on

The waiting game: Curtis Alexander (left) and David Dowell mulling over the day's severe weather forecast in the cab of a DOW radar truck in May 2004. © Mark Svenvold

the phone: he was the "Bob" in the sentence "Well, what does Bob think?" Alexander was just damn useful. He knew everything one needed to know about the radar equipment, the software, and forecasting. He was coauthoring several major papers with Josh Wurman, and beginning a new climatilogical study of tornadoes. On any given day, the three men could hold wildly diverging views about the forecast or the best area to target. None had veto power, which meant, practically speaking, that nobody was going anywhere until the three could reach consensus. This was in stark contrast to what went on in other scientific teams; Howie Bluestein, for instance, liked to spend the first part of the morning in his office, his door shut, until he'd decided upon a course of action. When Bluestein opened his office door, the weather briefing would begin and graduate students would crowd around his computer and listen to his thinking for the day. There was no genuine debate involved; if there was a consensus, it was that Howie was running the show and that everyone else was, more or less, observing the master at work. By contrast, Wurman had delegated the forecasting authority to three men who acted as if they had a stake in the matter. Consequently, we spent a good deal of time in parking lots, waiting around for the weather to shape up.

Today's parking lot was full of undergraduate meteorology students working with the DOWs. They seemed well practiced in the craft. They were mostly from the University of Oklahoma and Penn State, two big meteorology schools, and they were there to drive support vehicles and absorb what they could of field research. Just finished with their finals, they were flush in the knowledge of a new summer, new relationships, and a new chase season. They were only a few years out of high school, where they had been honor students and class valedictorians; they were so young that the "work experience" they listed on their résumés included "baby-sitting" or "camp counseling." One of them, a varsity cheerleader from Allentown, Pennsylvania, was just now walking around the parking lot on her hands. The OU and Penn State students were standing together in a small cluster, discussing music and movies, when one of them pointed to a trio of young women from the California University of Pennsylvania at Pittsburgh, who had roused themselves from their mid-morning nap to stroll across the lot.

The trio was young and girlish, and, in contravention of the storm-geek dress code—an androgynous uniform of shorts, sneakers, cap, T-shirt bearing an impossibly complex mathematical equation—they wore makeup and bikini tops and down below a garment that, in my junior high-school days, back in the seventies, was called hot pants. Only, the pants this season were somehow shorter than what I remembered, so that the sauntering by of the girls from California University of Pennsylvania at Pittsburgh became its own encapsulated moment in the day—a traffic-stopping, kinetic closed parenthesis of hip and buttock and pubic bone.

I went over to their van and introduced myself. Stacey was the darker of the two blondes. She had an oval face, a smallish mouth, and large, wide cheekbones that made her look as if she were peering shyly and a little fiercely out from behind a tribal mask, if such a mask wore mascara. Melissa had lighter hair, a narrower face, fuller lips, and a high forehead. She was likely to chew gum, or a Tootsie-Roll Pop, or a thumbnail, and her hair was pulled up. She, too, wore makeup and a black, strapless top.

The CUPP students were trapped by their own lives, by the invisible shackles of high school diplomas that meant little and car payments that meant more than they should, by a concatenation of events for which no one was singly to blame, but because of which these middle-class kids aimed lower than they might, undershot their potential, and strove modestly toward degrees in "broadcast meteorology." They were shunted off, or had shunted themselves off, to a lesser university that could not possibly prepare them for this encounter with the thoroughbreds from MIT, OU Meteorology, and Penn State—undergrads who'd aced Thermodynamics 1 and 2, who could do the math, who wore the math proudly on their T-shirts. The leader of the CUPPs was a professor named Swarn Gill, who had the best of intentions, of course: to show his students the actual practice of field research in meteorology. But it would have taken a mighty powerful personality, indeed, to breach the invisible barriers that had already been established around the DOW radar trucks. And if you did, if you walked up to David Dowell or Curtis Alexander in your black strapless top to inquire about the day's CAPE or convective inhibition or upper-level flow, you would be greeted politely and given a short, cryptic answer that would have taken an hour for Professor Gill to translate and explain, after which you'd need another month or two—perhaps an entire semester—to fully understand. So the CUPPs mostly stayed inside their van, snapping gum and listening to music, or lounged around motel lobbies; as the days wore on, the ensembles of the CUPPs meteorological beauties—one couldn't help but notice—became more outrageous, more revealing, like little salvos fired in quiet defiance from across an unpassable divide.

The parking lots of Nebraska were becoming the site of an ad hoc reunion that May of some of the best chasers in the country, and it said something about the goodwill Matt had built up over the years that they all came up to say hello. At one point, Matt introduced me to Jim Leonard, who had for decades chased tornadoes and hurricanes from here to Guam and was now running his own tour company. Leonard came up with a big smile, his face lined and worn by years of sun and wind, like an old fisherman's.

Others greeted Matt, too: Betsy Abrams, a short woman with a mane of Rasta-esque hair, and Matthew Crowther, who was thin, bespectacled, and bedraggled, smiling from ear to ear. They looked like a couple out of R. Crumb's comics, or the Fabulous Furry Freak Brothers, like two refugees from Bolinas, California, or from the Crosby, Stills and Nash standard "Marrakesh Express." They were happy, chatty grand doyens of the chaser circuit, who'd been letting their weather-freak flag fly for so long, they no longer cared what anyone thought about them. They were two of the dorkiest-looking people I'd ever seen, and I wanted to embrace them at the knees like the lost godparents I knew they must have been. That they were also two of the most senior meteorologists working at the Weather Channel was something not to be believed, and they seemed to anticipate my incredulity, to recognize that their own cavalier un-telegenic-ness might provoke some to doubt, but so it was. So it wonderfully was. This year, as in most years, they'd taken two weeks' vacation to drive from Atlanta and chase storms.

Still others arrived. Jeff Piotrowski, a high-strung man from Tulsa who took a penchant for doing several things at the same time—like driving at high speed while reading a map and talking on the phone—and applied it to selling high-end weather forecasting software and equipment to radio and television stations, managing his own photo and video stock archive of weather imagery, and consulting as a storm chaser for Pioneer Productions, perhaps the biggest of the big weather film companies that contract out to the Learning Channel, the Discovery Channel, National Geographic, and the BBC. Business was booming. At the National Chaser Convention, I'd asked Piotrowski if he wouldn't mind telling me for whom he'd be consulting that spring, but he demurred: "Oh, everybody. I can't really tell you." Meaning, apparently, that he was contractually obliged to remain quiet? This was big weather, indeed. I pressed him further. "Just everybody: books, magazines, movies, documentary films." I gave Piotrowski my card. Later in the afternoon he called me on my cell phone to give me a courtesy update on the weather. "There's a full blown storm west southwest of Holdredge, Nebraska, about forty miles. *It will move toward Lexington,*" he said quickly. This was followed by: "Okay, okay. It's going severe. *It's just gone severe.* I've gotta go." So, hurriedly, went Jeff Piotrowski.

Storm chasing was beginning to remind me of an outdoor version of

e. e. cummings's *The Enormous Room,* in which a series of characters enter a room and light up a cigarette. The room gets full and smoky, but nothing much happens. On this day, May 19, 2004, just east of Omaha, exactly nothing happened. Howie Bluestein had been right to declare the day down. A CAPE of 6,000 hadn't done much, by itself, to initiate storms. Matt and I had followed the DOWs across the Missouri River into Iowa, but by five P.M. Curtis Alexander and David Dowell were almost ready to throw in the towel. A football arced across the gravel parking lot. The DOW kids may have been able to explain the aerodynamics of a spiraling football, but they couldn't throw one to save their lives. They caught it and looked with bemusement at the seams of the ball, these students from two of the biggest football powerhouses in the country, and then they lobbed another dead duck into the air. That nobody could throw a football, it seemed, was a kind of dork's badge of honor, yet they kept trying even though each wobbly toss revealed to anyone who cared to look that in the world of ordinary youthful pursuits, these students, just now crawling out from under their thermodynamics textbooks, had a bit of catching up to do.

At 5:45 the DOW two-radio crackled, "Bogey coming in from the west": somebody had spotted Sean Casey. Soon the TIV pulled into the gravel parking lot, its rear hatch open, ducting air into the vehicle. Herb Stein began running alongside, giving Sean the thumbs-up and a cheer of welcome. Others followed Herb and gathered around Sean as he climbed out of his tank. Jena and Maiana gave Sean a hug, which he absorbed with an easy grace. Even the quiet, cerebral David Dowell walked up to shake his hand. Sean was much loved. Today was officially declared a bust and tomorrow a "down day." Tonight Sean and the DOW kids would have a party with volleyball, followed by swimming in the hotel pool. I felt a pang of jealousy. It was hard to be on the other side of all that fun. Back in Norman, Matt's wife, Mamie, was taking care of their daughter, Faith, and working nights as a waitress at a local watering hole. It hadn't been easy on her for me to take Matt away. My wife had called the night before, nearly in tears, because I hadn't thought to change my cell phone policy before leaving for Oklahoma, and, as a result of extra roaming charges made while storm chasing, we were looking at a phone bill that made my heart stop and my mouth go dry. It was the kind of figure that's best uttered at the tops of one's lungs, and Martha had done it justice. My nose began to tingle and my eyes to water. I walked across the gravel lot, watching Sean Casey enjoy the embrace of his companions. They were going to barbecue some steaks, drink beer, and watch the basketball playoffs, it seemed, for the rest of their days. *Life is not a summer camp,* I thought darkly, walking back to the van where Matt had been sitting all afternoon, watching the weather on a portable TV that he'd plugged into the cigarette lighter. At the close of the Channel 6 news, the anchors for the Omaha NBC affiliate conducted the following exchange, which Matt dutifully recorded:

Anchor 1: "Still a chance of severe weather tonight and most of the week."

Anchor 2: "And will we see those strange-looking vehicles around town?"

Anchor 1: "Yes. For the next few days, and when they're in town, we pay attention."

The waiting game brought to mind a phrase I'd heard a few days earlier from a client of Jim Leonard's named Olivier Staiger, from Geneva, Switzerland, who was on the second leg of a month-long tornado tour. Staiger, an affable man, traveled around the world pursuing solar eclipses—"anything, really, that has to do with the sky." The weather was his newest passion. He kept a daily Web journal on which he posted each day's triumphant sightings and was fairly bursting with excitement about what he'd seen so far and what was to come. Talking to him was like standing next to a cymbalist in an orchestra. *Crash! Crash! Crash!* He was the kind of person who, if he told you that leather tooling was one of the greatest hobbies in the world, you'd believe him. It had to be true. He had enough enthusiasm for two or three people, which may be why I simply forgot to ask why he liked storms so much. Eventually I wrote to him in Geneva.

"It's a little bit like music," he wrote back. "When you listen to quiet classical music, Mozart or Debussy style—that is nice quiet blue skies. Boring fall-asleep music.

"But when you get storms—lightning, hail, dark skies and tornadoes, then, you see—Rachmaninov, Tchaikovsky, Rimsky Korsakov. *Tadaaahh!!* That is energy. That is passion. That is life!

"Of course, there is the negative side of severe weather (destruction, death, etc) and I do not like that. But you can't have it all."

But I wanted to learn from this man who had come so far, why we were so focused upon the sky. This I did ask in person.

"We are paparazzi del cielo," he said with a smile, as he left the restaurant. The phrase seemed to capture a good deal of what was happening beyond the diner window, where the scene included scientists, media vans, tour groups, and teenagers in their trucks. Across the region, all of us, from commercial chaser to amateur chaser to storm spotter, were momentarily encompassed by a single phrase. All of us were lying in wait for the star of the hour, or era, to make its elusive, unpredictable, spectacular appearance.

SIX

Present Progressive

In my room, the world is beyond my understanding; But when I walk
I see that it consists of three or four hills and a cloud.
—WALLACE STEVENS, "OF THE SURFACE OF THINGS"

Everyone was bustling that morning, after a day's rest. Matt had called a local Omaha pharmacy to get a prescription that his doctor had phoned in. He explained that he was in the area from Oklahoma, working on a project. He didn't say what project it happened to be.

"I know," the pharmacist said. "You're the storm chasers. You guys are making me nervous."

An informal weather briefing was being held by David Dowell and Curtis Alexander in the cab of DOW 2, beneath the white fuzzy dice that hung from the rearview mirror. The dice, like other important talismanic objects, such as the Teletubby hood ornament, were part of a scientific forecasting regime that seemed to allow for a certain amount of voodoo practice. Jana Lesak, the athletic driver of DOW 2, was busy installing a cardboard sign: HONK IF YOU LOVE STORM CHASING. Sean Casey sat in between Curtis and David in the DOW truck, listening in. Curtis read aloud the "Day One Outlook" issued by the Storm Prediction Center: "Strong heating, rich boundary layer moisture contribute to extremely unstable conditions for the late afternoon." Every so often, Curtis would turn and explain a term of art for Sean's benefit. On a computer screen, Curtis was looking at what the computer models were predicting for a number of different storm "parameters." "Here's your low-level-shear vector for the area," he said, turning to Sean.

Low level shear, he explained, was a measure of how the winds can change in speed and direction in the lowest kilometer of the atmosphere. He turned next to the prediction for deep-layer shear. "The zero- to six-kilometer shear is a gage of supercell potential. You really want around thirty-five knots of shear up to six kilometers, and about twenty knots of shear up to the first kilometer—and we're certainly in excess of that."

The biggest puzzle today was that the SPC had predicted a slight risk of tornadoes over a huge area—basically all of Nebraska and Iowa—with a tornado probability bull's-eye of 5 percent covering the eastern two thirds of northern Nebraska and centering on the town of O'Neil, about a hundred miles northwest of Omaha. "Slight risk" and "moderate risk" are, as Matt had explained to me a few years ago on our first chase, relative to each other. A "slight risk of severe weather" was a significant risk. Because "slight" in fact expressed a greater likelihood of big weather than the word's commonplace meaning suggests, the SPC had begun attaching percentages to the "slight," "moderate," and "high" risk advisories, ranging from 2 percent to 25 percent. It was an attempt to bring specificity to what otherwise remained a qualitative estimate.[1] The basic concern, as David Dowell put it, was that storms might fire too far west of the best environment for severe weather, which was in northern Nebraska. The strategy that emerged would be to drift north toward O'Neil, staying on the eastern edge of the elongated, east-to-west 5 percent tornado risk area. This way, as Curtis explained, if storms fired off to their west as David thought they might, the storms would be carried east on the prevailing winds toward the DOWs, and the DOWs, charging west to meet them, would still have a chance of closing for an intercept.

After the weather briefing, I found Sean alongside the TIV. It had been nearly a week since we'd left Norman, but his meteorological instruments were still not up and running properly. "The computer on the DOW isn't recognizing me," he said. Earlier, in the trailer with David and Curtis, he'd been like the rest of us severe-weather initiates who had gathered to quietly and respectfully listen to the meteorological wizards discuss the forecast. Now, with the more familiar tools of his trade laid out on the ground before him, he seemed to have reacquired his usual imperturbable, amused detachment. He also seemed to have gained an acolyte. Maiana, the Scottish undergraduate from Duke University, was standing nearby, taking pictures of

High and low tech: Sean Casey with an IMAX camera and a roll of duct tape, May 2004.
© M. D. Biddle

"It's like fishing in a particularly fish-crazy community." Casey and chaser partner Gregory Eliason in front of the TIV, May 2004. © Davenny/Cote de Luna

Sean loading film into the IMAX camera, a big and clumsy piece of equipment with film and take-up reels positioned horizontally. Sean paused now and then to spit some chew into a cup. The camera case was open, exposing the teeth and gears and feeders and light baffles and the lens itself, as well as the diagram on the inside of the case to ensure that one fed the film properly. Each roll contained a thousand feet, three minutes' worth of film, at a cost of $1,200. "That is, if you buy it *new*," Sean said, spitting again. Using his hunter-gatherer, stuff-getting skills, he'd found some IMAX film from a project that had never gotten off the ground. "I got the film for about twenty-five cents on the dollar," he said, "about twelve thousand feet for thirty-five hundred bucks." The high cost of film and the fact that the camera was awkward to use affected the look of most IMAX films. "In a regular documentary you're using video or digital," he said. "You get to roll a lot. A lot of video. They get to roll, maybe, thirty minutes at a time. For us, it's really about keeping track of how much footage you've shot. With this format, you have to choose your shot and take it. So IMAX films tend to be very stagey."

The day before, as I sat glumly eating a bowl of oatmeal and thinking about my cell phone bill and how lucky Sean was and wondering, bleakly, whether I would even see a tornado, Sean had slid into my booth and had breakfast with me. To cheer me up, he'd taken a piece of paper from my notebook and drawn me a picture of the next-generation TIV that he would build that winter—the TIV 2, which would have giant steel plates that could be lowered to the ground like a skirt to prevent wind from going under the vehicle. It looked fantastic, a tank with wings. With any luck, TIV 2, he explained, would be included in VORTEX II, the next big, scientific tornado-intercept project, which would be the basis for Sean's ambitious IMAX film. Though Sean seemed completely sanguine about his chances of being included in VORTEX II, I wondered aloud how a stodgy committee of scientists would feel about TIV 2. Would it threaten to turn a legitimate scientific project into a spectacle?

"If the National Science Foundation is going to put money into a project like VORTEX II, they're going to want it to be shown," Sean said. "And also, the fact that we will have instrumentation will be an interesting angle.

Most filmmakers are never part of the science. And if they are, it's usually a silly part.

"This," he said, with a nod to the diagram of TIV 2, "is not so, *so* silly." He leaned into that second "so," to indicate his place in the scheme of things, a degree of remove, an order of magnitude, away from utter silliness.[2]

When it came to choosing the participants in VORTEX II, the largest field research project on tornadoes in a decade, there was no question that a case would have to be made, it seemed, for the inclusion of a tank with wings. I think that's what Sean meant by the phase "an interesting angle." But perhaps the gulf between him and the researchers wasn't nearly so wide as one thought. The DOWs, the crew, Josh Wurman, Curtis, David, and all the rest, were scientists, he seemed to be saying—*and closet adventurers,* in the tradition of Benjamin Franklin. To say that the DOWs were doing what they did only for the science would be, according to Sean, "a bit of a lie." The work was also tremendous fun, and it carried the whiff of danger and glamour. It wasn't like being an atomic physicist, searching for neutrinos at the bottom of a salt mine. Severe local storm research was sexy. It was cool. It put your name and your face in the public eye. You got yourself regularly on the national news. Russian film crews came to interview you. NOVA specials were made. Quasi-celebrity status was not necessarily something that one sought out as a scientist, but clearly it had its place. Even if nobody really wanted to talk about it, it helped pushed the science along. Conversely, it was not entirely true to say that Sean Casey was only—or even primarily—an adventurer, for not only could he serve a public relations function but also *it could be argued* that IMAX footage of actual tornadoes would be of genuine scientific value. By measuring objects filmed within a tornado and calculating the distance that those objects moved from one frame to the next, scientists could measure the wind speed in different parts of a tornado. The process was called photogrammatic analysis. Sean looked at me from across the table. By the word "lie" I don't think he meant real mendacity but rather a "cooperative or convenient fiction" that enabled both parties to get what they wanted: Sean, proximity to tornadoes; Josh Wurman and the National Science Foundation, public attention. "Their lie and my lie intersect," he said, "at the TIV."

By 1:30 P.M. the caravan of trucks, support vehicles, and assorted hangers-on was north of Omaha; the local radio station was jauntily playing Creedence Clearwater Revival's foot-stomping, apocalyptic tune "Bad Moon Rising":

Hope you have got your things together.
Hope you are quite prepared to die.
Looks like we're in for nasty weather.
One eye is taken for an eye.

It was impossible to hear this as just a nod to the weather forecast, this being Nebraska, the literal-minded heart of the Republican political base, impossible not to be struck by the looping back of history upon itself. Because this song, written so long ago, at the height of an extended period of national folly, deception, and disastrous military misadventure, now sounded more menacing than even John Fogerty could have imagined.

By the early afternoon, Matt and I had gone our own way, leaving the DOWs to themselves. We drove west and found, just south of St. Paul, Nebraska, a white van pulled off onto a dirt road. The van had a white radar dome on top, many different kinds of antennae, and Colorado plates. It belonged to Tim Samaras. For those unfamiliar with a certain recent *National Geographic* story on storm chasing, Samaras is a Denver-based engineer, longtime chaser, and organizer of the National Storm Chaser Convention. He is perhaps best known as the inventor of the HITP, the Hardened In-situ Tornado Pressure Recorder, an instrument that he likes to try to plant inside tornadoes. He does this by getting his white van very close—sometimes it's just a matter of a hundred yards or less—deploying his device, and then running away. The HITP, a heavy, flattened cone, like a Hershey's kiss that's been left in the sun, is virtually indestructible, contains no moving parts, and has been successfully deployed on several occasions, the most widely publicized of which—the one described in *National Geographic*—was the violent tornado on June 24, 2003, that erased the hamlet of Manchester, South Dakota, from the map.

Tim was in the driver's seat, studying his laptop. Electronically speaking, he was loaded for bear, with the latest weather forecasting software, the

Baron's XM Threat Net Weather Satellite Receiver, which emitted a steady pong, like sonar, all the radio communications equipment you'd ever need, and a portable TV tuned to the Weather Channel. With dark hair, glasses on a chain, short-sleeve shirt, jeans, and running shoes, he looked like an engineer on a dress-down Friday. With him was Carsten Peter, who had photographed the *National Geographic* story but was traveling with Tim this May on his own, freelancing. Carsten, who had his pick of beautiful, remote places to work in, had come to central Nebraska to chase storms. "The truth is, I'm hooked on this," he said, smiling. He'd had his own battlefield moment of clarity during the Manchester tornado. Tim mentioned one of the photographs Carsten had taken that day, a very high-resolution image of the debris cloud. "Essentially," Tim said, "you're looking at whatever is left of Manchester, suspended in the air."

Tim was also traveling with a chase partner named Carl Young, a friendly, dark-haired meteorologist from Reno, who had a habit of speaking at all times as if he were on camera in front of a green screen—lots of helpful hand gestures, excellent enunciation. At a cocktail party, for instance, broad, sweeping, skyward gestures of this sort might have been a distraction, but in the middle of Nebraska, as we stared at the cumulus clouds beginning to boil in the afternoon heat, Carl Young was, in fact, quite helpful. We were following a moisture tongue, he explained, that ran east and west along the Nebraska–South Dakota border into Iowa. There were two current areas of interest. One was to the north. He pushed his palms outward as if trying to stop traffic, the whole gesture taking in the cloudscape beyond the Missouri River toward Yankton, South Dakota. This northern environment and everything to the east into Iowa was like a powder keg. The trouble, as Curtis Alexander had explained earlier that morning, was the capping inversion that lay over all that unstable air. With the exception of the Twister Sisters, who'd called me that morning to say they were waiting for things to explode in Iowa, nobody, including the SPC, thought that storms would initiate that far east. But by 3:30 P.M., according to Tim Samaras's radar, the cap had broken east of Sioux City and storms were starting to fire.

"Looks like the Twister Sisters will be in business today," Matt said.

This made the storm to the north of our position particularly tempting. To play the north would take us into the best air, but then we would have to contend with a major obstacle—the Missouri River. Chasing was particularly sensitive to any sort of topographic perturbation, anything that interfered with one's ability to freely navigate along the regular latticework of road systems. Hills, gorges, lakes, and rivers simply created problems, especially at the golden hours between six and eight in the evening, when one was closing hard upon a storm. It was then that the Missouri River might suddenly, maddeningly, stand between you and your storm, the nearest bridge a half-hour away, forcing the kind of detour that killed a chase.

Carl Young swiveled to the southwest. Carsten and I pivoted on our heels to follow Carl's hands, which swept the entire horizon. A second storm was developing in that direction, he said. Already you could see the gauzy filaments of its advancing anvil moving our way. The choice was between these two storms, and we couldn't chase both.

Tim Samaras was out of his van, looking north. He turned around and squinted into the southwest, then looked north again. As he walked, the gravel crunched under his feet. Nearby, a meadowlark began singing.

"Oh," Carsten said, "the Tornado Bird is back."

"That's a very good omen," said the inventor of the Hardened In-Situ Tornado Pressure Recorder.

In the distance you could hear the low thudding of a Harley-Davidson. The driver pulled off the highway and headed onto the dirt road where we were parked, our doors open, blocking the way. The man came to a stop in front of us. "Expecting a storm?" he said.

Carl Young, who also served as an ad hoc community relations ambassador for the idle or curious, went into his on-camera meteorologist persona, giving the man a quick sketch of the forecast situation.

"Well," the man said, putting his Harley in gear, "that's enough for me." He nodded toward one of the open doors blocking his way. "Would you mind closing that, please?" The man drove about a hundred yards down the dirt road and came to a stop in front of his house. I watched him get off his motorcycle and go inside. Then I looked at us with our vans and our tripods and our rental car parked cattywampus, doors splayed open. We'd been blocking the man's driveway.

We headed north, listening to the American Farm Radio network. May, it seems, was National Beef Month. According to the Nebraska Beef Council, every dollar of beef sold brought six dollars to related industries. "We normally would now have Paul Harvey's *The Rest of the Story,* the DJ announced. "But because of technical difficulties, we'll be listening to Bob Wills and the Texas Playboys."

"Divine intervention," Matt said.

We'd been driving through the sand hill region of Nebraska—wheat fields, cows and a few pigs. It was Saturday. Farm auctions were in progress. Cows outnumbered people four to one in Nebraska. One out of five hamburgers was "grown in Nebraska," the beef booster association bellowed. We passed a farm where several dead hogs had been left by the road to be picked up by the rendering truck. I was eating an ice cream bar with my feet on the dashboard, tapping out the rhythm of the Texas Playboys. Matt looked at my ice cream bar and at the dead hogs.

"I wonder what kind of music the hog-rendering truck plays?" he said.

I was happy to see him in such a good mood. We fueled up at O'Neil, and then drove east on a secondary road, stopping every now and then to assess the situation. At six o'clock, about fifteen miles from Yankton, we paused on a dirt road. Matt showed me an old-school chaser trick, turning the radio dial all the way to the left, so that all I could hear was static. "If you hear a zip, that's a lightning strike," he said.

"Lightning?" I asked.

"The more lightning strikes there are, the more the storm is intensifying," he explained. "It's a cheap lightning detector." By contrast, Tim Samaras's van fairly sagged under its burden of meteorological hardware. At one of our stops I noticed that his Baron's XM Threat Net Weather Satellite Receiver was warning over and over, in a digitized voice like a fancy car alarm, "You are approaching a strong storm. Please exercise caution." The Weather Channel was still playing on his portable TV, and the National Weather Service radio chirped its warnings. Later, as we were driving east, Matt pointed ahead. Tim and Carl had stuck their hands out of the van windows.

"They've resorted to feeling the air with their fingers."

We stopped on a side road about fifteen miles south of Yankton. Tim stepped out of the van.

"Damn," he said. "No wind, again."

A tower to the south was shooting upward formidably.

"An SLC," he said. "Scary-looking cloud."

In minutes, as he knew it would, the SLC tore itself apart.

"I'm going to pull up a visual and see how the cloud tops look," Tim said. "To me, that's a real good indicator."

He stepped into his van and slowly brought up a real-time visual satellite image of the state of Nebraska, zooming in close so that he could see the boundary markers for each county. He was looking down into his lap at a screen that was looking at the cloud tops from 22,000 miles over our heads. We were in a classic situation, caught between two compelling storms. No amount of available information was going to help us decide which one to pick. It boiled down to intuition, experience, inclination. We had ventured as far toward the northern storm as we could without committing ourselves to cross the Missouri. The northern storm seemed to be dying out. "Well, we've saved Yankton from a tornado," Tim said, with a dark smile. Then he faced the southern storm. "Now let's go save Norfolk."

Matt, Tim, and Carl talked for a minute and decided to drift farther east for a while, just to make sure that the northern storm didn't suddenly intensify, and then we would drop south. But as they were talking, the southern storm exploded. Tim hunched over the satellite image. It was now as big as an entire county. "That's quite the tasty little mouthful," he said. Carl was already in the car, and Matt headed toward the van. "It's got shear, too." Feet crunched on gravel. Doors slammed shut. "I say we put on our catcher's mitt and catch it just north of Norfolk."

"THE NATIONAL WEATHER SERVICE in Omaha has issued a tornado warning for Knox County and Pierce County, northeast Nebraska. At seven-forty-two P.M., radar indicated a severe storm with a possible tornado." Matt spotted it instantly.

"There's the wall cloud," he said, nodding to the southwest as calmly as if he were folding clothes. He wore his dark sunglasses and his semi-ironic black fingerless driving gloves, and he seemed to have entered that zone I'd noticed so many other times before, a zone of tranquility, sending me a little dispatch from wherever the rest of him had gone. But that was wrong, of course. I knew it was wrong because I could feel a calmness beginning to work its way inside of me as well. People compare chasing with big game hunting, and I guess that analogy works up to a point. But how to describe the movements of the last hour or so, after the emotional momentum, after the long, steady buildup throughout the day of a movable opera whose stage was the earth itself, an opera that was reaching its climax? The hunting analogy was insufficient, a convenience for newspaper and magazine editors. Like most clichés, it pointed the way to a truth about storm chasing, but the truth kept skittering beyond its clumsy grasp.

For the reality of chasing wasn't so much that it was an "extreme sport" or a form of "adventure travel," but that it extended into middle age the adolescent American pastime of automobile cruising, of being in one's car without a particular destination but with the illusion of a sense of purpose one gets when moving over the landscape, behind the wheel. At one point in our lives, this had been a way of looking for something—for mischief, for girls, for weekend diversionary experience. The automobile had created a space in which we, as teenagers, did stupid things to make ourselves feel older. Now Matt and I were grown up, had children of our own and forbearing wives who, on occasion, vouchsafed us the old escape. We brought to it, of course, the scaffolding of research, and the nomenclature of meteorology, but mostly it was about endless bags of Doritos washed down with Mountain Dew. Mostly it was a form of being nowhere.

And all of it led to the true payoff of every chase, whether or not we saw a tornado—all of it led to this timeless extension into the present progressive, even as we moved through a transparent gauze and late afternoon blossomed into early evening, and the atmospheric heating was at its highest, and the cap had broken, and you could feel the convergence, and the tower that you'd finally chosen, after much deliberation, exploded into big weather—and it amounted to a temporary stay against the slant light waning into early evening, against time and the accumulation of grievances and resentments, against all the dashed hopes, and all the overwhelming responsibilities of midlife, the whole schmear reduced to a handful of important, elemental cognitive features. *Where was I?* The question so elemental, yet, as we zigged and zagged across a landscape that seemed to erase the cardinal compass points, its answer was not always forthcoming. *What was the storm doing?* Everything that seemed to have gone so terribly wrong for Matt—so many years on crutches, his daughter Faith learning how to embrace an arm-ful of metal; the abiding grudge against fate or God that had brought him his dark humor, a pessimism straight out of Lermontov; his love for those moments when things got a little chippy on the ice; the Ahab-like rage that I had witnessed now and then when the talk turned to politics and it seemed to both of us, as we leaned over bars late into the night, that weasels had taken over the world—all of this slipped away. Only then could I see that it wasn't so much that Matt had "gone" anywhere but that here, in the middle of nowhere, say, on a secondary highway somewhere between Pierce and Norfolk, Nebraska, at the center of a storm swirling around us, much of his life had been shed, unburdened for the moment in the golden hour at the height of the chase.

The voice of the weather radio continued, a vocalized ticker tape: "The most dangerous part of the storm is located east of Plainview and about twenty-seven miles northwest of Norfolk, moving east at twenty miles an hour." Dusk approached. We were headed south over open farmland, fal-low fields alternating with cattle grass and nothing to block the view in any direction, save for the gentle undulations, the crests and troughs of prairie topography, rollers in an open sea. The sky was gray with a low cloud base; and far to the southwest, a thin band of sunlight defined the horizon, glow-ing faintly. And there in the distance was the lowering that Matt was talking about. From fifteen miles away it was something one might have easily over-looked, appearing as the slightest dip of the clouds, earthward, but as I stud-ied it, even I could see that it was organized, as they say, and persistent, not like the raggedy scud that might momentarily present itself in an afternoon silhouette as a "wall cloud" and then vanish. This had substance. It had sym-metry. And presently a leaning finger descended from the lowering mass—a funnel cloud, and then another.

We were coming from the north, having abandoned a supercell whose vast overshooting anvil even now rendered that part of the day overcast and gloomy. Coming toward us from the south-southwest was our storm, a "tail-end Charlie," so called because there was nothing but clear sky to the south beyond it. We'd passed underneath its leading edge, where things got even gloomier, but in time we began to approach the storm's southern flank, and ever so slowly the horizon began to open up, the way a vista opens at the crest of a hill. Soon the wall cloud we'd been watching for miles took up most of our windshield.

"It's in the right part of the storm," Matt said.

But nothing came of it. Cold outflow air dropping from above and rushing along the earth undercut any potential for a tornado. No problem. With storms popping up everywhere on the horizon and the weather radio squawking its warnings, we targeted a second storm further to the south, toward the town of Norfolk itself, where the National Weather Service had issued a tornado warning, the storm in full view, lofting a stiff, vertical tower, a good visual sign of a storm's strength, illuminated in the slant light of the setting sun. We passed through some light hail and rain, then, two miles south of a little hamlet called Wee Town, we turned west on a dirt road. Matt did a quick U-turn, positioning the van so that it was headed east, toward the main highway, U.S. 81. If for some reason we had to flee, all we needed to do was jump in and go. He did not turn off the engine. I got out and watched Tim Samaras disappear westward down the road toward the storm. I'd be lying if I said I didn't wish I were in the van with him and Carsten, the German photographer, charging ever closer to the tornado. But this was as close as Matt wanted to get. The storm was approaching us, after all. Soon the wind began to pick up. "That's the inflow," Matt said. "The inflow is picking up. That's a good sign." He was out of the van, which I took as another good sign. If we stood quietly contemplating the clouds and listening to the birds on the telephone lines and feeling the inflow winds begin to buffet us, we did so for a very short time. Soon other vans approached from the main highway, passed us, did U-turns, and parked. Out of them spilled a couple dozen tornado tourists, all bearing cameras and camcorders, and tripods and other gear, some wearing rain slickers, some with cowboy hats, most wearing shorts and sneakers, each establishing a viewing position on the side of the road, pointing southwest across a landscape that buckled into gullies and draws lined with cottonwood and elm. You could hear the birds twittering and cameras clicking away, and the sound of Norfolk's tornado sirens carried on the breeze. Charles Edwards, Matt's longtime friend and owner of Cloud 9 Tours, approached us with a smile. Whatever was going to happen today was going to happen right here. Directly above us, the dark circular base of a mesocyclone rotated, and within its center, a needlelike condensation funnel began to descend. It looked to be about a thousand feet above us, and growing. As it grew, so did Matt's concern.

"Oh, shit," he said.

"What."

"We're going to have to go."

"What?"

"Well, we're not in danger, but I do *not* want to get cut off, so get ready."

"Okay. I'm ready," I said.

"You keep shooting while I get in."

"Okay," I said.

I was a little disappointed. I stood for a minute outside, as did Matt. Something had caught his eye. There were two dozen people lining the road, including Charles Edwards, and all of them were quietly looking in the same direction.

"Look on the ground for a debris cloud," Matt said suddenly, loud enough for everyone to hear. In that same instant, on the ground and many hundreds of feet beneath the descending funnel, a debris cloud kicked up. Charles Edwards thrust his arm forward, pointing, and yelled, "I think I see one right there!" And everyone drew a bead on a swirling veil of dust about a mile away.

I wanted to wait and let the tornado come to me. I wanted to have my tornado experience, whatever that might be, but Matt had other ideas, so I climbed in the van and Matt slowly pulled away. We were still north of an eastward-moving funnel. Ideally, we would drop below it, then follow the storm's natural eastward progress. The tornado would then be lit by sun against a dark backdrop. But if we stayed where we were, and if this funnel turned into a full-blown tornado and tracked east, we'd be cut off from our southern route, caught within the "backdrop," the worst possible part of the storm—its northeastern, advancing flank, the precipitation core, where rain and hail obscured visibility. Leaving made sense, but I still did not want to go. Neither did Charles Edwards, apparently.

As we crept slowly past the assembled crowd, one of Charles Edwards's clients, a bearded, bespectacled man in his forties wearing an orange shirt and a green baseball cap, his camcorder pointed to the wrong part of the sky, noticed that I was filming him watching the storm. He had the broad, self-congratulatory smile you see occasionally in people secure in the knowledge that they are having a prepackaged experience, one that had been advertised, mulled over, purchased, anticipated for months, and was now in progress, unfolding exactly as expected, all the mystery more or less siphoned out of it, the sublime become safari—which prompted him into the realm of non sequitur. "We were here," he said, more to my camera than to me, more to a "me" who would, at some point in the near future, it seemed, view this event, contemplate this experience-with-a-tornado that neither of us was having. For my camera was pointed at him and his tour group, and this had prompted him to step outside his tornado experience in order to leave a message for me, as if he were a high-tech video graffiti artist, uttering a slightly modified, latter-day version of the World War II phrase "Kilroy was here." I liked to imagine a soldier, perhaps one of the first to liberate Paris, in some moment of revelry climbing one of the Eiffel Tower's massive archways, in order to scribble that phrase and perpetuate a legacy, only to find at that giddy, dizzying height above the Tuileries, with Notre Dame in the distance, that he'd been out-Kilroyed by Kilroy. How different and difficult it was for Kilroy's descendants, all of us who had come after, destined always to live in the predicate, in Longinian ambivalence, to which the automobile offered the nearest, readiest, easiest antidote. Most of us could drive before we could buy beer, and the imprint was fierce—not the so-called American love affair with the automobile, but a need as fierce as an addiction. Indeed, it was a dark habit, and it was making the world darker than anyone wanted to recognize. But where else were we to go to put a little *avant* in our lives, to get a little forward feeling, to take the measure of reconquered ground?

"Hey, Charles," Matt said out his window, "I am bound and determined not to get cut off by this thing."

Charles Edwards looked at Matt and shrugged. And we turned south onto Highway 81. Everything else about the tornado that followed would be, in hindsight, and in a different sense than Matt had meant, bound and determined, it seemed, framed and refracted from the inside of a Dodge Caravan, contained within that shell of welded sheet metal, glass, and shaped plastic, its little electric noises *pong-pong*ing away, reminding us to fasten our seatbelts, the radio announcer reading off a list of counties affected by the tornado warning, the alarm from Matt's weather radio chirp-ing and squawking, the tires whining on concrete as Matt tried to get south of the tornado. I wasn't about to forget this experience anytime soon, but it wasn't exactly a Blakean encounter, either. The truncated cone, a slender white condensation funnel, descended against the gray of the parent storm to a perfect point, hanging about five hundred feet in the air. Beneath this it became almost perfectly transparent but for the wisps of debris that helped define a ghostly cylinder, spinning unimaginably fast, and then, near the ground, the fat debris cloud. Dirt by the cubic yard from the surrounding fields was being sucked up and launched into the air, giving the base of the tornado a heft. The ground cover and the trees and perhaps an outbuilding or two launched into the air helped provide a sense of scale, a sense of how violently things were being flung. Eventually Matt found a place to safely pull off and I climbed out of the car. I remember tasting the dust in the inflow, which was hot and blowing strong into my face. The debris cloud was straight west of us and seemed not to move. I panned upward with my video camera, following the slender funnel, which was being pushed south by the storm's outflow, stretching and roping out. Matt wanted me to get a shot of him with the tornado, which I did, and then he said it was time to go. I wanted more than ever to stay and watch, but as I got in the car I noticed something: the tornado had grown unmistakably larger in the few minutes that we'd been parked and was now about half a mile away. It had stopped tracking south and was moving east with the storm, directly toward us. Yes, it was time to go.

We dropped as far south as the hamlet of Hadar, just north of Norfolk, more of a crossroads than anything else, and Matt pulled over again. I filmed the tornado for a few seconds, and then, suddenly, it died. All the dirt sus-pended in the debris cloud just dropped to the ground.

And that was that—almost. Back at the turnoff at Wee Town, Matt had seen the tornado before anyone else, had directed all of us, counterintu-itively, to watch the ground and not the sky, and, as if on cue, the tornado had materialized. He'd remained one step ahead of it since it touched down, and now, when I thought the show was over and had walked back to the van, he was on the cell phone, reporting the incident to the local emergency management office. The tornado had already been reported, but it hadn't hurt to call it in, anyway.

The first thing I did when I arrived at the Super 8 parking lot in Norfolk, of course, was to walk up to a group of chasers and compare video footage with them. We stood in a tight circle under streetlights ooh-ing and ah-ing at storm footage. It was a fairly dorky thing to do, and while I recognized that I'd crossed a line into storm geekdom, I found myself completely unable to resist an impulse that seemed as old as hunting and gathering itself. If cavemen had had video cameras, they would have done the same thing.

And then it was time to eat steaks, following a tradition established by veteran chaser Tim Marshall, who made a point of eating steak after every successful chase, a ritual I was not prepared to violate. Word got out that we had video of a tornado, and soon people were approaching me for a look. A trucker who lived in town brought his little daughter for a peek, which I gladly showed her. The bartender asked whether she could go get the cook. Out came the cook from behind the double doors and I showed him my tornado video. It was horrifically bad camera work—lots of it was out of focus, and I'd forgotten to always include some part of the horizon in the frame, for scale, but there were a few seconds that were pretty decent, where the tornado was crisp, roping out in a broad, sinuous arc. And so, for the moment, in a franchise restaurant called Whiskey Creek, in Norfolk, Nebraska, I felt myself basking in a fraudulent glow of accomplishment.

Matt, because of his prosthetic leg, preferred to eat at the bar, where he could sit on a stool and eat comfortably. He was talking to two men, Ward Davenny and Jeffery Timander Cote de Luna, both landscape photographers and professors of art, who had asked permission to join Josh Wurman months ago and had been following the DOWs since the May 12 storm in Attica, Kansas. A few days earlier, Ward had shown me his video footage of that tornado. He was gray-haired and in his late fifties, with a handsome, weathered face in which one was liable to find a cigarette, and keen, sardonic eyes that seemed ever to be squinting beyond practical matters, to something higher, more rarefied, which is a way of saying that his life was a comfortable sort of shambles—he was tenured, at Dickinson College, which, as a friend once said to me, was a way of dying but not going to heaven *or* to hell; he was divorced, with three children; this spring, while he was chasing tornadoes, he'd broken up with his girlfriend; he told me he was emerging out of a period of deep isolation. This last had made conversation with him an interesting but sometimes halting affair, during which one waited around, as if for a bus, for the arrival of the predicate of a sentence, or for the name of an artist he wanted to recommend. I was drawn to him immediately. He liked to cut through all the crap and talk about art. You could see in him the price he'd paid for that allegiance. There was a gritty, unfussy quality about him. He'd flown to Norman to stay for two months but hadn't made any living arrangements whatsoever. On the day he arrived, he haggled with a slumlord and secured a dive that had been vacated—perhaps abandoned—by college students fleeing for the summer. He had absolutely no pretensions of being a chaser, no desire to understand forecasting. He wanted to capture the clouds after the manner of his predecessor, John Constable, but with a camera, and with the help of the DOWs. On the morning of May 12, his friend and colleague Jeffery had flown into town. Jeff was a young, handsome, charming department head who, after a week being on the Plains, was still getting his cultural bearings. He was liable to stumble into the kind of pre-dinner deliberations about wine, for instance, that one didn't often hear in beer country, with barbecued brisket in the offing.

On the afternoon of May 12, Jeffery was behind the wheel of Ward's rental car on the first chase of his life. It was late afternoon, and the two men were just south of Attica, on the main road leading into town. They had gotten separated from the DOWs and had stopped on the side of the road to photograph a wall cloud to the west. As Ward's video begins, one sees to the southwest the fat condensation cloud and the debris cloud on the ground that is the beginning of the tornado that would hit Attica, but Ward and Jeff seem more interested in a second lowering directly ahead of them that is passing over the road, where a group of storm chasers have stopped as well. Ward trains the camera on this second lowering, which soon disperses. You can hear Jeff's camera clicking and the wind blowing. A few minutes go by, and suddenly all the chasers down the road jump into their cars, making hurried U-turns northward toward Ward and Jeff and the town of Attica. "Let's go!" Ward shouts to Jeff, who can't seem to get the legs of his tripod collapsed. Ward pans to the southwest at the Attica tornado, which is now fully formed and coming right at them. Jeffery climbs into the driver's seat and does a quick U-turn as well, heading into town. But something weird happens. Ordinarily, most tornadoes track from the southwest to the northeast, but suddenly the Attica tornado shifts from its northeast course and tracks northwest, directly toward Attica, putting Ward and Jeffery on a collision course. Neither of them understands this at the moment. Jeffery is taking pictures out of the driver's window, while Ward steers the car from the passenger side, and, with his other hand shoots the video and shouts, "C'mon, man, step on the gas. Let's get out of here!" As soon as they get up to speed, it begins to dawn on Ward that something is terribly awry. He says, "I don't know, man. I think it's coming straight at us. Turn around." Jeff turns around and starts heading east again. The tornado now seems to take up most of the window frame. Their car has sped ahead of the tornado. By turning around, they seem to be driving in front of its path. You can clearly see the red clay soil spinning around the funnel. At this point, if they had continued east, they would have placed themselves completely out of harm's way, but Ward hasn't grasped that going away from town is good. Going northwest, toward town, is bad, very bad. "No, I'm sorry," Ward says to Jeff, "I think this is a mistake. Turn around." Jeff does another U-turn, again heading northwest toward Attica. They are now back on collision course with the tornado, and as the car accelerates Ward doesn't like what he's seeing. He's trusted his eyes all his life—and they do not betray him now—so he commands Jeff to make another U-turn, which Jeff does. By this point, the tornado is towering over them. "I could see red insulation from houses falling like snow on the ground all around us," he told me. The two professors of art and art history in their rental car now very much resemble a squirrel, darting back and forth in the road in front of an oncoming semi. A passing motorist leans on his horn, trying to warn the two men, but even though they are now headed east toward safety, Ward interprets the honking to mean that they are headed toward danger. He also sees storm chasers headed into town, and he makes the biggest mistake of the day—he decides that the storm chasers must know what they are doing. So he orders Jeff to turn around and drive north into Attica. "I'm sorry, man," he says, to Jeff by way of apology. "I'm just not equipped."

What an epitaph *that* would have made. Now, as the men enter the town with tornado sirens blaring and debris falling in the road, you can see the fear on Jeffery's face. And this is the part of the video that makes my heart race. There's a stop sign at the center of town, and here they run into a traffic jam of sorts—of chasers and assorted knuckleheads clogging the roadway. (All at once, like a revelation, I understood Matt's insistence on staying ahead of things—ahead of the storm, and most of all ahead of the circus of idiots who will one day clog some similar roadway, blocking all escape and getting people killed.) Somehow Jeff weaves through the mess and turns west. They find an underground shelter in an old folks' home, where they are received by the staff with Kool-Aid and cookies. There is a man, apparently dead, lying on a gurney. A couple of heavily tattooed orderlies, "obviously doing some time—you know, court-mandated community service work"— are loudly wishing destruction upon the town. After a few minutes, Ward and Jeff step outside. Most of Attica is still there. People are standing in the parking lot, shakily lighting cigarettes for each other. Somebody says, with half a laugh, "If that don't put the fear of God in you, nothing will."

It was as spectacular a bit of torn porn as I'd ever seen, caused in part by an aberrant tornado whose path nobody could have predicted. Ward grinned and shook his head. "We had no business being out there," he said. Later, he even sent me a copy of the video in the mail, but he wasn't particularly proud of it: "For as hard as it has made me laugh," he said, "all the while, I know that I'm laughing at an asshole."

SEVEN

A Citizen's Brigade

"Five-oh—Larry? What do you see?"

On weekends, Larry Ohs, a lawyer who has had a private practice in Lincoln for the last twenty-four years (mortgage lending, real estate, criminal court, juvenile court, wills), likes to pile his family into the Suburban and drive to Horseshoe Lake, just south of the Platte River, between Lincoln and Omaha. Larry and I have never met, but over weeks of e-mails and several phone conversations, I have come to know him primarily through his voice: unhurried, deliberate, and completely at ease with silence. When asked to describe himself, Larry, who is in his mid-fifties, will offer only that he is six feet tall, 200 pounds, and "sturdily built." He shows a middle American reserve, fleeing from talk of the personal as if from a fire, self-description giving way very quickly to a list of his favorite activities, which include a good deal of time spent in the great outdoors with his three sons, Ryan, Matthew, and Logan, all in their early teens. He sends me a picture that shows him surrounded in every way by the comforts of suburban American life, right down to the Chevy Suburban parked behind him, the freshly mowed lawns, neatly trimmed at the curb, the white, two-story houses with gabled roofs and large palladian windows, the driveways with basketball hoops. One imagines kids on bicycles, the sound of lawn mowers, the *tang, tang, tang* of basket balls on concrete, the smell of barbecue on the grill. Larry looks every bit the good neighbor and the active, participatory dad, with neatly trimmed hair and mustache, wire-rim glasses, a short-sleeve shirt that reveals the slightest paunch, cargo shorts, athletic legs, and active, outdoor-type sandals, the kind with Velcro fasteners. He stands smiling into the sun. Behind him, not a cloud in the sky.

Larry is alert to his sons' changing interests and enthusiasms. Ryan and Matthew are Eagle Scouts; he has been an assistant scoutmaster with Troop 12 for over five years, a role that has involved a fair amount of camping, hiking, sailing, biking, and the like, including, last year, a five-day, thirty-mile, twenty-one-day canoe trip in the Boundary Waters of northern Minnesota. Three years ago, his son Matthew, then fourteen, had returned from a Boy Scout National Jamboree with the desire to become a ham radio operator. Larry, in a way that seems typical of him, signed up for the course along with his son, and in a few months they were both licensed amateur radio operators. In the spring of 2003, they took storm spotting classes from which Larry emerged as an officially trained and certified storm spotter. (Matthew would have to wait until he was twenty-one before becoming fully certified.) But, during that busy season of storms, Larry was never available to respond to spotter activation. For a man who was spread a little too thin as it was—there were Scouting trips, and troop meetings, and training sessions for Scout leaders, not to mention his busy law practice—life simply got in the way.

The open end of Horseshoe Lake faces west, with Larry's cabin situated on the south side of the peninsula, looking across the lake a few hundred yards to shore, which is lined with trees and cabins and docks for swimming. No large boats are allowed, only canoes and paddle boats; a few people fish for bass or catfish, bluegill or perch. For fun, Larry's sons like to try hitting their friends in boats with a launcher powerful enough to send water-balloon projectiles in a watery cannonade arcing, almost, to the far shore. The Burlington Northern Line runs along the lake's western edge, just beyond the cottonwoods and burr oak. On any given evening, while he's cleaning up after dinner, say, or repositioning the sprinkler in the garden, or reading a magazine, Larry can hear the rumbling of the locomotives and the long train of coal cars rolling down the tracks eastbound into the night. Before May 22, 2004, it had never been for him an unpleasant sound, maybe a little loud at times, but something you became used to—the sound of something large and filled with benign purpose, moving over the landscape, on schedule, its

Dopplered passage moving with a rumble in the ground and a rhythmic knocking of wheels over track—*ka-thump, ka-thump*! The sound of the train at Horseshoe Lake seemed mostly to underscore how quiet the country was, pulling in its wake a powerful after-effect, a deepening silence.

Since May 22, however, the trains have an entirely different and altogether unpleasant effect on Larry. Something about the sound, perhaps the low-level vibration through bedrock, or the rumble propagated through the air, enters his brain, and in no time his heart is racing. His heart is racing and he has to sit down on the couch, or pull over to the side of the road, and breathe deeply, saying to himself, *Calm down, calm down.* Then he'll breathe deeply again; then he'll go through a litany of relaxing thoughts. *Everything's okay. Everything's fine.* Then more deep breathing and more peaceful thoughts. *Calm down. Calm down. Everything's fine. Everything's okay. It's not a tornado.*

"My heart starts to race *every time* I hear that train," he said to me over the phone one evening. Other things besides trains can trigger an attack. The sound of thunder can set him off. A storm blowing through. Recently, driving down the road in his Suburban, he cracked open a window. The wind rushing through set his heart galloping.

These spells last anywhere from two to twenty minutes and require Larry's full attention. "It's called post-traumatic stress disorder." He gives me a long Larry Ohs pause. "Yeah," he says finally, "I've got it," his voice trailing in a downward glide, as if he were talking about hay fever or a nosebleed.

On the morning of May 22, as Larry Ohs was relaxing in his living room, Matt and I, in a different part of the state, were getting our things together at the Super 8 in Norfolk. The word was already out that the Storm Prediction Center was calling for a big day. Austin Ivey, Matt's geographer friend, had called in the morning from New Mexico to wish Matt well. Matt lay in bed, going over the weather setup with Austin, who was convinced that today would be the biggest day of the year so far. Matt hung up the phone and watched the Weather Channel forecast for a moment.

"Today is going to be a different kind of hard," he said at last. ". . . . Hard to decide which storms to target. There's going to be so many." Because it was Saturday, the chaser circus would be out in force, the roads congested with weekend storm chasers; because it was harvest time for the winter wheat crop, caravans of harvesting crews would be lumbering over the landscape. Semis would be pulling oversize wheat combine harvesters on lowboy trailers, long-bed dump trucks transporting grain; there would be equipment trucks and RV trailers for crew living quarters. "They're going to make things interesting," Matt said.

By one o'clock, with a target area about a hundred miles west of Lincoln, just south of Grand Island, Matt and I set out from Norfolk, passing a U-Haul van that was moving either into or out of what a hand-painted sign identified as the "Johnny Carson Childhood Home." Matt was mulling over yesterday's tornado, replaying the chase, and shuttling into the discussion a little apology: "If I would have known that that tornado was going to be the only one we'd see that day, I would have probably driven right up to it," he said. If Matt was anything, he was observant, able to detect nuances in skies and in people. I must have betrayed a little impatience at his decision to keep ahead of the Hadar tornado. "I think there will be tornadoes today," he said, looking straight ahead into a Nebraska sky streaked to the south with cirrus, or mare's tails. "How do you want to go about chasing them? I mean, if it came to a choice between stopping for a nice lingering tripod shot of a tornado, or keeping ahead of the storm, what would you want to do?"

"I want to do what you would do."

"In that case," Matt said, "we'll be on the move quite a bit, mostly to protect ourselves from being trapped in a traffic jam of chasers."

We drove into an early-afternoon playlist of songs by the country superstars Brooks and Dunn ("Ronnie Dunn is from Oklahoma"), and Toby Keith ("He lives in Norman. I've seen him around") that lulled me into a lazy, Saturday-afternoon, toe-tapping, country-western nod and brought me to within a hair of putting a pinch of Skoal between my cheek and gum. There were, indeed, many harvesting crews, many with Canadian plates, moving in great caravans down long empty stretches of two-lane blacktop. Matt drove slowly behind them, and we stared at whatever wide load presented itself. I was lost in the vastness of the Nebraska horizon, thinking about farmers and karaoke, an unforeseen combination emerging as the hot new phenomenon that May. Not only were there radio advertisements and road signs announcing "karaoke night" at any number of local watering holes—taverns, bars, lounges, and VFW halls dotting the prairie—but the market for besotted, TelePrompted warbling seemed robust enough and of sufficient density even to support radio spots for *karaoke equipment sales*. A few days ago, at the motel lounge in south Omaha, karaoke night had been a bit of a disappointment: mostly regulars at the bar getting tanked on a school night, and a DJ, who, after it became clear that nobody was paying attention to him, began using the lounge's powerful PA system to heckle and hurl abuse at the crowd. It was an edgy approach, I'll grant you, that allowed for the occasional theater-of-the-absurd moment and whole minutes worth of silence between insults flung at the oblivious crowd.

As the Kansas/Nebraska storm-chasing campaign wore on, the unlikely pairing of farmers and karaoke found its place alongside a number of other oddball combinations that started to suggest a general pattern. You'd notice it in people's houses, or in motel lobbies, or on the road. That afternoon we passed a hockey rink where you could also buy "Amish Log Furniture," for instance. Yesterday, we'd eaten lunch at a franchise restaurant, an odd amalgam of Mexican and Hibernian called Carlos O'Kelly's. On the radio I heard an ad for a Lincoln, Nebraska, furniture store that seemed to have been written by a marketing team with its finger on the pulse of this emerging middle-American penchant for random mixing and matching. The store's interior design aesthetic, governed by a tornado, openly encouraged the merging of country kitsch, say, with Zulu battle gear. The unique selling point for the furniture store was "the juxtapose," a word snatched from a thesaurus, mugged, blindfolded, driven to a remote location in deepest Nebraska, then trotted out before a rural audience as a "high concept." People were free to do as they pleased, of course, but in many houses into which I'd been admitted, hospitably, graciously, the "juxtapose" aesthetic simply took my breath away. In Norman, I interviewed a well-known chaser in his house, which had been given over to this kind of manic collision. Ye Olde Grandma of the Prairie met head-on with Big Game Hunting in the Congo. Zebra-striped pillows. Cheetah-striped pillows. A big screen TV. Flowery prints. Statuary angels. Things that had curlicues. Filigrees. A huge, expansive, L-shaped couch on which entire families might have floated in comfort, as if on a raft, to Florida. Tchotchkes everywhere, a kind of tchotchke idolatry but for the countervailing pictures of Jesus, prominently displayed, looking a little like the country singer Kris Kristoffersen in a robe and sandals. Other homes had pictures of "His Hands," palms open, beckoning, or shepherd-and-flock pictures, sheep in the foreground, Christ appearing over a rise with his staff and a smile, or framed verses from the Bible—all of them giving the cherubim and the basketry and the dried flowers and the teddy bears and the doilies a firm, kindhearted shove toward everything that was nice and lemon-scented. Among all of this, there was scarcely a book to be found. "The juxtapose" wasn't so much a governing aesthetic, I came to think, as a form of anesthesia, an advanced compensatory mechanism suitable to a recent death in the family. Houses were overrun by an oppressive, animal-lover cuteness that made one want to run out and drown a sack full of kittens.

It was as if churchgoing, Bible-thumping middle America had found a harmless avenue of debauchery in interior decorating. "The juxtapose" became the key to unlock all the pent-up energy that came from abjuring the sinful life, but was now busting out all over the prairie, it seemed, as Carlos met O'Kelly for burritos and green beer, as ice hockey met Amish Log Furniture, as the Grange met for karaoke night, overtaking the local species of diversion—bingo, euchre—like a weed that could sing, like yodeling kudzu.

As we crossed the Platte—people were driving Jeeps right in the middle of the river—Matt's weather scanner began chirping and squawking, as it would continue to do all afternoon. At two, the National Weather Service forecast offices in Valley, in Hastings, and in North Platte, Nebraska, began scheduled conference calls with regional emergency management officers and media personnel. This happened only when the SPC was convinced that something big was brewing. Matt had been calling around, talking to Charles Edwards, Tim Samaras, Mark Herndon, and others. He sat down and drew me what he called a virtual synoptic map, based on these discussions. The map showed very deep moisture, which had been advecting north from the Gulf for several days, lying across the southern part of Nebraska, with CAPE values topping 4,000 joules per kilogram. A strong upper-level flow from the southwest created the necessary wind shear, lifting warm surface air aloft and increasing atmospheric instability. There were, moreover, strong easterly, or "backed," surface winds augmented by a low-level jet, and a dryline superimposed over a deep low that was sitting in the far western part of the state. All the elements were in place to get big, rotating thunderstorms. The question of the day was about initiation: where would the storms start? Here any number of chasers would second-guess the Storm Prediction Center, which seemed increasingly concerned about the southeastern corner of the state, near Lincoln, and decide, instead, to position themselves closer to the dryline, a few hundred miles to the west, right in the middle of the state, along the border with Kansas. This difference in opinion reflected a profound difference in point of view—or "forecasting bias." Chasers, of course, were monomaniacal—they wanted tornadoes that could be seen and photographed. The SPC, on the other hand, was concerned with all types of severe weather, including tornadoes, photogenic or not. SPC forecasts reflected this more encompassing perspective and thus, according to most chasers, required a little bit of "translation." Many chasers, including Matt, felt that today's storms would produce tornadoes early, right at initiation, then degenerate into giant overblown lines of thunderstorms—squall lines, which would make chasing impossible. The SPC was right to be alarmed by conditions in southeast Nebraska, so the thinking went, but if you wanted to actually *see* a tornado, all the action was out west. Matt and I decided to meet up with Tim Samaras near Grand Island.

All afternoon, the tornado watches and warnings came in fast and were spread out across the state of Nebraska; warnings were in effect in half a dozen counties stretching over 50,000 square miles. By early evening, Matt and I were about 200 miles west of Lincoln, moving north to assess the situation, then heading south, then farther west, then east, adjusting ourselves like an outfielder dancing underneath a high pop fly, but by eight o'clock we were losing daylight. I could feel the chase slipping through our fingers.

To our north, where we'd been a few hours earlier, a storm dropped a powerful, rain-wrapped tornado that derailed a Union Pacific freight train near the town of Fairfield and then continued northeast toward Highway 74, where two chasers—David Drummond and a woman I'll call Dorothy—were closing upon the storm from the east, slowing their van to a crawl.[1] Watching the raw video footage, which Drummond later sent me, one looks in vain for something to see beyond the steadily thumping windshield wipers. Rain mixed with hail and debris blows sideways, buffeting the van. Drummond pulls over to the side of the road and stops.

What is clear at the outset is that Drummond and Dorothy are chase partners only in the loosest sense—they are sharing a vehicle. Everything about their behavior suggests that they are on entirely different wavelengths. Drummond acts like a veteran chaser, his voice an easy Texas drawl, calm, collected; he describes storm structure in a steady, flat-line drone that wouldn't rise above a monotone even if the van were doing barrel rolls over the prairie. Dorothy seems like a chaser apprentice, equipped with some meteorological knowledge but not sufficiently experienced to have confidence in her observations. "Look at it! Look at it just spin around! We are, like, *directly underneath the meso,*" she declares at one point, then turns to Drummond with a hesitant "Aren't we?" The problem here, of course, as is so often the case when people die, is one of ambiguity—some dreadful, life-threatening thing shrouds itself in enough *maybes* to make us actually step toward it, or delay decisive action. Ambiguity, moreover, is to fear as gasoline is to a fire, and the mind begins to see things in the shape-shifting, rain-wrapped beast ahead, in the massive wall of wind and debris that fills their windshield, appearing and disappearing into the rain curtain, and reason drops away. At times Dorothy's voice seems fully ablaze.

Drummond knows he is perhaps a few hundred yards from something nasty, which is why he's brought the van to a halt in the first place. He knows *something* is crossing the highway in front of them and moving to the north. He knows, as well, that the best thing to do now is to turn around and drive east so that he can run parallel to it. But there's a bit of a problem: the person sitting next to him is going apeshit.

"It's gonna come down," Dorothy says. "If it's not down already, it's gonna come right down on top of us—David!" she says, angrily, as if David had fallen asleep just now and were somehow to blame for all of this. Her voice rises to an exasperated "Jesus Christ!"

David checks his anemometer, clocking the gust that's just hit the van at 54.8 miles per hour. The telephone poles in the near distance are rocking

*back and forth and appear on the verge of snapping. "I'm afraid to move,"
he says, "but we may have to." David still seems unfazed, as if he were
standing at the rail of a cruise ship watching a beautiful sunset.*

*"Oh, wow. This is incredible," he says; then he makes a U-turn, retreat-
ing from the storm. Dorothy seems disoriented.*

*"We're not going into an actual tornado, are we?" she asks, her voice
very small, as if she's retreated into a cave.*

*"No. We're going away from it. I think a tornado might have crossed the
road there, but this," he says, referring to the dirt blowing sideways from
right to left across the road, "this is all inflow and RFD wrap-around."[2]*

*As they pull away from the storm, it seems clear to both that the crisis is
over. Dorothy regains her composure.*

"How's that for an experience?" David asks.

*"That was awesome," Dorothy says, letting out a celebratory whoop.
She asks—jokingly, perhaps—whether they can go do it again. A few seconds pass.*

"What's that?" Dorothy asks, looking toward her right.

*"Ummm, that . . ." David pauses. The rain has made it hard to see any-
thing.*

*"That's something I don't think I want to drive under," says Dorothy.
"Are you going to drive under it?"*

"No. I'm going to stay back here."

"Oh, my God. It looks like it's going to drop on top of us," Dorothy says.

*What happens next will become a kind of cautionary tale for chasers
everywhere, and is, perhaps, best shown in transcript.*

Dorothy: Oh, my God, David [nervous laughter]. It looks like it's right
on top of us.

David: I'm going to resolve that issue.

Dorothy: It's right on top of us. I see it. I see it. I see it. Oh, my God! It's
directly on top of us.

David: Here it comes again.

Dorothy: Is it a tornado, or what is it?

David: It's all straight-line shit. It might be unpleasant, though.

[A wall of sideways-blowing dirt crosses the road in front of the van, then dissipates. For a moment, they seem to be in the clear again.]

David: That was awesome. [laughs] You'll never go chasing with me again, right?

Dorothy: Fuck, yeah! That was great.

Drummond, referring to the dirt blowing across the road, says that there's not much to worry about, unless the dirt starts to lift. "Then," he says, with a laugh, "you know you've got something to worry about."

As if on cue, a large cloud of debris begins to rise across the highway directly in front of them. Instantly, Dorothy seems to turn upon her mentor.

"Yeah, like right there?" she says, indicating the rising debris cloud, her tone withering, her voice stabbing at Drummond's aw-shucks nonchalance. "Right there, right there," she says, stabbing some more. Then—it's not exactly clear what's happening out of the frame—she seems to have jumped out of her seat and landed almost in Drummond's lap.

"Oh, hi," she says, a little embarrassed, "it's right there," as if pointing to a monster that has suddenly appeared at her window. "Oh, my fucking God almighty," she says, laughing suddenly.

They continue driving through the wind and rain. Out of nowhere, from the opposite direction, a fire truck approaches the van. Drummond slows down, perhaps to have a chat with the driver, but just as Drummond stops, the van's rear windows shatter.

Dorothy: Ouch! God! Dammit!

David: Settle down. We'll get out of here.

Dorothy: Oh, my God!

David: Just hold on. It's all outflow. It's not rotating. Fuck. I can't even see.

Dorothy: [frightened] Ooooh.

David: You all right?

Dorothy: No. Something hit my back.

David: It's rotating over our fucking heads. Right here.

Dorothy: I know. Would you just book it!

The van pushes its way through the debris cloud; soon they're in the clear, their emotions washing over them both in waves, followed by silence, then another set of waves, as they replay what's just happened to them, groping toward the conclusion that they must have just survived an impact with a tornado. They stop to examine the damage in the van. The rear and right side windows are broken, which, Dorothy seems to think, confirms that they've just encountered a tornado. Soon Drummond starts making phone calls.

Within minutes, the episode was being discussed on the chaser grapevine. Just after 8:30 P.M., Austin Ivey called Matt from New Mexico to tell him about it, and, indeed, as Matt observed after he hung up the phone, Drummond's close call evoked the chaser community's worst nightmare. A chaser getting himself killed by a tornado might be used as a pretext for drafting laws that prohibited or restricted the practice of storm chasing. The incident would provoke weeks of debate on chaser discussion groups, and in the wider world too.

It would divert attention from an even bigger story that was unfolding even now on the horizon to the southeast, where Matt pointed out a massive series of cumulus towers brilliantly lit by the setting sun—too far away to pursue, but pretty. Around those towers, just as the SPC had predicted, a drama was unfolding. We didn't know it then, as we drove across the landscape in our own little sphere of recirculating air, preoccupied with the dwindling prospects of the day, but the storms in the distance were about to destroy Hallam, Nebraska. At dusk, Matt spotted a wall cloud to the south that we followed into Kansas. It was 8:46 P.M. We'd driven eight hours and over five hundred miles when, just off the van's right side and about three miles away, a tornado dropped from the sky and plowed up a field for about thirty seconds. We followed the mesocyclone for a mile into the darkness, slipping and sliding along a greasy road, when I saw in the sudden flash of lighting, the unmistakable form of a second, bigger tornado ahead of us, pulling away from us, slowly moving off into the night.

We stopped at the only bar in Belleville, Kansas, The Lone Wolf, to sit out the heavy rains. A real gully washer was under way, sheets of rain roaring down. The TV above the bar was tuned to the local station and everyone was glued to the screen. Nothing was yet known of Hallam, but the storm-as-reality-show programming was at full steam, satellite trucks providing live feed from locations across Nebraska, reporters filing their stories from distant, rain-bespattered corners of darkness, then tossing it to the weather anchor back at the studio, who stood next to a Nebraska map that fairly sang with alarm, with 3-D graphics, pixelated Doppler radar scans, visual satellite loops, blinking watch/warning boxes, and a continuous crawl with warnings going up from county to county like a souped-up version of the war room "Big Board" in *Dr. Strangelove.* Storms may have been tracking across the state, doing whatever storms do, but that night at the Lone Wolf Bar, having driven over 2,700 miles in the last seven days, I was done. I was done with the weather. My dinner consisted of peanuts and Pepsi. I had had it with anything weather-related. In fact, I was altogether finished with the weather. The weather could go screw itself for all I cared. The walls of the Lone Wolf were dominated by life-size posters of famous stock car racers and oversized softball and bowling trophies. Next to the pool table, someone had pinned up one of those big yellow ribbons inspired by the 1973 song "Tie a Yellow Ribbon Round the Old Oak Tree." The ribbon was surrounded by newspaper articles and photographs of boys from Belleville and Concordia, some smiling, some grim and determined, all with a fairly good chance of getting their ass shot off or blown up somewhere in Iraq. In a few months, the number of U.S. military personnel killed in the conflict would top a thousand. Was it just me, I wondered in my distemper, staring blankly at the ribbon, or was this the saddest, stupidest, most pathetic, most tragically inept public symbol ever to materialize and gain currency, anywhere? Who were we, if we were a nation that, from among all possible choices, had settled upon Tony Orlando and Dawn as the appropriate messengers for the remembrance of those lost or in harm's way?

I walked over to the pool table and chased the eight ball around for a while, then sat down next to Matt, who was drinking a beer and chatting with some local boys.

"Concordia has the highest rate of sexually transmitted disease in the country," one of them said.

"That's just a statistical oddity," Matt said, taking a pull from his beer.

"Paul Harvey even said so."

Leave it to Paul Harvey to jump on that one, I thought. "Look," Matt said, "there's probably only four cases in the whole town—probably traceable back to one person—but per capita that helps make Concordia have the highest rate of disease."

Matt had set his weather scanner down on the bar, then walked over to the jukebox and selected Bob Segar's "Against the Wind," which I took for another semi-ironic gesture, made for my benefit. Matt returned to the bar and looked at me. He understood instantly what I was thinking.

"He's from Detroit," Matt said.

"Oh."

I stepped outside for a moment, pausing in the doorway, and found myself leaning into Bob Segar's song, and the song, a bittersweet, melancholy air, leaning into me. We were like two drunks propping each other up on the dance floor. Segar's voice ran headlong into the torrent outside. Matt's weather scanner wasn't a prop. We were still in the hook of a very big storm and anything could happen. If it did, Matt would know about it. Main Street was completely submerged, an occasional truck sloshing slowly by. I still didn't know it—nobody in the Lone Wolf Bar in Belleville, Kansas, knew it, not even Matt—but out there, the lives of hundreds of people had been changed forever. Meteorologists for the Weather Channel were already being dispatched to Hallam, and the news wrote the next day's headlines in the *Lincoln Journal/Star* and the *Omaha World-Herald*. The tornado's damage path stretched over fifty miles.

Just after seven that evening, a call had gone out from the Emergency Operations Center in downtown Lincoln to Reynolds Davis, the emergency radio coordinator for the Lancaster County Skywarn Network, a Nebraska chapter of volunteer storm spotters operating under the auspices of one of the oldest radio clubs in the country, the American Radio Relay League, or ARRL, the national organization of ham radio operators. The Skywarn system divides Lancaster County, which is shaped like an upright cereal box, into six spotting sections of equal size. From the top of the box, a center line divides the county longitudinally into a western and an eastern half. Two equally spaced lines of latitude then create the six spotter sections—Sections 1 and 2 in the northern third of the county, Sections 3 and 4 in the middle third, and Sections 5 and 6 in the southern third. Each spotter who reports for duty is assigned a two-digit station number, the first digit identifying the county location, the second the exact position within that section. (The spotters are issued maps that tell them how to get to each location and where to look for the small metal sign—stamped, say, to a telephone pole, that tells them where they should pull off for the best view, etc.) At 7:15 P.M., Lancaster County EOC engaged the spotter network, a "tone squelch" alarm system that alerts all ham radio operators to begin calling in their availability.

Larry Ohs had been at home with his family getting ready for a late supper. As the skies grew dark, his ham radio began to squelch and squawk. It occurred to Larry that he had absolutely nothing going on that night, so he picked up the radio handset and announced his availability. Reynolds Davis assigned him to the position 5.0, in the southwestern corner of the county.

Matthew Ohs, hearing the transmission, grabbed the portable radio and left to install it in the Suburban. Larry talked to his wife for a few minutes, flipped through the Lincoln Emergency Management Office manual to find his spotter's position, then went outside. Matthew had installed the radio and was waiting for his dad, in the passenger seat, buckled in.

"I'm going with you!" Matthew said.

"No, you're not."

There ensued a short debate that required all the skill Larry Ohs had gained in his twenty-four years of arguing cases before the Lancaster County Criminal Court. The long and short of it was that Matthew unbuckled his seatbelt and walked the length of the unfair, stupid, boring driveway back through the garage, back into the unfair, stupid, boring house, where he plopped himself down, eventually, in a chair in the radio room, to listen to what was happening *out there.*

In the basement of his house in southwest Lincoln, Reynolds Davis, who now assumed the role of "net control," in amateur-radio-speak, fielded incoming calls from available spotters. At 7:28, the first spotter had checked in, and within twenty minutes all of the thirty-two fixed points in the county had been assigned, with spotters, among them Larry Ohs, en route to their locations. In addition, five spotters were in position at the area hospitals; four were in place at the local television and radio stations; one was at the airport; one was in downtown Lincoln, at the Emergency Operations Center; and one was acting as a liaison relaying relevant information to neighboring county EOCs on a regional frequency. All of them were connected directly via ham radio to the local National Weather Service forecast office in Valley, Nebraska, where a forecaster and ham radio operator could ask any spotter, or any cluster of spotters, through Reynolds Davis, to look in any direction in order to confirm radar signatures, the characteristic profile as seen on Doppler radar of tornadic storms. Thus, someone like Matthew, listening in at home, might hear Reynolds Davis ask a spotter in Position 3.8 to "look to the southwest and report what you see." Davis, prompted by the NWS in Valley, might also ask the spotter in a neighboring position to look toward his neighbor—to the southeast, for instance—and report what he saw. "When you hear that on the radio," Larry Ohs told me, "you know that Valley is seeing something on the radar, and that they're trying to get a visual confirmation using the spotters." In twenty minutes, a command and communications system, one that ran parallel to but that was—importantly, purposely, and entirely—*off the electrical grid,* had established itself around a perimeter stretching 120 miles.

The spotters were from every walk of life. They were off-duty policemen and volunteer firemen; they were teachers and government bureaucrats; they were house painters and laborers; they were factory workers and car salesmen; they were a citizen's brigade standing to, their eyes on the sky to the southwest section of the county, in Section 5, where something large and dark and powerful was moving. Among them was Larry Ohs, on his first spotting mission, Larry Ohs, lawyer and solo practitioner, of Larry Ohs, P.C. He was now heading west, toward Section 5, through driving rain on Hallam Road.

Peggy Willenberg and Melanie Metz, the Twister Sisters, were west of Wilber, about 10 miles southwest of Hallam, at full dark when they realized that something unusual had happened—more unusual than the damage they noticed in the town itself. It came to them sideways, as it were, and it wasn't that the power was out, which it was, or that there were bricks and tree branches in Main Street. These things they'd seen before. What caught Peggy's attention was something that happened when they were just east of town, when she noticed that the winds were coming *from the south.* It was a fact that would have gone unnoticed by most people, who would have been distracted by the Black Angus cattle set loose on the road by downed fences, or by roadside trees and telephone poles that looked as if they'd been cut by a scythe.

The road they were on, Highway 41 into Wilber, runs east–west. As they'd entered the town on this road, the winds had been blowing *from the north.* Now, as they left Wilber, the winds were blowing *from the south.* The only possible inference was that they were dealing with the remnants of a cyclonic wind field—one capable of knocking down brick buildings and shredding large trees. Another word for "cyclonic wind field," of course, was "tornado." But surely, they thought, this must have been the meso-cyclone, the "mother ship" from which tornadoes emerged. Even so, as they moved cautiously forward through the driving rain and debris, it was diffi-cult to get their mind around the evidence before them: according to the odometer on their van, they had just driven through a damage path that was at least two miles wide.

Minutes earlier, Will Togstad, covered in mud and mortar, had emerged from the basement of his parents' home, a large two-story farmhouse that had just been lifted entirely off the ground and moved a few dozen yards, where it crashed into and uprooted a large oak tree. Will's brother, Terry, and Terry's two teenage friends Missy and Lacy Bostock were trapped in the basement behind the furnace. An hour before, Will had been upstairs asleep, dog tired from working cattle since 5:30 that morning with Dan Vilda, his ex-girlfriend's father. His mother, Cindy Togstad, who manages the family business in Wilber, had called repeatedly to warn Will of the approaching tornado and had finally sent Terry to the house. Missy and Lacy had simply gone along for the ride. At the house, Terry nudged his brother awake. Will stared in annoyance at Terry, who was making a goofy show of their mother's concern. "Get up!" Terry said, waving his hands around in mock alarm, "Get up! There's a tornado coming!"

Will buried his head in the pillow. He'd just been jostled from one of those deep daytime slumbers that can descend like a coma and seemed to require a sling-and-pulley system to climb out of, slowly, arm over arm, as if from the bottom of a hole. "Where is it?"

"It's by Western," Terry replied. The town of Western was about twenty miles to the southwest.

"That ain't ever gonna reach *here,*" Will muttered into his pillow. There was a pause, during which they could hear the rain falling outside. Down-stairs, Missy and Lacy were making themselves comfortable, having a snack in the kitchen. There was something strange about somebody standing there watching you try to sleep, even if it was your kid brother. Will rolled over and looked again at Terry. "Why'd you come out here?"

"Mom wanted me to come warn you," Terry said.

Will rolled out of bed, put on some shorts and a shirt, and walked downstairs. His cell phone rang. It was Dan Vilda's wife, Kathy, who'd been following the spotter reports on her scanner. The tornado, she said, was within six miles of Will's house. Even then, Will was disinclined to worry; he suggested to Kathy that the tornado would probably pass to the west. But Kathy knew what she knew. The Emergency Management Office for Saline County had deployed its spotter network at 6:35 that evening across forty-two locations. A big, rotating storm had gone up in Thayer and headed almost due north until it hit the Saline County line, where it split, one part of the storm continuing north. The second part of the storm, a strong "right-mover," the kind of storm that gets everybody's attention, began tracking east-northeast at 6:51, dropping multiple funnels like a piston on a cam. At 7:42, spotters reported two funnels south of Western, which triggered the sirens at Western. Spotters in Sections C and D, in the middle of Saline County, described a large, rain-wrapped tornado moving in a steady, unwavering path. At eight o'clock the windows of the Emergency Management Office in downtown Wilber began to bow outward and the office was evacuated. Everyone—the emergency dispatchers and all the other personnel in the Wilber city hall—ran downstairs, crossed the street, and took refuge in the basement of the city jail. "At that point," said Emergency Management Director B. J. Fictum, "the Emergency Operations Center for Saline County came to a complete stop." "It was complete chaos," said Shawn Kyker, a dairy and hog farmer who kept his eye on the radar, dispatched radio traffic, and otherwise held down the fort with three other people—the manager of a hardware store, a college student, and a nursing home employee—until it was time to flee. Kathy Vilda, who heard the Wilber EOC sign off, didn't need a map to tell her where the tornado was headed.

"Will," she said, with a directness that dislodged a few cobwebs, "it's headed straight for your house."

Will Togsted sent his younger brother and friends down to the basement, then opened the front screen door and looked southwest, past the driveway, past the horse barn, and farther along a valley. It was a view he'd grown up with. On a clear day, you could see anything coming for ten miles. "There was a greenish sky, and then, in the blink of an eye, everything turned black," Will recalled. "Then it got real quiet." And then came a thunderous downpour unlike anything he'd ever seen in his life. The wind became very strong, and to the south, though he couldn't discern the shape of a tornado, he saw debris sailing sideways very high in the sky. Terry was struggling to get the family dog, a Rottweiler named Buddy, down the stairs, but the dog wouldn't budge and the house was starting to shake. Terry fled down the basement stairs and turned around. As Will descended, Terry saw the screen door fly away.

Soon the entire house was airborne. From his position near the furnace, Will felt a sudden, tremendous pressure drop, his ears popping repeatedly, painfully hard. He looked up and saw above him the floor joists, row upon row of support beams upon which the first floor was anchored, all of them suddenly moving as one *to the northeast.* The house lifted and sailed off with the storm; the brick wall that divided the basement in half cascaded down upon Will, knocking him unconscious. Eventually, he made it out onto the gravel road, where, through the driving rain, he saw a pair of headlights.

In the van were Peggy and Melanie, the Twister Sisters, slowly making a detour north on the road leading to what was left of the Togstad house. Melanie Metz saw a young man stagger into the headlights and trip over a downed telephone line. He was big and husky and completely caked in mud. He'd been hit in the head by a brick, and could just barely squeak out that his brother and two others were trapped in the basement of his house. He pointed down a driveway and Peggy shined a flashlight through the rain at a pile of boards lying on the ground like scrap wood waiting to be burned. She walked toward the pile. In the beam of the flashlight she saw a scattering of 45 rpm records; a large air conditioner; and a long string of tiny white Christmas lights stretching off in the fields as far as the beam of her flashlight would go, at the end of which lay a denuded wire mesh reindeer. Peggy looked down at the pile of boards and junk, and did something that might have seemed odd had you stumbled suddenly upon her in the rain. She yelled at the pile of wood. Then she yelled again. Nothing. A volunteer fireman showed up and walked around to the other side of the pile. Broken

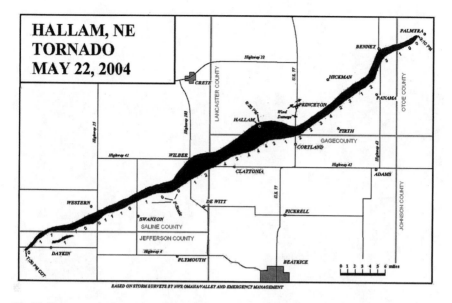

The Hallam tornado damage path. © Omaha National Weather Service forecast office

propane lines were hissing and leaking gas into the air. Then a figure appeared, caked in mud with dark, matted hair: a young girl. Peggy walked *onto* the pile and met the girl; the two of them walked carefully through the shattered wood and nails and Sheetrock. The fireman now appeared with two other figures, all muddy and shaken. And they were brought back to the vans where their mother, who had shown up in the meantime, was waiting. Buddy was never seen again.

The storm that flattened the Togstad house had knocked out most of the electrical grid by the time Larry Ohs drove through Hallam, just after 8:32, according to Lancaster County EOC records. The town was in complete darkness. No traffic lights, no sirens, no street lights, no porch lights, no house lights, no lights in the storefronts, no lights from the railroad yard, no big broad lights above the grain elevator. There was no glare or refraction; there were no streaks, none of the multicolored spidery whorls that one sees when driving at night anywhere in America in the rain—no blurry beer signs, no NAPA auto parts signs, no International Harvester signs, no lonely motel signs reading VACANCY in red. It was perfectly quiet but for the windshield wipers of the Suburban flapping rhythmically as Larry Ohs, the last

A freight train toppled for as far as one could see. © Kenneth F. Dewey/High Plains Regional Climate Center

In town, the grain elevator resembled a soft sculpture by Claes Oldenberg. © Kenneth F. Dewey/HPRCC

This old house: most of the homes in Hallam were destroyed or lifted and moved off their foundations. © Kenneth F. Dewey/HPRCC

The aftermath of the widest known tornado in history (2½ miles), in Hallam, Nebraska, on May 22, 2004. © Kenneth F. Dewey/HPRCC

person to see Hallam intact, passed the buildings of the town, where not a soul was to be seen in any direction.

West of town about half a mile, still in driving rain, Larry Ohs turned the Suburban onto West Fifty-eighth Street, a gravel road; he traveled a little less than a quarter mile, put the truck in Park, and turned off the engine. The truck was facing north into a hard wind that blew sheets of rain up and away from the windshield. Then the engine of the Suburban suddenly seemed to race wildly, as if he had his foot on the accelerator. But Larry Ohs was holding the keys to the truck in his right hand. He cracked open the window and heard the sound of the racing engine that was not his engine, and he knew that it was the sound of a tornado. A not-very-far-away tornado, but a tornado that was not like a freight train coming over the house, either. This was how people who had had their houses blown up described it: "Yep," they would say, "the train went right over the house." But while Larry Ohs was hearing this strange, faraway sound, objects were hitting his windshield—gravel, hail, tree branches; he wasn't sure—and this sound, a sound one wanted to pay attention to, wasn't getting any louder the way it would if it were coming over the house.

"Five-oh, what do you see?" It was Reynolds Davis, calling Larry Ohs.

That's funny, he thought. Usually, if Reynolds Davis asked for a visual report, he'd ask you to look in a particular direction, *toward* something.

Larry spoke calmly into the microphone, reporting debris hitting his truck and winds of about 80 miles per hour. But apparently nobody heard him amid all the radio traffic.

"Five-oh—Larry? What do you see?"

There, Reynolds Davis did it again. No request for Larry to look in any particular direction. *Jesus.* That could only mean the tornado was right on top of him. Larry tried to open the door of the Suburban, but the wind was so strong, the door wouldn't budge. The rain and rocks popped the windshield like firecrackers, as if somebody were taking a tire iron to the truck.

In a few minutes the wind had subsided, the truck stopped rocking back and forth, the gravel stopped flying. He looked east toward the town. In the lightning flashes he could see, from half a mile away, that most of Hallam was gone.

The following morning, the Weather Channel was broadcasting live from what was left of Hallam. The outbreak had produced eighty-four tornadoes touching down from Wyoming to Michigan, half of which fell upon sixteen counties in central and southeastern Nebraska. But Hallam was the main story, the aerial photos showing F4 damage in most of the town—a brick church completely destroyed; a pair of steel grain elevators collapsed; a freight train derailed, and 95 percent of the structures lifted off their foundations or just plain flattened. The post office was a jumble of collapsed brick. Trees were uprooted and trucks tossed a country mile. The contents of Hallam had been sucked into the clouds and lifted into the night, where they began drifting in a broad, southeastern plume across the rest of the state. Things began falling from the sky over Lincoln—sheet metal, vinyl siding, shingles. Checks from the bank in Hallam were found as far away as Omaha.

Hallam had taken a direct hit, the damage path there as wide as the town itself, about half a mile across. Beyond the town, the path exceeded two and a half miles in diameter, which, if confirmed by damage-survey reports, would make the Hallam tornado the widest in recorded history. There was one fatality, Elaine Focken, a seventy-three-year-old woman who was struck by debris when her house was lifted up, then collapsed upon itself. In the days to come, hundreds of volunteers would arrive to begin the long cleanup, Larry Ohs among them, shuttling workers from the amateur radio clubs in a large van to Hallam and to the surrounding farms, many of which had also been leveled. Ohs recalled driving a group of volunteers to one such farm near the town of Wilber one weekend after the storm. The van was filled with teenagers, mostly, talking and chatting and joking. For most of the kids, it was their first experience cleaning up after a tornado, so they expressed interest in driving through Hallam to see the wreckage. As a scout-master, Ohs knew a thing or two about object lessons and how to deliver them. He was a man who had trouble sleeping at night because the sound of a distant train reminded him of a certain other sound that he wanted to forget but couldn't. The kids he was shepherding around that day seemed to want a piece of that, and so he obliged them and drove through Hallam. And as they passed through town, the van of gabby teenagers was brought to a complete and utter silence that lasted the rest of the trip.

EIGHT
Goodbye, *Wakan*

*Nothing is more characteristic than that precisely this most
intimate and mysterious affair, the working of the weather on humans,
should have become the theme of their emptiest chatter.*
—WALTER BENJAMIN

few notes about emptiness. First of all, I could not sleep. Matt and I had sat in our motel beds for a good long while, our heads propped on pillows, in a state of Weather Channel–induced narcosis, like a pair of retirees blathering about the state of the world. There was the whole global warming thing, for instance. It was impossible to have a bigger weather story than this, and yet, until recently, the Weather Channel had assiduously avoided the topic, as one might avoid bringing up a murder in the family. The network wasn't alone in its reticence. For a time, CNN had aired a weekly environmental series, which fizzled out. Climate change was not as sexy a topic as natural disaster, it seemed. You couldn't fit global warming into the television frame as well as you could a tornado, or a dog howling on a rock in the middle of a flooded river. "Communicating climate-change science via television is difficult," the Weather Channel's recently hired climatologist, Heidi Cullen, told a reporter, "because the subject typically lacks the visuals of other stories."[1] More sensitive still was the question of human agency, or "anthropogenesis." "They don't really want us to talk about the causes of global warming," Weather Channel meteorologist Buzz Bernard told a reporter in 2000,[2] even though world scientific opinion on the subject had been leaning heavily toward anthropogenesis ever since the Intergovernmental Panel on Climate Change (IPCC), an international group of more than 2,000 climatologists, made its first pronouncement on the likely causes of global warming, in 1995.[3] Further research among this group, which one observer described as an "impossibly contentious world . . . of atmospheric chemists, physicists and climatologists," had only strengthened the consensus.[4] In 2001, the IPCC's third and most recent assessment, strongly endorsed by the National Academy of Sciences, a group not known for rushing headlong into things, stated unequivocally that "most of the warming observed over the last fifty years is attributable to human activity."[5] Yet, according to Robert Henson, a historian of broadcast meteorology, the subject of global warming was "still in the closet." Media executives, according to Henson, "feel uncertain about how they should position themselves. They don't know who they might offend."[6]

The Weather Channel's official position on global warming, announced in May 2004, was a slight revision of earlier statements. This new one had "evolved," according Heidi Cullen, "to objectively represent the state of the science," but when it came to clearly stating the likely causes of climate changes the Weather Channel's "new" position was fraught with obfuscation.[7] For one thing, it was front-loaded with equivocation of the sort one might expect from the corporate hacks at ExxonMobil. It was, Dr. Cullen wrote, "difficult to determine precisely to what extent the current warming is due to human activity." This, of course, was not *exactly* untrue, but as an opening salvo addressing the biggest problem shy of nuclear annihilation that humankind had ever faced, the announcement, with syntactic sleight-of-hand, drew attention to the *difficulties of precise measurement,* while burying the substantive news—namely, that natural cycles of climatic variation notwithstanding, humans were, in all likelihood, the most significant cause of global warming. Indeed, Dr. Cullen's statement was comparable, in its spirit and effect, to a document produced by ExxonMobil, containing primary research that had arrived at an opinion entirely at odds with the consensus view of the IPCC. The company, despite a proxy vote in 2004 by its own shareholders demanding that ExxonMobil explain its minority opinion, would not release its research for review. "There continue to be substantial and well-documented gaps in climate science," the report stated. "These gaps limit scientists' ability to assess the extent of any human influence on climate."

Blindness, too, might *limit my ability to assess* that a freight train, for instance, was coming down the track toward me. But despite that *substantial gap* in *my ability to assess* the situation, the larger truth would make itself felt in any number of ways—in the sound of the engine getting louder, in the ground beginning to rumble and vibrate, in the blast of the train whistle—and these signs, although incomplete and indirect, would strongly suggest a course of action. In the penultimate paragraph of the Weather Channel press release, of course, the truth did finally emerge, Dr. Cullen pointing to "strong evidence that a significant portion of the current warming is a result of human activities"; but, of course, the opening lines, which now had the imprimatur of a climatic expert, her, had already done the work they were meant to do. They had clouded and distracted and soft-pedalled the issue, reflecting the Weather Channel's desire to maintain a position of expedient detachment about the role of human manufacture and consumption—our role—in exacerbating the biggest weather story of our time.[8]

A world economy based on the ever-increasing production and consumption of fossil fuels had led to significant increases in the discharge of greenhouse gases into the atmosphere. These gases trapped more of the sun's energy than was required to sustain life, so that the earth had warmed more in the past century than the previous thousand years. The process had begun during the Industrial Revolution, had worsened in the last hundred years, and had demonstrated, in harrowing fashion, the interconnectedness of all things—what "ecology" had always meant, of course, though it had always seemed to be about something else, like being kind to spotted owls. The *global warming thing*? It kept slipping to the bottom of the agenda we'd been meaning to get to.

According to the National Academy of Sciences, the global temperature would increase anywhere between 2.5 and 10.4 degrees Fahrenheit by the year 2100.[9] About 40 percent of the predicted warming would be caused by greenhouse gases, the remaining 60 percent by various processes of self-acceleration called ecological feedback loops, whereby, for instance, the seven gigatons of carbon emitted into the atmosphere each year warmed the earth's surfaces, accelerating the hydrologic cycle of evaporation and precipitation. Suspended water vapor, according the Academy of Sciences report, produced the most important feedback loop in the predictive models. The increased quantities of suspended water vapor raised temperatures further still,[10] and when combined with the ice-albedo feedback loop—an increase in atmospheric heating caused by the melting of reflective ice on the earth's surface—these two feedback loops alone amplified by two and a half times the greenhouse gas heating.[11] The earth's poles heated up faster than anywhere else, and the thawing permafrost released previously trapped methane and other greenhouse gases, which further warmed the atmosphere. Higher temperatures speeded decomposition and leaching in the vast tracts of low-growing vegetation blanketing Alaska, Canada, and Russia above the Arctic Circle—the so-called "carbon sink" of the treeless tundra—and now seemed to be releasing more CO_2 than it absorbed.[12] The collapse in a month's span of the Larsen-B Ice Shelf off Greenland in 2002, the melting of inland glaciers, and all the other melting going on "freshened" the North Atlantic and threatened to slow the North Atlantic conveyor, the thermohaline circulation system of deep ocean currents that brought cold water south and warm currents like the Gulf Stream northward in a great global heat exchange.

Changes to the ocean's salinity that were "unprecedented in the relatively short history of the science of oceanography," according to William B. Curry of the Woods Hole Oceanographic Institute, threatened to slow or stop the conveyor. It was the cessation of the conveyor, and the subsequent loss of the heat exchange that was thought to be the causal link between "global warming" and a dire, perhaps counterintuitive consequence: the onset of an ice age. Scientists believed that this pattern—a period of intense warming followed by a great cooling—had happened at least eight times within the last million years. If carbon emissions continued apace, the planet could become hotter than it had been since the Eocene epoch.[13] In its general import, none of this information was particularly new. It was the stuff of grade school book reports and of recycling drives conducted by the children who would be burdened with the mess we had made of the world.

There were new wrinkles, though. A study published by the Pentagon in 2003 made headlines because, for the first time, it seemed, Americans—at least two of them—had thought to frame the uninterrupted pursuit of happiness at any cost as a security risk for the United States. The authors of the Pentagon report, Peter Schwartz and Doug Randall, wrote a "quick freeze" climate scenario that was based on an event occurring 8,200 years ago, when a slow period of increased global warming was followed by a relatively sudden, headlong pitch into a one-hundred-year period of shivering in the winters, sweating and starving in the summers, and running away from uncontrollable forest fires, among other entertainments. The Pentagon's updated version saw the Netherlands reclaimed by the ocean, California's Central Valley turned into a brackish inland sea, and Europe looking like the set of *Dr. Zhivago*. Famine and flood depopulate Scandinavia to the north and Africa to the south, leading to widespread disease as whole populations start moving. The western and southern United States are a gigantic dust bowl. Major cities on the U.S. East Coast are slowly flooded. As bad as they get in the United States, with few exceptions matters are far worse everywhere else, so the nation turns into a fortress as it increasingly becomes a target of worldwide resentment. As a foray into the future, the Pentagon study was not an apocalyptic fantasy but an extrapolation of patterns that were already being seen. And while its authors fully acknowledged that the likelihood of their scenario's coming to pass was remote, the fact was that, however you wanted to dress it, it remained solidly within the realm of the plausible.

And even conservative estimates of the dire consequences of global warming were fearsome beyond any scale of reference in human history. No plague, no war, no famine, and no combination thereof could compare. This was the gist of the situation; it occasioned the kind of catastrophilic dread that I had not experienced since Cold War days, when mutually assured destruction was official government policy. In such moments, fueled by how much sense *even the Pentagon* was showing, I sometimes imagined archaeologists sifting through the ruins of our civilization, perhaps the Weather Channel headquarters itself—after the city of Atlanta had become a desert—and stumbling upon a press release that spoke of difficulties determining "precisely to what extent the current warming is due to human activity."[14]

"Once you say global warming is caused by human means," observed Stu Ostro, a senior meteorologist at the Weather Channel, in 2000, "you have to say whose fault it is. And then you're in a very difficult political situation."[15]

For nearly twenty years, the Weather Channel had shown a profound disinclination to address stories that moved beyond empty weather talk, urging caution on sunny days ("You might want to put some extra sunscreen on if you're out at the beach today!") or bundling the children up during a cold snap. Years before a certain sitcom made the phrase popular, the Weather Channel had drawn up its own charter, its own bizarre premise, to which it had remained true-blue, earning itself an ardent audience: it was the ultimate "show about nothing." Its natural state was to be a "Cartoon Channel," as Matt liked to call the network, with lots of baubles for the eye—weather graphics galore, weather vixens like Kristina Abernathy, hunky heroes like Jim Cantore and Bill Keneely, endless satellite loops, the grand overview of the North American continent. The godlike survey of weather patterns moving over a nation in the eternal present made manifest what cultural critic Jody Berland calls "the gorgeous, metaphysical triumph of the technological sublime."[16] The Weather Channel maps offered a Promethean comfort, like watching a crackling fire, yet in this map-friendly format, as another Weather Channel critic has observed, one noted the complete absence of the kind of map that might jar a viewer into thought: "there are no maps of acid rain damage, deforestation, oil spill concentrations, toxic dump locations, or downwind nuclear zones."[17] This wasn't a programming complaint, of course, but an observation about an intentional omission from content that amounted to a description of the very product the Weather Channel so faithfully delivered—a weather narrative that remained forever in the present progressive tense, that had been, by design, completely decoupled from the consequent world of the predicate, where global warming lurked.

Now that global warming had breached the walls, however, the network still carefully manicured the subject, keeping politics at bay; coverage was limited to the science and remained silent on issues of policy. "The simple fact that they are discussing the issue means they are not going to avoid the politics," observed Roger Pielke, Jr., director of the Center for Science and Technology Policy Research at the University of Colorado. Pielke wondered publicly, and perhaps a little dreamily, whether the network might soon broadcast shows that addressed "climate change adaptation and mitigation strategies," which would be analogous to the safety tips the network often featured when covering hurricanes, tornadoes, and floods.[18] A Weather Channel show on CO_2 "mitigation strategies," however, would require mention of the unmentionable—that viewers needed to change their behavior as consumers—but, of course, an advertising platform like the Weather Channel simply could not afford to do that. It would happen, as they say, when hell froze over—a possibility that, one imagined, contingency planners were even now addressing somewhere in the labyrinthine halls of the Pentagon.

Movies have a way of foregrounding large, looming anxieties in the cultural dreamscape; the blockbuster natural disaster movie *The Day after Tomorrow,* which premiered in May 2004, while Matt and I were on the road, featured, it seemed, the Pentagon's predicted "quick-freeze" climate scenario. The movie played to a fear writ large—call it a folkways hunch about the elephantine, gas-guzzling SUV parked in America's living room—that mankind had, perhaps irrevocably, knocked the planet out of balance, had exposed itself, finally, to the possibility of a vast and terrifying retribution. The Weather Channel had a big part to play in the movie, appearing, according to its own press release, "as the trusted expert during the most severe situations . . . one of the last networks on-air amidst the chaos caused by the catastrophic events."[19] It was a star turn, in fact, the movie offering the ultimate corporate fantasy, inflected for our time—not so much the dream of dominance envisioned, say, by Standard Oil in the previous century and nearly achieved by Microsoft, but a heroic going-down-with-the-ship scenario in which the Weather Channel, as "one of the last networks on-air," sheds its lowly cable status and steps boldly into prime time, "where the game is played," as an advertising executive for Saatchi & Saatchi told me. In the dream role, the Weather Channel thus fulfills both its public service mandate and, as everyone else succumbs to the crashing, oceanic floodwaters, a final ecstatic paroxysm of market positioning that Noah himself might have captured—had Noah thought to be a weather channel.

The studio 20th Century Fox first approached the network in August 2002 about the possibility of its playing a major role in the movie.[20] The company was enthusiastic, but the opportunity also presented a degree of public relations awkwardness for a network that had for so long glossed over political complexities and avoided discussing the human impact on the environment. Within months of making the movie deal, the Weather Channel hired Heidi Cullen and began airing the *Forecast Earth* series. The new focus came not a season too soon, for in a year that saw hurricanes homing in on the coast of Florida like colossal Frisbees, it became impossible for anyone to ignore these extreme weather events and what they seemed to evoke in the public mind, for good or ill, about global warming. By then, the Weather Channel had established its climatological bona fides, while hopping daintily over thorny issues of public policy. *Extreme Weather Theories,* for instance, the craftily ambiguous title of a program timed to coincide with the release of *The Day after Tomorrow,* managed to dodge the most substantive and troubling facts of global warming (theories of extreme weather) in favor of the quick-freeze climatological fringe (extreme theories of weather) that fueled the movie and furthered the Weather Channel's ambition to be a leader in the commerce of awe.

The Weather Channel seemed to have discovered in catastrophilia, in the growing culture of awe, yet another method for avoiding troublesome content. For awe is emotional—that is, antidiscursive. People in a state of awe are silent, as Larry Ohs discovered when he drove the vanload of volunteers through the flattened town of Hallam. Like God, or the Big Bang, awe obliterates anything outside its own position. In its beginning is its end. By foregrounding awe, moreover, the weather became, in Marita Sturken's useful phrase, "a story without blame." The audience enthralled by a never-ending series of natural disaster effects, like horrific baubles, could remain untroubled by the elision of their causes.[21]

The merest peek at causes, of course, was a recipe for despair, an entry point into a world owned entirely by the forces of oil and energy, forces that had helped reelect a Republican president from Texas whose administration had undone, in many more ways than can be enumerated here, more than thirty years of environmental law. It was a world whose economy had long been based on a steady flow of oil; consumption was currently 25 percent of global supply, and the demand would only grow, domestically and abroad, in the emerging powerhouse economies of India and China. Big oil and big energy, in short, needed people to continue doing what they were doing, to consume without a care in the world—and, frankly, so did the Weather Channel.

The ideal "weather citizen," according to cultural critic Andrew Ross, sounded a lot like the kind of ideal consumer upon which the present petroleum-based economy depended, that skittish possessor of disposable income, the "consumer" whose "confidence" economists worried over like obsessive parents. He or she was not someone mucking out a barn stall, mind you, or pouring you a cup of coffee behind the counter, but someone "comfortably off, white-collar, with cars, boats, vacation options, families, and gardens and homes that require extensive upkeep."[22] All the specialty maps on the Weather Channel—"fishing maps, business travel maps, picnic maps, indoor relative humidity maps, tanning maps, allergy maps . . . each sponsored . . . by the manufacturer of an appropriate product,"[23] all of these indices fairly sang to an ideal consumer and were geared to his or her pursuit of happiness. This business-class traveler, this delicate professional soul who needed a UV Index and an "Aches and Pains" index, was more likely than not sheltered in daily life from any actual weather encounter, yet for that person the Weather Channel became a kind of courtier, a way to gently and continuously emphasize the consumer's sanctified place in the scheme of things. The Weather Channel draped its arms around this demographic—"an audience of uniquely engaged consumers consisting of over 20 million adults with household incomes above $75,000, over 17 million college graduates, and 52 million homeowners."[24] It was simply not possible to fawn and dote and indulge and worry and fuss *too much* over this consumer. There was an implicit flattery, too, in this focus on the upwardly mobile, whether you were "one of the more than one million business leaders and professionals," according to a network press release, who "get a jump on their day" by tuning in to *First Outlook,* or whether you were just a guy getting off his third-shift factory job, eating cold pizza for breakfast before nodding off for a couple of hours. Either way, *First Outlook,* with "business-savvy Kim Perez, Nick Walker, and Dennis Smith," spoke to you *as if you were* a master of the universe.[25] "Weather is a dream weaver," Wonya Lucas, the network's executive vice president of marketing, told me one morning over the phone from her office in Atlanta. We'd been talking about how the network's coverage of the weather appeals to the imaginative life of its audience—how, for example, somebody who lived in New York might "look at the weather in Phoenix all the time," Lucas said, "because five years earlier he'd almost taken a job there." The report of weather in Phoenix, as the phrase "dream weaver" so aptly suggested, offered many more viewers than there were actual business executives a fantasy of escape down the road not taken.[26] Just so, I thought, on my own little fantasy excursion; who *wouldn't* want to be a "business traveler," after all, flying around, doing deals, with a personal weather valet at one's side, murmuring in your ear how right it was to be you? And while the slobs back in coach had to *buy* their lunches, which came in a box, the weather valet handed you your glass of Chardonnay on a tray—"Your weather, sir"—and, with any number of helpful signs and gestures, smoothed and soothed you. It was all about as necessary as a maid in a fancy hotel, coming in to "turn down the bed." Of course you could do it all by yourself, but that mint left on the pillow—now, *that* was nice.

Meanwhile, in our Super 8 motel room on a Kansas border town, Matt and I watched and snickered—it was a laughter less mirthful, perhaps, than the product of a habitual grimace—before turning to an assessment of various on-camera meteorologists, or OCMs. At the top of Matt's list was Jill Brown, "the one that got away," a woman with serious meteorological chops and great beauty, who dazzled many, then jumped over to CNN, a loss that Matt was not alone in lamenting. "Now that Jill Brown is no longer on," one viewer wrote, "my relationship to the Weather Channel is strictly professional." Among the world's many distractions were Weather Channel chat rooms in which one could discuss favorite or despised meteorologists, like the bland Marshall Seese, whom Matt liked to call Marshall Deceased, or get up-to-the-minute fashion critiques of OCM Kristina Abernathy's wardrobe. When OCM Sharon Resultan was pregnant, Internet discussion groups tracked her progress according to the latitude her belly reached on the U.S. weather map.[27] There were websites dedicated solely to the Weather Channel ladies—"Kristina actually showed some leg today," one observer wrote, warmly. "It wasn't as much as Kim Perez shows, but it still was something."[28] Another viewer, Matt Marron, of Omaha, Nebraska, seemed to have dedicated much of his junior and senior years in high school identifying the *music* played on the Weather Channel, the smooth, finger-snapping, jazzy George Benson–esque pabulum that accompanies the "Local Weather" segment for two minutes, six times an hour, every hour of the day, it would seem, until the world comes to an end. Maybe this is what gets played on the elevator ride to heaven, something a little perky by Spyro Gyra, say, to put a lift in your step. Steve Hurst, the network's music programmer who, over the years, had smuggled the Rolling Stones, Eric Clapton, and the band Phish into the playlist, received more than 400 CDs a year from avid listeners, some of whom, like Russ Korins, a corporate lawyer in New York, made compilation CDs of "Weather Channel music" as gifts for his friends.[29]

I pondered Weather Channel groupies for a while; watching Stephanie Abrams glide in front of a weather map to recap the day, I had to admit she was *a bit of a hottie.* If you doubt me, you can go to a website—www.kaptured foryou.com—that features endless screen captures of weather babes like Stephanie Abrams in mid-pucker. It was by no means an accident that there were so many beautiful female meteorologists gesturing in front of the chroma-key. In the subterranean realms of Weather Channel fandom, weather—as titillation—was a notion that was treated, more or less, as a point of fact. In an article entitled "Am I Watching the Weather—or Porno?" one viewer wrote, "The female meteorologists on TWC are porn stars. Period. I don't know who decided to mix hot chicks with weather forecasting, but it was genius." The essay went on to consider Alexandra Steele—"Okay, that's a bona fide porn star name if I've ever heard one"[30]—as well as Stephanie Abrams, Kristina Abernathy, Heather Tesch, and Hillary Andrews, among many more. Others besides this viewer—paid professional thinkers and observers of culture—had long noted the weird similarities between broadcast meteorology and pornography, observing, for example, that in both realms the stars routinely change their names to reflect a greater commitment, as it were, to the craft. "The only other profession that comes to mind," writes Marita Sturken, "for which people change their names (such as Frank Field, Storm Fields, and Dallas Raines) as signifiers of their work is pornography."[31] In a *New Yorker* article on the Weather Channel, John Seabrook actually used the term "weather-porn," without arousing in that magazine's punctilious copy editors a sense that something needed explaining.

Seabrook's usage referred not to the babes of the Weather Channel but to a new fact of contemporary life, the watching of weather disasters in particular—catastrophilia—which has played a pivotal role in the success of the Weather Channel. "It was the coverage of a hurricane—Elena, in 1985— that first brought the Weather Channel widespread public attention," Seabrook notes, adding that the network noticed a tremendous "ratings spike" whenever a big storm came along. Indeed, 1985 was a watershed year for the network, which faced extinction unless it could convince cable franchises to pay a fee for its service (its advertising revenue had been woefully overestimated). The response to the fee-for-service caught the network off guard. The cable franchises didn't seem to blink. They wanted the Weather Channel. They couldn't imagine not having it. Just as the revenues began kicking in, along came Hurricanes Elena (1985), Hugo (1989), and Andrew (1992), which, for all the damage they caused, could not have come at a better time for a company in the business of reporting the weather. A host of other factors also led to the general turnaround, but it is indisputable that weather disasters, and a better understanding of how to manage and market and program and play big weather (soberly, earnestly, continually) helped save the network. Today, the network still attains its biggest audiences during disasters. As Hurricane Frances headed for the Florida coast, the Weather Channel outperformed all other news and information cable networks for the day, with over 1.5 million homes viewing the event, reaching a high of 2.7 million homes as the hurricane made landfall.

Yet for years the network has successfully avoided the perception of weather-mongering, if not the actual fact. This was made easy since its interest in severe weather was but an amplification, appropriate to each new situation, of an overall, abiding interest in all types of weather. Disasters were just part of a continuum of coverage. Thus, the Weather Channel has continued to enjoy a special public relations advantage whenever the network trucks arrive on the Florida coast to cover a big hurricane. The public perception has been that the Weather Channel *should* cover hurricanes, as a matter of course—that was its regular beat. Whereas for the hordes of other networks an approaching disaster was just another sensational opportunity, the Weather Channel's coverage—which remains comprehensive and, more recently, has included special "weather-triggered" advertising features for its clients—still seems to *belong,* in the minds of most viewers. The network has kept what might be called a vow of sobriety regarding weather events, while at the same time, maneuvering more and more toward the ecstatic modes of catastrophe and awe. This balancing act has included, of course, common programming practices, for example the placement of very attractive females, like Stephanie Abrams, in front of the camera.

Matt and I watched the weather for a while, and then, using the unspoken signals of men now familiar with each other's habits, we switched off the lights and went to bed, though not to sleep. Matt rarely slept well. He'd slipped his headphones on and had gone off into a nocturnal world of weather freakdom; I stared at the ceiling, forced to address a crisis that had lain in wait for me all day, while I found ways to distract myself from an uncomfortable fact that had hovered over this trip and that now had me in its grip. At some point I got up, slipped on my sneakers, and left Matt there, softly breathing the air-conditioned air.

I made my way down a dirt road until I got beyond the reach of lights in the motel parking lot. With wheat fields to my left and right in the darkness, under stars, with gravel crunching rhythmically under my feet, the prairie wind met me, buffeting my body and frisking my T-shirt. The wind brought my anxiety into relief. I had been on the road more than a week, ostensibly "storm chasing," pursuing a natural phenomenon, steeped in the weather, and yet, surrounded as I was by weather fanatics, weather instrumentation, and nearly nonstop weather talk, with the Weather Channel constantly in the background of every motel room I entered, I had never felt so removed from the weather in my life. On my midnight walk, I felt unusually alert to the promptings of the elements, as if I were emerging from an extended bout of sensory deprivation. Indeed, for the last 3,000 miles, I had been wrapped in recirculating air, the Dodge Caravan a cocoon of sheet metal, plastic, Doritos, and vulcanized rubber. Some part of me had had enough and had kept me awake that night until, in a moment of anxiety, I had escaped this self-imposed gulag of interiority and taken the extraordinary step of *going outside for a walk.*

What I found was the always blowing, always oncoming wind. If the prairie wind had been a person, we would say that it had a problem with boundaries. If it were a god, it was a god that was too proximate. The Sioux had a word for the force that underlay the wind, and the wind's mystery, and the mystery and power of all things in nature: *wakan.* Tonight, the wind seemed like some gruff, overly familiar *wakan* intermediary. It had one thing to say, as I crunched my way down the road, and it said it loudly. Or maybe this was the only certain way of getting my attention, the way discomfort draws the mind to what's needed, a demiurge pointing the way to something bigger. I imagined the early white settlers to this part of the world, working outside with this great invisible blowhard, this unrelenting wind, all day, every day. It was easy to see how the constant wind could become a sickness, a wind weariness, easy to see how one might look for relief. It led some to madness, others to God. And now? What was I after, with all this weather? In addressing the weather as directly as I could, in chasing after it, my subject seemed to have completely eluded me, the way God vanishes upon becoming the target of contemplation. I wanted to stop moving. I felt I had a better chance of finding what I was looking for if I let the roving weather marauders, radar trucks, and weather junkies go where they would. It would be impossible, of course, to follow this impulse, to let Matt go, to let Sean Casey and the TIV go, to watch the DOW trucks and the DOW kids and the girls from California University of Pennsylvania at Pittsburgh recede into the distance, to sit here, in the middle of the country, and watch the weather ebb and flow.

Just ahead of me that night on the gravel road near Belleville, Kansas, lay my answer. I met it there, but I did not have the wisdom to recognize it. I was looking for storms, after all, for the big dramatic truths therein, so that when the biggest part of big weather arrived quietly, modestly, in a kind of murmur, I mistook it for something small. One hears the truth, after all, the heart of a story, the deepest part of oneself, and then, in response, perversely, one decides to play something preposterous such as ABBA's greatest hits, loudly, on the stereo, or to fall asleep to the gentle burbling of the television.

I had walked about a quarter mile when I came upon a stand of cottonwood trees by the road. Something about them made me stop in my tracks. A transformation had occurred in the rising moonlight. I had entered a wind shadow, the cottonwood splitting the wind's one dull note, which had seemed like a finger stuck in my ear, into a thousand voices a few paces away. It was a wind plume, with a modest sweep, a gently rising and falling shimmer, a sheen. "What is this?" Angel Clare asks Tess at the end of Hardy's *Tess of the D'Urbervilles,* the law closing in as the two fugitives reach Stonehenge. It is the dead of night. Tess, who does not recognize the place but understands what she feels and hears, says, "It's a temple of the winds." Just so. Something was moving through the cottonwoods that a Druid or a Sioux would have understood. Life, out here, was lived, always, on the horizon's terms, which were the terms of the absolute, the individual erased, absorbed by the sky and the vast undergirding *horizontalisme* of the Plains, but a tree was a momentary stay against all this. A tree resisted that erasure, and made by its act of resistance a spot on the vertical, a place, a temple in which to dwell, and to hear, or perhaps fleetingly to imagine hearing, *wakan.*

And that was all there was to the Belleville Epiphany. I was struck by a moment of grace, but by the time I'd crunched my way back on the gravel road to the motel, it—whatever it was—had morphed into something else, perhaps a greater appreciation of National Arbor Day. Something had happened out there, and then had covered its tracks, though in my journal that night I left a cryptic entry, which read, the next day ("Write history of National Arbor Day!"), like a lost connection, the telephone yanked out of the wall in the lobby of the Super 8.

The world has a way of distracting us from moments like the Belleville Epiphany, and bringing us back to the Weather Channel, for instance.

There were important business decisions behind all of the success of the Weather Channel that seemed completely, outrageously unpropitious at the time, beginning in 1977 with the counterintuitive vision of John Coleman, the *Good Morning America* weatherman, that people would actually watch a cable network dedicated to the weather, but extending into the operating partnership between Coleman and Frank Batten, whose Landmark Corporation bankrolled the whole enterprise. Landmark, you'll recall, is a big Virginia communications company that has for the past four decades specialized in decidedly unglamorous but extremely profitable businesses. Founded by Batten's uncle the legendary newspaperman, Samuel L. (Colonel) Slover, who in 1905 bought the Norfolk, Virginia, *Public-Ledger,* by 1933 Landmark was a regional newspaper empire of small second- and third-tier Virginia dailies—the Newport *News, Times Herald,* the Richmond *Times Dispatch,* the Portsmouth *Star,* the Petersburg *Progress Index*—that left Slover awash in cash. Colonel Slover purchased WTAR, the first radio station in Virginia, and in 1948 purchased a television license, going on the air with WTAR-TV in the spring of 1950. By then, Slover's nephew had graduated from Harvard Business School and was put to work in the circulation department of the *Ledger-Dispatch.* Four years later, Slover appointed Batten, then just twenty-seven years old, publisher of his newspaper conglomerate, responsible for 500 employees and gross receipts of $8.7 million in 1954 dollars.[32] In the next forty years, Batten would become a king of the invisible pot of gold—of cable companies (TeleCable, 1963); the Weather Channel, (1982) that nobody else had seen as even remotely necessary, and of free automobile-ad leaflets (1995), the kind displayed in grocery stores. It was Batten who discovered that if you applied the economies of scale to the unprepossessing auto trader and amassed, say, nearly 700 of these crappy little rags across the country, you could make some serious money.[33]

The decision to move into the unheralded cable market began in 1963. Cable, or CATV as it was then known, offered a new way for rural communities to watch the *CBS Evening News with Walter Cronkite,* for instance, along with the rest of the country. To do business, you had to secure a franchise from a local community, then build a "head-end," a glorified antenna to receive distant signals, which were then routed through a network of coaxial cables all over the countryside, through valleys and across distant plains hitherto unreachable by transmitters, and then directly to people's homes. The head-end, the construction of a cable network, and the leasing of telephone lines, to name only a few expenses, was capital intensive, but these tax-deductible costs also worked to Landmark's advantage, shielding the profits of the parent newspaper conglomerate and building tremendous value from new businesses, developed at a steeper discount than if they had been purchased as preexisting franchises. And since everyone was clamoring for cable, each new franchise created a reliable revenue stream.

TeleCable secured franchises in places like Columbus, Georgia, and Kokomo, Indiana, where they provided regular network programming and an assortment of channels that offered oddball local fare—one channel might have news from the AP wire scrolling across a screen, another a stationary camera aimed at an array of weather dials, another a bingo game or city hall meeting, broadcast in its entirety, while still another might feature a bowl with a goldfish swimming around in it—all rather dull, of course, but each, one can't help but notice, containing the germ of what would become the Weather Channel's success. People loved the goldfish, for instance, as Frank Batten recalls in his memoir. And if by chance someone, perhaps a janitor, accidentally moved the goldfish bowl out of the frame, the American people, viewers of a nascent cable empire, spoke up, calling the station to complain bitterly.

By the mid-seventies, the famed coverage of the 1975, Ali-Frazier boxing match, "the Thrilla in Manila," brought satellite cable coverage into the public eye, and the way was paved for nationwide cable networks with specialty programming, such as CNN's all-news format, HBO's pay-per-view special events, ESPN's all-sports network, and MTV's groundbreaking music video format. It was in this competitive climate, when cable programming was emerging as a new and potentially lucrative business, that Batten was approached by John Coleman, the *Good Morning America* weatherman, with his proposal for an all-weather channel. Batten saw in a network that broadcast both national and local weather an opportunity to advertise both nationally and locally, and he agreed to fund Coleman's idea, provided that the "national/regional/local" advertising scheme was an integral part of the business plan. The ability to hit national and local markets would, among other things, exploit "cooperative advertising" funds allocated by large corporations to regional franchises, and would become an important part of the Weather Channel's future success.

Batten knew a few other things, too. Cable franchises had a limited number of channel offerings at the time, anywhere between twenty-four and thirty-six channels, all of which were dedicated to carrying either one of the major networks (ABC, NBC, CBS), one of the budding cable networks (CNN, HBO, QVC, ESPN), or local fare (the goldfish bowl, or the weather). Batten intended to offer his Weather Channel as a replacement for—and a significant improvement upon—what the thousands of local cable franchises were already offering their customers. His business plan did not ask the local franchises to give up anything, only to improve something that already existed, usually a shabby local weather format, by substituting a shiny new, professionally produced weather channel—for free. Batten guessed correctly, and made three large bets—the equivalent of going "all in," three times in a row, in a game of Texas Hold 'em. First, in a bidding war to secure the rights to lease a satellite transponder that would provide the all-important national signal, he made a preemptive $12 million bid—huge money in the early days of cable. He won. Next, he bet that he could solve the immense technical puzzle of bundling local weather information for every county in the United States into the national satellite feed, and then routing it properly so that Seattle's weather didn't appear on TV sets in Weehawken. This led to the company's invention of the Satellite Transponder Addressable Receiver, or the WeatherSTAR. Last, Batten bet that he could convince the National Weather Service—a service owned by the American public, with a network of forecast offices, each its own little fiefdom, with its own way of transmitting weather data to the home office—to standardize its data transmission across the entire agency. Because of the technical requirements of the WeatherSTAR system, the cooperation of the National Weather Service was essential, but it was by no means clear why a privately held company should receive a sweetheart deal from the U.S. government, changing the way the NWS did business so that a single company might emerge from its shell, fledge, and fly—straight to the bank.[34]

But Batten shrewdly took advantage of the political climate. The Reagan administration, citing "big government" as an evil second only to the Soviet Union, routinely targeted the NWS's budget, threatening to close forecast offices, fire staff, reduce research, and, in short, slash and burn until there was nothing left of the agency, but a squeaky weather vane atop the Department of Commerce building. Batten gambled that under these circumstances Richard E. Hallgren, the agency's director, would agree that it was in the NWS's best interest to help create a media empire—a broadcast network fueled entirely by repackaged National Weather Service data. The Weather Channel, it could be argued, would be a unique platform by which the NWS could further its mandate to protect life and property. Cable television would enable wider dissemination of National Weather Service data. The arrangement also made the National Weather Service seem more visible, more valuable—less expendable. So the NWS used the Weather Channel as a highly visible media shield, protecting itself from the media-conscious legislators on Capitol Hill, while the Weather Channel and Landmark Communications received a tremendous corporate gift. Some would call this an example of corporate welfare; others would say it was the granting of a monopoly. In an era so set against "big government," it was big government itself that completely bent over backward to usher a cable giant into the world.

A giant that, though it couldn't control the weather, had proven, perhaps as nothing else could have, that the weather can be effectively marketed. The company, which now earns nearly 40 percent of Landmark Communications' annual revenues of nearly $750 million, has remained intimately familiar with its target audience, famously commissioning a psychographic segmentation study in 1998 that parsed the Weather Channel viewership into three distinct categories. The "weather engaged," the largest segment at 41 percent of the audience, were complete weather junkies. Matt was perhaps a near and supreme exemplar. The second segment were "planner people," 28 percent of the audience, who used the Weather Channel to plan events (golf trips, picnics); the final 31 percent comprised "commodity people," who just want to know the current temperature.[35] The nagging question for the Weather Channel had long been how to cultivate the planners and commodity people without alienating its weather-engaged base. The answer seemed to involve a three-ball juggling act. The first ball was simply to remain true to the network's original forecast formula. The second ball reached across segments to attract crowds the way a car wreck will do. It required an intensified effort in natural disaster programming—houses sagging into the sea, twisters gobbling up small towns. The third ball also reached across viewer segments by reinventing the weather as a kind of lifestyle cipher.[36]

In May 2001, the Weather Channel began a $15 million integrated marketing campaign, ushered in with the catchphrase "Live By It," that began a new phase of the corporate business plan, the transcription of weather into "lifestyle" programming—"to build meaningful relationships," a company executive intoned, "with audiences across all TWC platforms—cable, Internet, wireless, radio." Wonya Lucas, who inherited the "Live By It" branding initiative, wanted to throw another other ball into the air—the "awe aspect"—while at the same time building upon the "lifestyle" agenda. A second marketing campaign, which might have puzzled more than a few of the network's loyal base of weather wonks, emerged in April 2003, during the annual "upfront," a week of courtship during which media buyers come to see what each cable network has to offer as an advertising vehicle for corporate America. The night happened to be the first such "upfront" for the network. And so, cast in the role of the debutante, in a trendy Manhattan club called Splashlight, with the pop diva Michelle Branch performing for a youngish crowd of media executives, one heard for the first time a catchphrase for a new "programming initiative" that was a little unusual for a company called the Weather Channel: "It's not about the weather," the Weather Channel declared. "It's about life." This suggested that the network had come a long way from its original plan in 1982. The message, Wonya Lucas, assured me, would never be heard on the Weather Channel itself: it was meant for the ad buyers' ears alone. "We did it for a very specific business reason," she told me. "In the advertising community there are a lot of younger buyers who don't see the relevance of a network like the Weather Channel. We wanted to show that our product was not so much about the weather, per se, but about what you do with the weather." She paused. "It was also a provocative statement for the Weather Channel to make."

It was time, it seemed, for the staid organization nurtured by Frank Batten, king of the free auto-trader, to move over—time for a little youth-oriented provocation. "We were falling off people's radar," Bill Burke, the then president of the Weather Channel Companies, told a reporter.[37] It was time to loosen up, time for the network to point at the chest of the key 18-to-49-year-old demographic and, when the demographic looked down, to tweak its nose. Time for Dr. Steve Lyons, the balding and esteemed hurricane expert, to strap himself inside a wind tunnel to demonstrate the power of hurricane-force winds during "Wind Warrior," an episode in a new five-part hurricane series entitled *Into the Eye*. It was time for *Road Crew*—in adspeak, a show appearing as "two-minute, branded interstitials" between longer programs to take viewers to "entertainment and sporting events like NCAA football games." It sounded like fun, but it wasn't clear how that key demographic would respond to hanging out with "a charismatic host" at the Kentucky Derby, say, or the New Orleans Jazz and Heritage Festival.

No matter; the network could count on a second successful year of *Storm Stories,* probably the hottest thing to hit the Weather Channel since Stephanie Abrams began broadcasting in a tight, V-necked sweater.

According to Nielsen Media Research, the network still enjoyed its biggest audiences in the mornings, as the planners and commodity people got their weather info for the day. Yet most of the advertising revenue remained in the prime-time market, which was still dominated by the major networks. "A popular show like *Everybody Loves Raymond* might get a rating approaching nineteen or twenty percentage points, which is huge, and not uncommon for that show," a Saatchi & Saatchi executive told me. "That means over twenty million pairs of eyeballs are watching the show during that time slot": big money for network advertising sales. By comparison, the

Weather Channel was clearly in the minor leagues. On its best day, the network might attain a Nielsen rating that topped 1 percent, but the usual was some fraction thereof. Patrick Scott, the executive vice president and general manager of programming, operations, and distribution for the company, crowed about the effect of *Storm Stories* on its eight P.M. time slot, which had captured a recent Nielsen rating of 0.3, or about 300,000 viewers—up 50 percent from the previous year.

Hence the big push to prime time and toward "reality-based" content. It was time for a little awe to kick in, like the catastrophilic shot through the body politic by which "shock and awe" had become a movie-trailer catchphrase for the bombing of Baghdad. Coincident with that war came a renewed commitment to the commodification of the sublime, the Weather Channel warming to the business of catastrophilia. The network wasn't alone, of course: every storm-tossed region had its own version of Weather Channel coverage, perhaps nowhere more than Tornado Alley.

For at least three months of every year, Oklahoma City TV stations became miniature versions of the Weather Channel, dedicating much of their programming to the spectacle of severe weather in Tornado Alley. Ground troops—freelance storm chasers—fanned out, captured, and sold storm footage or contracted out as stringers for a news agency specializing in severe weather footage, Breaking News Video Network. BNVN, a Minneapolis-based business, founded in 2001 by the chaser Doug Kiesling, received up-to-the-minute digitalized storm footage from chasers in the field, who then paid Kiesling to negotiate contracts and to collect fees on their behalf for material that media outlets such as the Weather Channel wanted to use. The BNVN stringers expected only to make enough over a three-month season to help finance their hobby, but there were occasional exceptions. David Drummond's explosive encounter with a wind gust outside Fairfield, Nebraska, which played nationally as a "Storm chasers versus tornado" story, presented an unusual windfall; after subtracting a percentage for Dorothy and for Kiesling, Drummond earned a little more than $8,000 in total licensing fees. His first customer? The Weather Channel. Other chasers, Charles Edwards of Cloud 9 Tours and Jim Leonard of Cyclone Tours among them, led tour groups as small as six and as large as a few dozen people, each of whom paid over $2,000 for a week. In a good season, Edwards might gross nearly a hundred grand. Bigger money, as Warren Faidley had proven, came to those who patiently built up a library of weather stock photography. Fewer and far between were the consulting gigs for production companies—clients from movies, television, documentaries, and publishing. In general, business was booming.

Indeed, Norman in the springtime was becoming a little like Hollywood, with absolutely everyone in search of a piece of the action. All the local stations engaged in an annual springtime campaign, known locally as the weather wars, during which the stations constantly trumpeted their forecasting prowess. If KOCO (Channel 5, the ABC affiliate) had a "First Alert Doppler Radar," then KFOR (Channel 4, the NBC affiliate) responded with "The Edge," which featured satellite imagery and street-level photos from rooftops to help "Get you closer to the storm," and this new development would prompt Gary England's KWTV ("Count on Gary to get you through the storm") to introduce VIPIR, a graphics software for radar that, according to one observer, "turned perfectly understandable radar into Disney-esque cartoon dramatizations of Armageddon with spinning meso-cyclone icons." Channel 9's secret weapon of the moment seemed to be something called MOAR, or Mother of All Radar, a new, high-resolution system whose name seemed to wink at the parochial absurdity of the weather wars even as it raised the ante further still. How the competition would answer this new development, how anyone would out-Doppler the Mother of All Radar, only another spring would tell. The competition was so fierce that Oklahoma stations felt obliged, it seemed, to jump on each gust of wind as a "developing story"—the clouds rolling over the countryside, the television stations stringing the story along, with interruptions for commercial sponsors, like carnival barkers in front of rival sideshow tents.[38]

For its part, The Weather Channel was offering a welter of catastrophic specialty programs. There was *Nor'easter Season* and *Winter Storm Season,* of course, each with its own array of rain, snow, and flu-season advertising tie-ins, which brought us all, as the earth moved unerringly around the sun, to the main disaster lineup of the year. In the blessed order of the universe, the Weather Channel's *Tornado Season* happened to correspond to the media-wide period known as "sweeps week," which The Weather Channel tackled head on with *Tornado Week*. But tornado-centric reality programming continued from March all the way to June. It was followed by *Hurricane Season,* which, as John Seabrook noted, lasted "almost as long as hockey season, from June 1st to November 30th." Then there came an onslaught of *Storm Stories, Raging Hurricanes,* and *Supercells,* plus bouts with the *World's Worst Weather.* Such programming pulled strongly in one direction, and it seemed to require a countervailing force. "We have to be careful that we don't go too long without our bread-and-butter forecasting products," Bill Burke told *Adweek,* "which are what bring people to the network day in and day out."[39] It was left to Burke, it seemed, to trot out the standard vows of seriousness and decorum that draped and wrapped and anchored the station, like tethers holding down a blimp that the wind threatened to blow away. Catastrophilia still accounted for only a small fraction of the network's programming, which, as Burke suggested, would remain mostly bread, mostly butter, mostly true to the blandness of weather talk.

But what, really, was the Weather Channel, anyway? Many had tried to say, but something important kept slipping off the page. There was the ontological explanation, a kind of assessment of the emptiness of American houses, and the need to fill that up with something. The weather on the Weather Channel offered a "calming effect . . . a zen-like state of being," according to Jerry Gentile, of the marketing firm Chiat/Day. Jeff Masterson of the Weather Underground, a weather forecasting website, suggested that the Weather Channel provided a sense of casual community, with a dose, perhaps, of Metamucil. The network was "a way of being connected to other people" without "being stimulated greatly. . . . The weather just passes through you." Perhaps it offered, according to a *Washington Post* article, "a murmuring accompaniment to life." A darker explanation emerged as well. "The old world order was breaking down," suggested Seabrook, writing a few months before 9/11, "and the new order would be less stable, more chaotic—more like weather." Against this troubled world, the Weather Channel seemed to provide a parallel universe of "safe" discourse, a world without politics, like the coma-inducing escapist television fare of the Vietnam War era.

The more I read of the marketing initiatives of the Weather Channel, the more the network began to resemble a fiefdom within the world of fashion, another realm in which emptiness had been transcribed like a seasonal Rorschach. "The Weather Channel was an entire outlook on everyday life," Andrew Ross wrote over a decade ago, and the network, after many millions of dollars in market research, seemed to concur. "It's not about the weather. It's about life." Maybe weather had become, in one weather watcher's memorable phrase, "a floating signifier . . . like God after the death of God."[40] Weather was Frank Batten's goldfish in its bowl and the yearly, $300 million gold mine that it became—the dream of every marketing executive, a vehicle with infinite tie-in possibilities, perfectly malleable, everywhere and everything for everybody, like water, taking the shape of any vessel into which it was poured.

NINE

Weather Risk
and the Great Folly

We're history's actors . . . and you, all of you,
will be left to just study what we do.
—UNIDENTIFIED SENIOR ADVISOR TO GEORGE W. BUSH, 2004

n October of 1998, a violent tornado swept through the city of Moore, Oklahoma. It approached the house of a man named Donald Staley, who climbed into the bathtub with his wife. The force of the tornado peeled off roof shingles and swept away his carport. From across the street, a neighbor's carport smashed into a tree in Staley's front yard. Had there been no tree blocking the way, the flying carport would have cut through Staley's house like a scythe. Over the next few weeks, he began repairs, filled out a battery of local, state and federal disaster relief forms, and then, like most Oklahomans similarly affected, tried to put the tornado behind him. The following spring, in the early evening of May 3, 1999, Staley was working alone in his garage, entirely absorbed in a carpentry project, when the lights began to flicker. He stepped outside. Like so many others who have described the event, Staley was momentarily stunned by what he saw: automobiles sailing around inside a mammoth tornado that was approaching his house. He stood there in awe until an engine casing from a tractor landed next to him. He was soon cowering in his bathtub with two cats and a German Shepherd, as winds from the single most destructive tornado in U.S. history, the F5 that damaged or destroyed 10,000 homes in Oklahoma City, crossed Northwest Seventeenth Street and ripped off the roof of his house.

It was time for a change, time to relocate and start anew, which is just what Donald Staley did, making his bid for a new life in another house—all the way across town. This strikes most people who are not from Oklahoma as odd. People find it peculiar that the Staleys, twice clobbered by tornadoes in as many years, did not remove themselves to some climatologically less perturbable spot—to San Diego, say, where the winds, if they come at all, arrive as the most sanguine sort of zephyr parting one's hair of an afternoon. *Wouldn't that,* people seem to want to say, gently but firmly, *make more sense?* But Don Staley was happy where he was. And, anyway, though he didn't think of it at the time, it would have seemed, to anyone who knew about such matters, that Staley had statistical probability on his side. Tornado season in Oklahoma can be seen as a reverse lottery, with everyone wondering *Who will get it this year?;* the chances of being hit by two tornadoes in successive years are about one in a million. This unlikelihood, of course, had come to pass. The odds of a *third* tornado striking the same place in Staley's lifetime were spectacularly long. It was more likely that, in a coin-toss marathon, Staley would succeed in flipping thirty-one consecutive heads than that he would be struck by another tornado. Staley had burned up all the bad luck that anyone could ever expect to have.

But living through tornadoes does things to people, bumps the improbable into a closer orbit, so Staley had an above-ground bunker of reinforced concrete—a safe room—installed in his backyard. It had just enough room to stand or lie down. Its door slid sideways on rollers. In this big concrete block, this ugly time capsule, this temple of preparedness, Staley placed a cot, bottled water, a flashlight, and extra batteries. The world had twice knocked him flat, and Donald Staley had gotten back up. But if big weather were to come for the third time, however long the odds, he would be ready to bear witness. The third time around, he would bring his video camera.

Four years later, on May 8, 2003, a tornado completely demolished Donald Staley's third home. Before it hit, Staley fled into the safe room. Minutes after the tornado passed, he emerged, his camera rolling. It's shaky footage. The wind is still blowing him around, and he's stepping over broken glass, shattered wood, nails. Live power lines are strewn about like spaghetti. Broken natural gas pipes hiss loudly. There's nothing left of Staley's house. He zooms in on the safe room that has more than likely saved his life, then pans back for a broader shot. Smoke from a fire rises in the middle distance. The prairie wind keeps pushing him around. You can hear him shout "Hello!" to a neighbor across the street, who does not offer a reciprocal hello, or even an "Are you all right?" but says, only, "You're unlucky!" Which is so obviously and so painfully true that it seems to catch Staley off guard. "Well, *yeah,*" is all he can muster at the moment.

Serial destruction of this sort, visited upon a single human being, inevitably offers itself up for contemplation like something out of the Old Testament, Staley's verbalized shrug—"Well, *yeah*"—the sort of thing Jonah himself might have offered to the angry crowd amidships, every accusing finger pointed his way. But Jonah, of course, was a man on the run from God. Staley, in work boots and jeans, with kind eyes and a firm handshake, had nothing to hide. He was just a guy trying to make his modest way in the world. Yet there could be no doubt that Staley was singularly unlucky. How bad, indeed, could bad luck be? Could such misfortune be quantified?

I called the National Severe Storms Laboratory, in Norman, and spoke to Harold Brooks, a specialist in severe weather risk analysis. Brooks, an affable man who often fields questions from the media, launched into a monologue that seemed designed to throw cold water on my budding interest in Donald Staley. The tendency to look for significance in stories like his, Harold Brooks said, was an example of something called the "multiple endpoint fallacy," a sort of tabloid mentality, a tendency to become unduly focused upon some remarkable outcome—someone struck by three tornadoes in six years, or the birth of quintuplets, for instance, which, from a statistical standpoint, when viewed against the world's population of tornado victims or of women giving birth, is not nearly as remarkable as it is inevitable. "Given this larger framework," he said, "we know it's going to happen to someone. We just don't know who that someone is going to be." Well, it seemed, we did now.

Harold Brooks had recently calculated the most accurate "return frequency," or "recurrence interval" for violent tornadoes (F2 or higher) for any individual location in North America. After running his computer model 40,000 years into the future, he had calculated the probability of getting hit by a single violent tornado of the kind that damaged or destroyed each of Staley's three homes as 1 chance in 4,000 years, which seemed like pretty steep odds against such a single event, even in a tornado-prolific

*Donald Staley and his concrete,
aboveground bunker near
Newcastle, Oklahoma, May 2004.*
© Mark Svenvold

region like Oklahoma. The multiple end-point fallacy notwithstanding, the
tabloid part of my brain was still hungry for a Las Vegas–type number to
apply to Donald Staley, and this, after a few minutes, Harold Brooks supplied. Having your home destroyed three times in six years, it turns out, was
a 1–in–3 billion chance. But what did *that* mean? I groped around for a
practical example and found Bart K. Holland, an epidemiologist and author
of *What Are the Chances?*, who spoke to me from his home in New Jersey.
Suppose, he said, that someone from one of the following regions—China,
India, and Europe—steals my wallet, and suppose that my method for finding the thief is to choose one of the regions at random—China, say—and
then get on a plane and *fly to Beijing*. If, at the airport, I confront the first
person I see, and she hands me my wallet, then that, Holland said, would be
a good example of a 1–in–3 billion chance.

The world had barely enough people, it seemed, to supply the number of
extras needed to satisfy scenarios at this end of the spectrum of unlikelihood,

a hardship post *waaay* off on the end of the bell curve, where, I imagined, a small contingent of unlucky people, perhaps not enough to fill an elevator, stood scratching their heads, a cohort of misfortune for whom luck was more or less uniformly bad, like the difference between *flammable* and *inflammable*. And when it came to tornadoes, Donald Staley was, even among them, a singular instance, arguably the unluckiest man on the planet.

I met him south of Newcastle, about twenty minutes south of Oklahoma City, in his fourth house, located a few yards off Highway 15, a busy four-lane arterial dotted with cattle, microwave repeater towers, and auto body shops. He sported a baseball cap and a neatly trimmed goatee, and he posed stiffly as I took a picture of him in front of his tornado shelter, hands poised over his groin as if to foil a foul ball, or a meteorite falling from the sky. As we watched the video of his destroyed third home on the wide-screen TV in his living room, he rattled off the details of a story that, after so many television and radio interviews, now bore the unmistakable signature phrasing of the well-polished sound bite. Staley, the erstwhile construction worker, had become media savvy. His name and circumstances had been circulated as an extremely rare anecdotal gem. And he had helped the story along, having gone through a midlife career change, putting down his carpenter's hammer and now selling aboveground storm shelters. He appeared in local television ads that showed him standing alongside the concrete bunker that had saved his life and which he was now selling and for which he received a commission from Oz—Oz brand aboveground storm shelters. Staley was fast becoming a survivor celebrity, one who, I couldn't help but think, if he ever relocated again, would add new meaning to the phrase, "There goes the neighborhood."

If Staley had taken his spectacularly bad luck and found a way to trade up, shedding the tools and long hours of the carpentry trade for a day job selling storm shelters, many others had discovered money in the troubled skies. The housing and construction industry in Oklahoma, for instance, was as robust as it had ever been, a fact with a straightforward, easy-to-fathom correlation to the tornado outbreaks of the last six years, which had created in their destructive wakes a surge in the demand for demolition, cartage, remodeling, and rebuilding—an unrivaled construction boom in which nearly 10,000 houses were constructed in the Oklahoma City area alone. Smelling of spackle and paint and newly laid wall-to-wall carpeting, they echoed as houses do that are empty of possessions. For the tornadoes had scattered people's belongings across the state—refrigerators, televisions, water heaters, dinnerware, beds, sofas, lawn mowers, garden hoses, and sports equipment—all the accumulated stuff of early twenty-first-century American life. As the insurance checks were cashed, people began flooding the retail malls, furniture stores, and car dealerships, and flocking on weekends to the monolithic purveyors of stuff—to Wal-Mart, Target, and Home Depot, where the stuff-getting, the demand to fill empty houses, created economic microclimates that cleared the shelves and boosted profits. Not that there was anything *wrong* with that. It is a fact of commerce, a fact of the grim science of economics, a fact of any era, any cavalcade of ages—the Enlightenment, the Age of Reason, the Age of Exploration, of Colonial Empire, the Industrial Age and its offspring, the Age of Consumption—that one person's misfortune was another person's boon. This remained true, especially at the end of the Age of Consumption, which was where we were now, though we didn't like to think about it. Many different features of the cultural landscape were brought to bear, it seemed, to distract us from thinking too much about the new era, whose contours one felt vaguely as one feels a change of season. Now was the arrival of the predicate, the arrival of limits, of "carbon constraints," of the consequences of consumption, of what the climatologist James E. Hansen called "humanity's Faustian bargain and the payments coming due."[1] The predicate asked something of Americans that we were not yet ready to give, fixed as we still were upon earlier assumptions, dreams that others before us had lived and enjoyed, of getting in the car and hitting the road. History had long revealed that ages, like empires, collapsed, yet continued on their own colossal momentum, so that during the difficult interregnum an entire culture could proceed for decades, for perhaps a hundred years, as if nothing had happened—might steam ahead at full speed, for instance, even as a new age was at hand—the Age of Risk.

PERHAPS DONALD STALEY was the new age's emblematic figure, the World's Unluckiest Man, resourceful enough, however, to capture for himself the smallest share of a new, rising economy of misfortune. Call it the weather risk franchise, a realm whose first cause was risk itself—the fact that hail, or frost, or drought can kill crops, that hurricanes and tornadoes can destroy property. Risk, of course, was inherently "securitizable," as they say on the trading floor. Somebody is afraid of something bad happening, so somebody else invents a way to allay that fear, for a price. Mankind had long known that foreknowledge of weather risk was valuable. Weather forecast information had been at a premium, perhaps, since Thales used his study of the heavens to predict a poor olive crop, prompting him, in 586 B.C.E., to become one of the first in recorded history to act in anticipation of a predicted shortfall caused by the weather, and thus corner the market in olive presses. Today, a staggering portion of the U.S. economy—nearly a third of the gross national product, or $3.8 trillion—is at risk each year due to the weather.

It was by no bureaucratic fluke that the National Weather Service made its administrative home not, as logic might suggest, in the Department of the Interior, or of Agriculture, or even of Defense, but in the grand building that houses the Department of Commerce, on whose edifice the single most abiding fact of contemporary life is etched, tellingly, in language fueled by a metaphorical storm. "Commerce," as the nineteenth-century American historian George Bancroft observed, "defies every wind, out-rides every tempest, and invades every zone." I liked to think of Donald Staley, the world's unluckiest man, selling his above-ground storm shelters in Newcastle, Oklahoma, as someone occupying the bull's-eye of the weather risk franchise, the smallest zone, a tiny speck in the center of the country, perhaps no bigger than a storm shelter itself. From that damp, musty cell, I would travel outward into concentric circles of expanding interest and influence, zones of capital expenditure, and estimates of annual gross receipts for all business in the United States dealing with weather consulting, weather risk management, insurance, reinsurance, and all other forms of alternative risk transfer that amounted to an annual figure of just over $100 billion.[2]

Staley addressed risk in a literal way, as did a few other, oddball companies like Dyn-O-Mat, a company that made "environmental absorbent products," in Jupiter, Florida. Dyn-O-Mat claimed to have used a patented cloud-seeding process to erase a cloud from the sky, like Mr. Clean on bathroom tiles,[3] but most of those in the first realm of the weather risk franchise were information brokers—consultants offering accurate information about the weather and the means of producing assessments of weather risk. Bloomingdale's, for instance, hired a meteorological consulting company to help calculate the demand for long winter coats. The Movie Gallery, with almost 2,000 stores in North America, depended upon long-range meteorological information to calculate, up to a year in advance, how bad weather will influence its inventory of movies and video games. The PGA Tour pays a meteorologist to track thunderstorms, and every year at Thanksgiving, Macy's uses Brett Zweiback, a Metro Weather Services meteorologist, who, from inside a clear plastic tent on the corner of West Seventy-seventh Street and Central Park West, and with 2.5 million people awaiting his decision, gives the crucial "go/no go" signal for the launching of the annual Thanksgiving Day Parade balloons.

It was a world in which the weather had become "monetized," according to Joe Schaefer, director of the Storm Prediction Center, who also presided over the American Meteorological Society's certifying board for private-sector meteorologists. It was a relatively new market that had grown substantially as computers and computer software and Internet access made weather data more accessible, so that anyone with a degree in meteorology and a computer could enter the fray.[4] Schaefer spoke of a man, for instance, named Mike Smith, of Wichita, Kansas, whose specialty was to forecast the weather for railroad companies. "There's big money along railroad tracks," Joe Schaefer said. In the back pages of the *American Meteorological Society Journal,* one could find ads for forensic meteorologists, who testified as expert witnesses in civil and criminal cases; companies specializing in "optimized vessel routing" and "TV weathercaster training"; companies that brought their meteorological expertise to bear upon "noise and dust." Accuweather, a privately held company based in State College, Pennsylvania, was an example of a successful, medium-sized player in the consulting business. From the company's visitor's balcony, one can observe a scene very much like the one located above the humming Chicago Board of Trade: a veritable hive the size of an airplane hangar, with dozens upon dozens of junior-grade meteorologist drones applying themselves in earnest to any number of Accuweather niche markets: the forensic division, the ready-for-air television graphics division, the worldwide weather forecast division, the Internet division, the educational division, the weather derivatives division, and the newspaper division, where weather information was fed directly into high-speed printing presses of 851 newspapers in the United States and around the world.

Beyond the realm of weather consulting lay the more rarefied realm of weather derivatives, financial compensation contracts that allow weather-sensitive companies to straddle the unknown, to hedge their bets against weather uncertainty. For an inherently weather-sensitive company like Six Flags Great Adventure, the outdoor water-slide conglomerate, unseasonably cold summers can really hurt the business. But as a public company, with profit forecasts to make, Six Flags can hedge against the threat of a cool summer using weather derivatives. Each summer, the company can buy a contract for a certain number of heating degree days (HDDs) that it is afraid of losing. Payments are triggered after the loss of a predetermined number of heating days. If the summer is warm, the extra gate receipts offset the cost of the weather derivative contract. Contracts for cooling degree days (CDDs) can also be written for companies, like ski resorts, for instance, or utilities companies, which depend on cold weather in winter for much of their revenue. Derivatives allowed companies to outwit fate, to calculate in advance their minimum income and factor out any weather-related sales volatility. "When weather-related loss is no longer a factor," according to Randall Dodd, of the Derivatives Study Center in Washington, D.C., "companies can concentrate on what they do best."[5]

It's all about "insurance" in its broadest sense, "hedging" against bad news, or, in the case of catastrophe bonds, against *really* bad news. "Cat bonds" are almost universally issued by insurance or reinsurance companies to protect themselves from being wiped out by an unthinkable natural disaster. In Florida, hurricanes are the primary threat of catastrophic proportions. A company like USAA, for instance, which does a great deal of business in Florida, might seek a "risk spreading mechanism" to decrease its exposure to tremendous losses by issuing a bond for, say $100 million. Call it Blammo Capital Ltd. USAA creates a secondary company whose sole function is to facilitate the sale. A hedge fund sinks $10 million, as a "premium," into Blammo Capital. The secondary company takes the $10 million and invests it in Treasury bonds. In return, USAA pays the hedge fund a much higher quarterly return upon its investment than it would receive for almost any other sort of bond, plus it receives the interest payments on the T-notes. USAA, on the other hand, considers the interest payments to the investors a small price to pay for having $100 million at the ready—just in case. In this simple example, the bond is issued for three years, with certain weather parameters—wind speed, for instance—in mind. In the unlikely event that those parameters are met during those three years, a payout is triggered and USAA receives its reserve of $100 million to offset casualty claims. The investors of Blammo Capital are left holding the bag.[6]

You don't need a weatherman, the song says, to know which way the wind blows. What you need, of course, is a banker. A banker, and a credit risk officer, and, perhaps most of all, someone from a large reinsurance company. If you can get them together, and if you can get them to talk about what they worry about, then *that* is which way the wind is blowing. Insurance and reinsurance companies were the biggest players in the field of the weather risk franchise, with that whopping $100 billion in annual premiums. The insurers, of course, were worried about big weather.

Insurance and reinsurance companies were the canaries in the mine and were likely to feel the effects of catastrophe soonest and with the earliest signs of its dire consequences. The annual changes in big reinsurance contracts suggested not only which *way* the wind blew, but also its frequency and its intensity and what damages it caused. It's thanks to the insurance industry that we know, for instance, that damages from weather catastrophes from the 1980s through the 1990s rose exponentially, from $4 billion to $40 billion annually, and that in the 1990s, Federal Emergency Management Agency (FEMA) payouts for disasters quadrupled.[7] According to financial reporter James Surowiecki, in 1992, "insurance premiums in South Florida rose 200 percent."[8] And that household and property insurance rates had increased by 2 to 4 percent per year because of weather risks.[9] Scientists and environmental groups might say all they wanted about global warming, but when the insurance companies raise their rates or limit the coverage they offer, they affect the pocketbook and the bottom line. And that, it seems, was what got people's attention.

Swiss Re, the second largest reinsurance company in the world, had not so quietly become a partisan in the global warming debate ever since it issued its first report on global warming in 1994. Every year for the last five years, the company has sponsored a Greenhouse Gas Conference, which gained notoriety in 2002 when it published a report announcing that losses as a result of natural disasters had doubled every decade and had reached $1 trillion in the past fifteen years. "The human race can lead itself into this climatic catastrophe," the conference report said, "or it can avert it." The environment was beginning to emerge, not just as *an* issue, but as *the* issue of the age, perhaps "the greatest security threat of the 21st century, eclipsing terrorism," as one news agency noted.[10] More recently, Swiss Re had held conferences on emissions trading and developed an extensive education campaign, underwriting a three-part documentary produced by the Discovery Channel, *The Great Warming,* and announced wherever it could the most alarming figures to emerge from the 2002 Zurich conference—that "the cost of climate change could reach $150 billion per year by 2010 with insurers facing $30 billion to $40 billion in annual claims."

There were any number of reasons for Swiss Re's vigorous vanguard effort to educate the world about the potentially catastrophic economic impacts of global warming, and most of them, of course, were self-serving. Still, it afforded one that rarest of visions: a multinational corporation looking after its bottom line *while also trying to save the world*! A corporation that had, on its own, without prodding from anybody, intuited the connection between its bottom line and the possible ruin of the only world we'll ever have. Call it a Renaissance moment, if you like, but elsewhere the global corporate oligarchs were catching on.

The regulation of greenhouse gasses, as stipulated by the 1997 Kyoto Protocol and its 106 signatories, the first international treaty to address climate change as a global issue, officially signaled the end of the era of unbridled consumption. It made no difference that a key participant, the United States, was missing. The global will had made itself felt. As Chris Walker of Swiss Re explained, "For Europe, global warming is a foregone conclusion. They're dealing with a carbon-constrained future." Emissions trading in Europe would begin in 2005, at which time companies that were in compliance with emissions standards would earn valuable credits, or trade credits with other companies that had yet to bring their greenhouse gas emissions under control, or be fined. For companies that hoped to compete in the global market, emissions standards, emissions trading, and the threat of climate change litigation were becoming "market drivers."

At home, fourteen states had asserted their right to climate protection in lieu of any effective federal policy, and several state attorneys general, including New York's Eliot Spitzer, had filed the first climate-related lawsuit in the United States. Large institutional investors, religious institutional investors, and others controlling $250 billion in voting stock filed proxy resolutions with major energy and oil companies demanding to know what the companies planned to do about global warming and the risk it posed to their investment. The strategy was working, and by the spring of 2004, only one giant oil company, ExxonMobil, based in Irving, Texas, had failed to disclose to its shareholders the financial risks that global warming posed for the company's bottom line.

The believers now included John Browne, the CEO of British Petroleum, who, in a 2004 speech before the Council on Foreign Relations, stated that "certainty and perfection [had] never figured strongly in the story of human progress. Business, in particular, is accustomed to making decisions in conditions of considerable uncertainty, applying its experience and skills to areas of activity where much is unknown." Business, he concluded, "will have a vital role in meeting the challenge of climate change."[11] A few lifetimes ago, when I was an undergraduate, I spent my summers as an Alaska tour guide, driving Greyhound-sized buses filled with gray-haired retirees all the way up the Haul Road from Fairbanks to Prudhoe Bay. It was, as we used to say, a big tour, with plenty to learn: the natural history of the Alaskan interior and the Arctic climate zones; petroleum geology; the discovery of oil at Prudhoe Bay; the Native Claims Settlement Act; the construction of the Trans-Alaska Pipeline. I would occasionally pull over to let everyone stretch their legs— old men and women, husbands and wives who came of age during World War II, gingerly fanning out onto the tundra to try and take it all in. I remember getting a special tour of the British Petroleum facilities at Prudhoe Bay, looking out toward the Arctic Ocean at a sun that would burn steadily above the horizon for the next few months, and looking at wellheads dotting the tundra for as far as I could see. There was no bigger place than this, and yet it was all, entirely, subsumed—drilled, plumbed, and pumped—by a force bigger even than it. Here, in a place as hostile as could be found anywhere on earth, the human will to have oil had asserted itself in a breathtaking technological and industrial sublime. I had entered the beast itself, it seemed, the maker and destroyer of the world. Workers flew in from Texas and Oklahoma for seven twelve-hour shifts, said "y'all" to each other and ate lobsters and steak every evening, then flew back home without ever once stepping outside or touching the ground. If anyone knew what it meant "to meet a challenge" it was British Petroleum, which had recently announced that emissions reduction activities had saved it $650 million.[12] The smart money, it seemed, had accepted global warming as a fact of science, and was ready to benefit by it.

Rather than acknowledge the risk as British Petroleum and ChevronTexaco had done, ExxonMobil had funded a campaign of pseudo-scientific misinformation, sponsoring studies whose conclusions gave the appearance of challenging the overwhelming consensus on the anthropogenic causes of global warming. ExxonMobil had contributed heavily to help elect George W. Bush, and the company could not have been unhappy with the appointment of Republican senator James Inhofe of Oklahoma, the second biggest recipient of big oil and energy campaign contributions, as chair of the Senate committee overseeing greenhouse gas legislation.[13] Presiding over a major senate hearing, "Climate History and Its Implications," Inhofe taunted climatologist Michael E. Mann, the lead author of the 2001 report by the Intergovernmental Panel on Climate Change, which the administration had taken great pains to discredit, and coddled two scientists: Willie Soon, an astrophysicist with *no* climatological credentials, and David Legates, director of the University of Delaware's Center for Climatic Research.[14] The proceedings were a piece of legislative theater, in which the players sat themselves down at nine in the morning of July 29, 2003, and read through their lines in front of microphones. Nobody wondered aloud about a basic disproportion of witnesses—two people representing a marginal scientific point of view, one witness representing the consensus view, a ratio that gave a procedural advantage to the marginal view—two, it almost went without saying, being exactly twice as many as one. No matter what one voice said, no matter how sensibly Dr. Mann presented his case, there would always be two voices to countervail the sense, to besmirch and befog it, especially if Inhofe, as chairman, in the interest of "fairness," gave each speaker an equal amount of time. Nobody asked Willie Soon or David Legates, moreover, about their intimate working relationship with the oil lobbying group the George C. Marshall Institute, whose own president was a registered lobbyist for ExxonMobil. Nobody observed the correlation between Dr. Soon's funding source for his report—the American Petroleum Institute—and its purported scientific conclusions about global warming, which served the interests of the American Petroleum Institute's benefactor, ExxonMobil.[15] Nobody mentioned Dr. Soon's work as "science director" to another Exxon-Mobil beneficiary, the conservative think tank Frontiers of Freedom, where Dr. Soon had recently busied himself with a paper purporting to offer scientific evidence against the EPA's decision to more stringently enforce mercury emissions.

"My name is Willie Soon," he began. "About a month or two ago, I became a very proud and grateful U.S. citizen. I just cannot believe where I am sitting today."

If Dr. Soon, in his introduction, apropos of nothing, nearly fell over himself to express his gratitude to all parties concerned, if he was momentarily overwhelmed by the endless opportunities that being a newly minted American citizen afforded the opportunistic man of science, and if he seemed, caught up as he was, to forget himself, to fairly bend low and kiss the ring of his benefactors, those in attendance, including Senator Inhofe, let that awkward moment pass. *Note to self,* one imagined Inhofe saying. *Hired help needs some polish.* Dr. Soon's position, based on a review of "approximately 1000 researchers and hundreds of peer-reviewed papers," cast doubt on the consensus view's most basic observation: that warming had increased substantially during the twentieth century. When he finished his opening remarks, Senator Inhofe seemed almost to pat Dr. Soon on the head.

"Dr. Soon," he said, "we appreciate that excellent opening statement. You did not even take all of your time. That is very unusual."

Dr. Mann established his credentials to speak on the subject of climate variability and its causes and provided a precis on the consensus view of global warming, then briefly pointed out the flaws in Dr. Soon's research—basic methodological errors that would have made a graduate student blush. David Legates followed, challenging, among other things, Dr. Mann's use of "proxy" climate records (tree rings, ice cores, etc.) along with instrument records, the combination of which was "the scientific equivalent to calling apples and oranges the same fruit."

What followed was a round of tag-team witness badgering and baiting orchestrated by Senator Inhofe, who misrepresented Dr. Mann's 1999 study as outdated research compared to Dr. Soon's study, conducted in 2003. "I think," Inhofe observed, "that the timing [of the two studies] would mean something because I know that [climate change] is not a static target. This is a moving target."

"Excuse me. That is not correct," said Dr. Mann.

Inhofe ignored this objection and engaged in a dialogue with David Legates that generally impugned the work of Dr. Mann. Having let Dr. Mann simmer away for a few moments, Inhofe then confronted Dr. Mann.

"Since you have characterized your colleagues . . . in several different ways as nonsense [sic], illegitimate, and inexperienced, let me ask you if you would use the same characterization of another person. . . . I would like to call your attention to the recent op/ed in the *Washington Post* by Dr. James Schlesinger, who was Energy Secretary under President Carter. In it, he writes, 'There is an idea among the public that the science is settled. That remains far from the truth. . . .' Do you question the scientific integrity of Dr. Schlesinger?"

Dr. Schlesinger's views on global warming were not published in a peer-reviewed journal, of course, as environmental writer Chris C. Mooney later observed, but in an op/ed column, a forum that had been used with great success by the Bush administration and by the energy industry to befog the scientific consensus on global warming. Schlesinger's career as the former director of the CIA, the Department of Defense, and the Department of Energy during the Carter administration was at a far enough remove in the public mind to make him an authority, whose name people recognized and whose opinions carried more weight than they should have. In this particular piece of political stagecraft, nobody thought to mention that Dr. Schlesinger currently sat on the board of directors for Peabody Energy, the largest coal mine in the world.[16] To Inhofe's suggestion that Mann had done Dr. Soon a professional discourtesy, Mann replied:

"I do not think I have questioned scientific integrity. I have questioned scientific expertise in the case of Drs. Willie Soon and David Legates with regard to issues of paleoclimate." As for Schlesinger, Dr. Mann dryly asserted, "I am not familiar with any peer-reviewed work that he has submitted to the scientific literature."[17]

Dr. Mann had given the world the famous "hockey stick" graphic that illustrated in dramatic fashion a slow, steady increase in greenhouse gasses over thousands of years, followed by a sudden, abrupt elevation in the last decade. It was this diagram that the White House had insisted upon omitting from a 2003 EPA report, inserting in its place a reference to a contrarian paper funded by the American Petroleum Institute and authored by Dr. Soon and Dr. Sallie Baliunas, whose conclusions would have made their way to the dustbin of history, had they not been cherry-picked by the administration and used to counter the global warming consensus. Dr. Mann was unsparing of his scientific colleagues' clumsy efforts. "It is the collective view of our entire research community," he said, of Soon and Baliunas' basic methodology, "that this is one of the most flawed papers that has appeared in the putative peer-reviewed research in recent years."[18] The morning wore on, the committee's time ran out, and the debate, such as it was, became part of the public record, became reportable, and was reported upon. In the newspapers, the minority view of Dr. Soon and Dr. Legates was given equal weight with the consensus view on global warming. But science, as Chris Mooney notes, is not democratic. The truth of science is that some ideas are, in fact, better than others. They were better because they withstood the hard and careful scrutiny of rival and often contentious colleagues who, nevertheless, share the same standards of scientific procedure, of objectivity and peer review. "The only way to have real success in science," as Nobel laureate Richard Feynman once observed, "is to describe the evidence very carefully without regard to the way you feel it should be. In science, you learn a sort of standard integrity and honesty." It was difficult in the extreme to square this with the work of Dr. Soon, which, if the opinions of the ranking climatologists in the world meant anything, were less the findings of an inspired maverick than the deeply flawed conclusions of a man who seemed unaware of or was unconcerned about the use to which his work was being put.

By late November 2004, after the red, evangelical heart of the American republic had spoken on the issue of its next president, and the American energy lobby was rejoicing at the promise of a second installment of George W. Bush, Inc., the East and West Coasts sat stunned, bluer than blue. For those who pondered the environmental depredations that lay ahead, the gates of the kingdom of a common inheritance seemed to have been left open and unguarded by the very citizens who stood to suffer most from mega-polluting coal-fired power plants, for instance, which were the nation's second largest source of nitrogen oxide pollution, after automobiles.[19] In 1999, the EPA, citing egregious violations of the 1970s Clean Air Act, brought suit against seven utility companies that had been polluting the skies of the Republican Midwest and south with an aggregate 2 million tons of sulfur dioxide per year and 660,000 tons per year of nitrogen oxides for nearly twenty years, until the Bush administration's "Clear Skies Initiative" made the punishing of these corporate crimes practically impossible, and, as if in baptism, washed all their sins away.

This was just the tip of the iceberg, of course, a phrase itself that was swiftly becoming obsolete. Imagine students, in a hundred years, asking themselves, "What's so special about the tip of an iceberg?"—through no fault of their own completely missing the point of the metaphor in the first place, that the bulk of something deadly lay hidden from view. In just the same way, phrases like "Clear Skies Initiative" and "Healthy Forests Initiative," "sound science" and "science-based policy," in a pattern of singularly Orwellianly turns of phrase, hid a massive campaign to pollute the skies, clear-cut the forests, and pass off as legitimate science the views of contrarians financially in the pockets of oil and energy companies.[20] A great folly was at hand, rendered, perhaps, no more emblematically as on an April evening in 2004 when Senator Inhofe was presented with an award from the Annapolis Center for Science-Based Public Policy, an institution that receives the bulk of its funding from the National Association of Manufacturers and ExxonMobil, in recognition of "rational, science-based thinking and policy-making." Senator Inhofe had recently helped defeat the McCain-Lieberman Climate Stewardship Act, which would have begun to put the United States on track to take its share of responsibility for polluting the world's atmosphere. It was Inhofe who said, famously, and in the face of overwhelming scientific evidence to the contrary, "Could it be that man-made global warming is the greatest hoax ever perpetrated on the American people?"[21]

Ours was a world in which the terms "rational," "science-based," and "thinking" had become rather like helium balloons that a child had let go. Those who came after, in years or decades hence, would see that "sound science" had come to mean "pro-corporate," "anti-environmental" science. "Rational" had become, more than anything else, a fog-bin of deceit, a reservior of fallacious argument, of sophistry, of passing counterfeit truths. As for thinking, perhaps it had become one of those good habits we'd grown out of.

I can only attest, as a poet grown accustomed to addressing posterity, that when it came to global warming, we were faced with two clear choices, one short-term, one long-term. The short-term position argued with great alarm that the immediate costs of emissions reductions, for instance, would be tremendous, and that the benefits would not be felt for decades to come, if ever. This was all completely true, yet the great folly of it—that it seemed like a cost/benefit analysis performed by accountants on the deck of the *Titanic*—seemed somehow beyond us. The long view asked of us something we could not readily imagine without sinking back in fear, as the balloons of truth drifted over the capital, growing smaller and smaller, rising through the atmosphere. Those who still held out hope understood that the choices were stark, but bracing: to be lauded for heeding the good advice of our best scientific minds or studied and remembered hereafter as counterexamples— as paragons of hubris, of a colossal failure of imagination. There would always be more to a study of our legacy than that, of course—volumes more—but here would be as good a place as any to start.

TEN

How Firm Is Your Foundation?

*The Lord is slow to anger, and great in power, and will not at all
acquit the wicked: the Lord hath his way in the whirlwind and in the
storm, and the clouds are the dust of his feet.*

—NAHUM 1:2–3

Mid-morning in Manhattan, Kansas: Matt and I had stopped for gas at a convenience store. I was a little groggy and in need of a powerful jolt of caffeine. Manhattan being a college town, I went inside and asked the man behind the counter where I might find a coffee shop.

"We've got coffee here," he said, pointing to an array of percolating machines.

"I had a cappuccino in mind," I said.

The man nodded again toward the coffee counter. "We've got espresso right here."

He was referring to a small machine of the sort that has an inviting picture of a steaming cup of cappuccino but which, experience has taught me, dispenses a dark dollop of espresso-flavored goo into a cup of lukewarm water. Matt was loading up on Diet Pepsi and chips, listening in. I asked the man if he wouldn't mind directing me to a coffee shop; he gave me a long, complicated set of directions and then I paid my bill and went outside to the van. After a few minutes Matt climbed into the driver's side, a big grin on his face.

"What?" I said.

"Want to hear what that guy said after you left?"

"Go ahead."

Matt pulled his sunglasses down the bridge of his nose and looked at me, then, in his best Bob Dole voice, laced with derision, said: "Guy wants to drive all the way across town for a three-dollar cup of coffee."

It was $3.25, actually, and worth every penny. Though, indeed, we did drive all the way across town, under tree-canopied streets, past yards with plastic outdoor play toys, swing sets, lawn sprinklers arcing water jets into flower beds, dogs in fenced-off yards giving chase to our van. "Basement," Matt said, passing one house. "Basement," as we passed another.

"Basement . . . basement . . . basement," he said, pointing left and right as we drove from block to block.

"How do you know those houses have basements?" I asked.

"Check the windows built into the foundations. How often do you see that in a house without a basement?"

"Oh." Now basements seemed to blossom everywhere. "Basement," I started saying. "Basement again." Then "Large concrete stairway going into the ground—basement!"

"In Kansas," Matt said, "you'll hear people say that they've never actually seen a tornado but that they've *spent some time down in the basement,* which is a phrase you'll never hear in Oklahoma." He took a swig of his Diet Coke. "The geology is basically the same here in Kansas as it is in Oklahoma," he said. "But in Oklahoma, of course, they don't have basements."

This was true. It was a peculiarity of Oklahoma, the most tornado-prone spot on earth, that it had so few basements in which to take shelter in the event that a tornado came barreling down on your house. You may recall that I had met this puzzling feature of Oklahoma during a tornado warning in El Reno, with TV meteorologists urging people to seek shelter. The motel clerk had sneered at me and said, "We don't have a basement here." The question of basements, or the lack thereof, in Oklahoma had preoccupied me ever since; during the doldrums those first two weeks of May, with nothing else to do, I spoke to a number of building engineers, building contractors, and home owners in pursuit of an explanation.

Richard Mize, who covers real estate for *The Daily Oklahoman,* acknowledged the strangeness of the situation and offered a pet theory. "The first thing that the early settlers of this territory did was to dig a hole in the ground and live in it," he told me one day over the phone. "So there may be a cultural hiccup of some sort against holes in the ground." Mize gave me the name of Brian Coon, of Coon Engineering, who, Mize said, was "highly regarded as a dirt-moving engineer," which sounded promising. Mr. Coon seemed to have heard this question many times before. He began by addressing the two main arguments commonly made against basements in Oklahoma: the high water table and the presence of too much sand and clay in the soil. He dismissed both arguments categorically. "Sometimes the water table might be too high for a basement," he said, "as it might be anywhere, but the water table in general does not prohibit the construction of basements." As for the vagaries of sand and clay—"expansive soils"—"With adequate drain lines, there was no real reason not to have a basement built today."

Alan Kirkpatrick, a structural engineer in Oklahoma City, added another dimension to the basement question. "We can't afford them," he said with a laugh. "It's an economic thing. It costs more to dig a hole than to pour concrete on the ground." Indeed, on the flight to Oklahoma City I'd sat next to a mechanical engineer who had worked in housing construction back in the early eighties, and he told me that he'd never once seen a basement dug. The foundations were mostly slab on grade, "because it was fast and cheap," he said.

What a socioeconomic wrinkle: an entire state, more vulnerable each spring to the ravages of the wolf-wind than anywhere else on earth, that had failed to grasp, or perhaps could not afford to implement, the salient lesson of "The Three Little Pigs." At construction sites in Moore, Oklahoma, a suburb of Oklahoma City that had been flattened by a tornado on May 3, 1999, and in other residential neighborhoods damaged by the outbreak of May 8, 2003, I walked among newly or nearly completed houses, each one a replacement for an earlier house that had been destroyed by a tornado. Most of the houses *seemed* to be made of brick. You could see the bricks stacked on pallets on the construction sites. But as I walked *through* the houses, from room to room, between the joists and the electrical ducting, like a ghost walking through walls, I saw that the load-bearing exterior walls of every single house were made of wood, usually particleboard slapped onto joists, with Tyvek waterproof material and insulation stapled onto it. On top of this came a brick façade, which looked sturdy but was entirely ornamental, like clapboard or shingle siding. This was true of every building site I visited. Here, too, were the cheap slab-on-grade foundations, the houses themselves basically stapled into the concrete, and not a basement to be seen anywhere. I mentioned this to Dave Gastgeb, a professional engineer with Acme Brick, in Oklahoma City, who specializes in residential investigation. "You've got your finger on something there," he said. "You wonder if we've learned anything."

In almost every respect, and in every way that such things can be measured, including housing values, Oklahoma was at or near the bottom rung of things.[1] People had grown used to making compromises, sacrificing safety to appearances, for instance, in the construction of their houses. The crippling thing about long-term economic hardship such as the kind experienced in Oklahoma is this: it grinds you down; it grinds institutions down, it works its way into your system. It works its way into *the* system. The most talented people fled these hard-luck places. Those who remained had to choose, constantly, between the lesser of two evils, had to compromise at every turn; this had the effect, over time, of lowering standards, of lowering everyone's expectations, of increasing cynicism, and of increasing the likelihood that even good people would resort to favoritism, corruption, and fraud. And, yes, it got to the point where, if someone wanted to build a basement, he had to contend with certain systemic problems—inferior building materials, design, engineering, and labor, and a general lack of expertise about such things. This was not, mind you, rocket science we were talking about, but a hole in the ground.

"I think we just got out of the practice of it," Brian Coon finally said.

AS A POET, without a profession or an inheritance to lean upon, I'd been poor for almost half of my adult life. From the age of twenty-one, when I left the protection of my parents, until the age of forty, when I got my first, serious career-type job, I patched things together, month to month, hand to mouth. Being poor turns you into a gambler. For long stretches, I gambled with health insurance and car insurance, for instance, betting that in the near term I would beat the actuarial tables. Poverty also made me selfish. I didn't want to think too much about the consequences that my gambling might have to others—the cost to family, friends, or the state in the event I suffered some catastrophic injury or illness. In my heart, that is, I recognized the choices people seemed to make in Oklahoma. I had gambled with my life as many Oklahomans seem to gamble with tornadoes. Basements are expensive, after all. That's where fate or faith comes in—the law of probabilities, or God's all-knowing dispensation toward his children.

Oklahomans were not out of practice with respect to the *idea* of a basement, or with respect to a good foundation *as a metaphor* upon which one might reflect, say, during Bible study at the Moore First Baptist Church, which was where I found myself one Sunday morning during the first week of May 2004. The First Baptist Church sits across the street from Highland Park, a residential subdivision that was devastated in the May 3, 1999, tornado and then struck again on May 8, 2003. The church had been used as a triage site during the first outbreak, so it seemed a likely place to engage people in the discussion of their tornado experiences. I arrived late that morning, parking near the church's towering, asymmetrical brick façade, walking across a parking lot as big and as full of automobiles, trucks, and minivans as any Wal-Mart on a busy weekend.

Inside, I was directed to a Bible study for middle-aged adults, and, after wandering the halls for a little while, found a classroom full of men and women, mostly married couples, sipping coffee and watching a videotape of the senior pastor, Kevin Clarkson, addressing them on the theme "Serving My Church." As the church program announced, this was part of "a continuing series of messages from Pastor Kevin," a seven-week program of instruction developed by the Southern Baptist Conference and entitled "Building Life on the Seven Pillars of God's Kingdom Family."

Everyone but I had a copy of the "Seven Pillars" workbook, but a man I'll call Glenn handed me his own, marked-up copy.

"Don't you want this?" I asked.

"No, no. Take it," he said.

The cover of the workbook, published by LifeWay Press in the very capital of the Southern Baptist Conference, Nashville, Tennessee, showed a construction worker, trowel in hand, putting a piece of cinder block in place on the foundation of a house. I thumbed through the pages. The book used the construction metaphor throughout, beginning in Week One, "Your

Foundation: The Unseen Essential," Day One, "How Firm Is Your Foundation?" I understood, of course, that I was being guided metaphorically in my spiritual development, but on Week One, Day One, of my month-long visit to a region where violent storms regularly swept houses from the face of the earth, in this setting, so famous for its literal interpretation of the Bible, it was difficult not to pursue the question of foundations along a more literal line.

The workbook contained scriptural quotations (Luke 14:28, for instance: "Which of you, wanting to build a tower, doesn't first sit down and calculate the cost, to see if he has enough to complete it?") followed by exegeses. One of the pull quotes in the page margins read, "Nothing is more critical to a building than its foundation." A passage from Matthew (7:24–27) warned, "Everyone who hears these words of Mine and doesn't act on them will be like a foolish man who built his house on the sand. The rain fell, the rivers, rose, the winds blew and pounded that house, and it collapsed. And its collapse was great!"

"Seven Pillars" had activities and quizzes, charts and fill-in-the-blank questions and other promptings—"Are you confident that you have genuinely experienced God's love and forgiveness in Christ?"—that Glenn had dutifully answered, in this case checking the box marked "Yes." In the section "Take Your Spiritual Temperature," Glenn had duly notched his spiritual temperature using a handy thermometer, supplied in the margin, scoring himself fairly high ("I know Christ, but I live in disobedience to Him in some areas of my life"). The Southern Baptist Conference dominated the cultural landscape of the South, with nearly 16 million members, almost all socially and politically conservative in the extreme. The Southern Baptist Conference was, in short, the base on which every Republican president who ever hoped for success depended, as the 2004 presidential election would so plainly demonstrate. The "Seven Pillars" workbook was distributed by the hundreds of thousands to Bible study groups all over the land, yet what to make of its trope of "foundations" except that, at least here in the wind-blown and bedraggled state of Oklahoma, the faithful seemed to overlook a fundamental disconnect between words and deeds? By and large, the actual, physical foundations upon which Oklahomans built their houses were shoddy. *They had no basements.* What Oklahomans had, instead, was a brand of faith that demanded, per Pillar Number Two of the "Seven Pillars" workbook, that they "submit to every

authority." Somehow, despite the opinion of every expert to whom I had spoken, word had gotten around that basements couldn't be built in Oklahoma,
and so there were none. It was just that simple.

Glenn was leading the Bible study this morning. He was an uneasy
teacher in training, a rookie, setting out under the watchful, encouraging eye
of Ron Dunkin, a man I'd met in this very room the previous January. In his
mid-fifties, balding, with a big nose and a bit of a paunch, Ron had a dry,
self-deprecating wit that I recognized in many Oklahomans, a head-scratching
befuddlement that was often a setup for a singularly penetrating insight,
often amusing, always understated. I called it the Okie put-on, and it made
each of its practitioners, from the very first model, Will Rogers, a cowboy
Socrates. Ron had a way of loosening everybody up. That January, illustrating the sin of gluttony, he'd mentioned how, the previous Thanksgiving,
he'd pushed himself slowly away from the table, got up out of his chair, and
said, "I'm going to go lie down in the yard and unbuckle my belt." That got
a big laugh. He made the morning sail along.

Glenn was struggling, but everyone smiled and nodded as he quoted
Psalms 122:1 "I rejoiced with those who said to me, 'Let us go to the house
of the Lord.'"

"I looked up the word 'house' in the dictionary," Glenn began, "and
found that the word referred to many different things." He scratched on the
blackboard the word "House," and "a dwelling place; a legislative assembly;
a family; a business firm; an audience; a theater; a dynasty; a school resi-
dence hall." "Any one of these," he said, pulling the string that tied it all
together, "can be applied to a church." The church and a house were syn-
onymous, Glenn concluded. "Personally, when I go to church," he said,
"this is my home."

But did your home have a basement? I wondered. The Bible study was
soon over, and Ron Dunkin walked with me down the church corridors
which soon filled up, like a high school's between classes, as people in their
Sunday best made their leisurely way to the "worship center," a vast semicir-
cular auditorium with long rows of cushioned pews narrowing to a proscenium at the front of which was a single lectern. Directly behind the stage was
an impressive music section—the Celebration Choir and Orchestra, piano,
drums, bass electric guitar, strings, and horns—that had already launched

into a soft-rock toe-tapper, "Come to the King," while adults helloed each other from across the pews, and teenagers milled about in groups that congealed and scattered and reformed. Behind the band, the Celebration Choir, perhaps fifty people in burgundy robes, swayed together on risers. Directly above them, stood the centerpiece of the auditorium, an immense crucifix perhaps thirty feet tall, on either side of which were mounted two giant stadium-sized TV monitors, the lyrics to "Come to the King" scrolling down them. Pastor Chris Malone, a slight man with a voice out of all proportion to his size, a choirmaster, sergeant-at-arms, and cheerleader, whose official title, "Minister of Music," sounded like a discarded James Brown epithet, brought "Come to the King" to a close and then greeted the congregation.

"Are we glad to be in the house of God this morning?" His voice boomed over the public address system. The congregation was still talking, milling about, sitting down in their seats. Chris Malone said again, this time a little louder, "I said, *Are we glad to be in the house of God this morning?*" To which the congregation responded, a little more compliantly than passionately, with shouts of "Amen!" and applause.

"Sing to the King," Chris Malone said. "Let's bring blessing, honor, glory and power to the only one who is worthy." Then began another bouncy hymn, "Ancient of Days."

To the right, Dr. Kevin Clarkson sat on stage in a comfy wing chair of a style I'd seen in living rooms all across Oklahoma. Here it represented the same "living room" look you'd find on Pat Robertson's *The 700 Club*—overstuffed chairs, end tables, flowers, doilies. Pastor Kevin was handsome and athletic looking, like a football coach, which was a valuable attribute in Oklahoma, where the twin passions were pervasive and conflated; I saw a T-shirt once that tried to realign the priorities: "Jesus B 4 Football," it read. Pastor Kevin wore a gray blazer and pullover, like the sort favored by the hunky football commentator Howie Long. In his chair, in a faux living room, symbol and site of American interiority writ large, with the Celebration Choir and Orchestra breaking into another upbeat number, Pastor Kevin exuded godly energy and enthusiasm, though it seemed against the manufacturer's specifications to do so in a wing chair. Soon, the Minister of Music enjoined everyone to stand and sing, which, while giving Pastor Kevin a little more room to maneuver, opened up a whole new can of worms. He couldn't exactly *get down,* of course—this wasn't a sweaty Pentecostal church, not a bunch of Holy Rollers; nobody was passing live rattlesnakes from arm to arm in *this* house of the Lord—but he did make a few moves to the beat, to show his support for the program. Then he smiled abstractedly, at his fingernails.

After a few initial announcements and prayers came the "ordinance of baptism," which was performed high above the choir, just beneath the gigantic crucifix itself, upon a boy and a girl. One at a time, in their baptismal gowns, they waded into an elevated tank of water, which you could hear sloshing. The pastor introduced each to the church and then got to the business at hand, the business that Baptists are, more or less, known for: the backward, no-look, full-immersion dunking.

"Married with Christ in baptism"—*kaplush!*—"rising to walk in a new life." The newly baptized were then led away, as the congregation, perhaps 400 people in all, burst into long, rolling applause.

What were they being baptized into? According to Larry Eskridge, associate director of the Institute for the Study of American Evangelicalism, the Southern Baptist Conference had a long tradition of inculcating obedience, not only to God but to all authority figures. "They take the Bible very seriously," Eskridge said, citing Romans 12 and 13, in which Paul enjoins his readers to respect authority. "They're liable to take that very literally." Indeed, in the "Seven Pillars" study book, after the prompt to read Romans 13:1–7 and "write any significance [this has] regarding the area of authority," Glenn had noted: "Submit to those with authority over you since God has authority over all and he has placed them there for a purpose."

This *was* the heart of the Bible belt, after all. But America at large seemed to be rising, as if from slumber, into a religiousness of a particularly strident and evangelical slant. Since 1960, the number of Pentecotalists had increased fourfold, while the number of Episcopalians had dropped almost by half.[2] Americans in general were three times more likely to believe in the miraculous (the Virgin Birth of Christ, for instance: 83 percent) than in the theory of Evolution (28 percent). A staggering 47 percent of *non-Christians* in the United States believed in the Virgin Birth.[3] Sixty percent of Americans said they have "never doubted the existence of God."[4] "Submit to Every Authority," the "Seven Pillars" enjoined its readers,[5] underscoring the point with a helpful quiz on 1 Peter 2:13. Glenn himself hadn't gotten this far in the catechism, nor had I, but, reader, I offer this as a cautionary hint of the theocratic lesson plan for the years ahead. "Everyone must _____ to the governing authorities, for there is _____ authority except from _____, and those that exist are instituted by _____."

MAY 3. That was all you needed for people around here to know what you were talking about. The forecast that morning was nothing to raise anyone's eyebrows. Dave Imy, the branch operations chief at the Storm Prediction Center, finished his day shift and went with his sixteen-year-old daughter to buy her first car. "We had a very unstable air mass . . . we had sufficient shear and an upper-level trough approaching from the west," he recalled. These are usually indicators of an approaching storm. But a big shield of cirrus covered a good portion of the state, and that, to nearly everyone whose job it was to make decisions about the weather for the public good, meant that the chance of severe storms was low. At seven A.M., the outlook was for a "slight risk" of severe thunderstorms and tornadic activity. By 11:30, the field of play was narrowed to central Oklahoma, and the outlook modified, accordingly, to moderate risk. Gayland Kitch, the director of emergency management in Moore, remembered that the change from slight to moderate risk that morning had impressed almost nobody. The area had been under a "slight risk" outlook for almost three weeks. Kitch had been aware that there was a chance for a storm, but it was "a dime-a-dozen sort of awareness," Kitch said. "When I stepped outside, it was muggy. The air was moist. The outlook had called for potential severe weather and it was no big deal."

Even so, an armada of research vehicles from the National Severe Storms Laboratory, just down the road, had been dispatched to an area southwest of Norman. They were "mobile mesonets," "vehicle-borne weather sensors," awkward-looking sedans tricked out with so much sensitive weather instrumentation that each looked like it was set to troll for salmon. These "probes" measure position down to 1/1000 of a degree, as well as temperature, humidity, barometric pressure, and wind speed—all the while on the move. Two of the vehicles were responsible for deploying "turtles," portable, low-profile "instrumentation packages" designed to withstand a tornado. A turtlelike device had been a plot element in *Twister,* but to date, no turtle had been successfully deployed.[6] The movements of the probe fleet were directed by Erik Rasmussen of the Severe Storms Laboratory. The Verification of the Origins of Rotation in Tornadoes Experiment, or Project VORTEX, was a long-range study begun in 1994 that actually sent vehicles into storms to determine why some developed tornadoes and why others, nearly identical, did not. It was a dream project to more than a few with a passion for storms, a happy conflation of weather-geek gadgetry—fast-response thermistors, X-band scanning Dopplers—and flat-out, ballsy, Ben-Franklin-on-a-horse tornado chasing.

Greg Stumpf, whom I interviewed in his office at the National Severe Storms Laboratory (NSSL), had been encouraged by the change to "moderate risk." Greg, a specialist in cartography, computer design, and storm damage assessment, spoke to me in a cramped little cubicle about storm chasing, an off-duty obsession he shared with many colleagues. "Typically, I would have already gone out several times before that, but life and work had distracted me," he said. Greg showed me a new map he'd made on his laptop that integrated and superimposed satellite imagery, meteorological data, and a vast array of damage assessment data to depict the paths of all the May 3 tornadoes, right down to contoured F-scales. As he spoke, he zoomed in and out on the map, retracing his route that day.

He and a friend named Jim LaDue had taken the day off for what looked like an easy day's storm chasing within the Oklahoma City area. They brought a portable ham radio and made their way over the countryside, monitoring the other probe vehicles in the VORTEX fleet. (They dubbed themselves the Rogue Probe.) It was very cloudy, windy and warm, with an on-and-off drizzle that ended later in the morning.

Spotting the layer of cirrus above, Greg and Jim became pessimistic about seeing a tornado, so they headed southwest toward Altus, Oklahoma, where a little hole in the cirrus had opened up. "And I'm talking about a little hole," Greg said, "like about the scale and size of a county or less. And a storm popped up under this hole, just southwest of Lawton, and so we decided, Let's target this storm."

At three P.M., they received a call on the ham radio. The Storm Prediction Center had just revised its afternoon outlook to a "high risk" of severe weather and tornadoes. The announcement made Greg and Jim sit up in their seats. They were witnessing the birth of what would be called Storm A, sitting directly under it, in fact. Storm A would produce the single most violent and damaging tornado in recorded history, and it would be broadcast nationally, live, on CNN. But at that moment, in a little town called Geronimo, beneath the towering cumulus, the first thunder of Storm A seemed hardly worth noting. "We didn't know any of the details," Greg recalled, "but we thought, Well, they must be seeing something we're not."

Indeed they were. Dan McCarthy, meteorologist in charge at the SPC, had been analyzing upper-air wind profiles from instruments based in White Sands, New Mexico, and he hadn't liked what he saw. Across the street, at the National Weather Service forecast office, meteorologist in charge Dennis McCarthy (no relation) had similar misgivings. At noon, he'd ordered an additional weather balloon sounding, to take measurements of the winds aloft. Both men concurred that the severe wind shear recorded by these instruments indicated a "high risk" of tornadoes and severe thunderstorms.

Outlook; watch; warning. The Storm Prediction Center had been moving in the right direction all day: the outlooks, first issued early in the morning, had changed as the day wore on from slight to moderate to high risk of severe weather, until, at 4:45 P.M., the center raised the ante yet again, issuing a tornado watch for the entire central Oklahoma region. Normally, a tornado watch means "Keep your eye on the sky"; many people now turn on a radio or a television for weather updates. Normally, too, an hour or two might pass between the issuance of a watch and the time the first tornado hits the ground. On May 3, *two minutes* passed between the watch, which was an expression of probability, and the tornado warning, which was an exclamation point of a fact. Dozens of positive sightings began flooding the National Weather Service office.

Over the two-way radios, Greg Stumpf heard the probe crews calling in confirmed tornado sightings. You could hear in the voices of these scientists the sudden, unmistakable mixture of fear and excitement. "Twice that day," remembered Matt Biddle, who was driving Probe 2, "we had tornadoes on *both* sides of our chase car. It was surreal." Greg relayed these sightings on his ham radio to Scott Curl and Cheryl Sharp, the two warning forecasters on the day shift at the NWS forecast office in Norman. By this time, Dennis McCarthy, the meteorologist in charge, had asked Doug Speheger and Kevin Brown, the evening shift forecasters, to report to work as backup. McCarthy had also called in Chris Sohl, another NWS forecaster, and David Andra, the science operations officer. It just so happened that Liz Quoetone was also present. Quoetone's regular job was to train forecasters in the use of new technology, which required that she visit NWS forecast offices regularly to observe how forecasters work in the pressure cooker of severe weather outbreaks. She would have no better opportunity than today to make her observations. Storms were building strength rapidly as they moved over south-central Oklahoma. Dave Andra began pacing the office. Near the town of Chickasha, a large tornado plowed through a local airstrip, demolishing planes, lifting up cattle. It would carry the 350-pound wing of a Cessna nearly seventy miles north.

By 6:30 P.M., the NWS Norman forecast office was processing a flood of confirmed tornado sightings, including two large tornadoes heading straight for Oklahoma City. Both of the latter were being broadcast live on local television. No warning bulletin could possibly convey the magnitude of the danger facing the city's nearly 500,000 citizens. So at 7:00 P.M., Andra sat down at a computer station and opened up a software program called WarnGen, which contained the standard severe-weather boilerplate. This he tossed aside. Quickly, he began composing a historic warning; nothing like it had ever before been issued by an NWS office.

Tornado Emergency in south Oklahoma City metro area. At 6:57 pm a large tornado was moving along interstate 44 west of Newcastle. On its present path this large, damaging tornado will enter southwest sections of the Oklahoma City area between 7:15 and 7:30. Persons in Moore and south Oklahoma City should take immediate tornado precautions! This is an extremely dangerous and life-threatening situation. If you are in the path of this large and destructive tornado, take cover immediately. Doppler radar indicated this storm may contain destructive hail to the size of base-balls or larger.

At six o'clock that evening, twenty miles due south of Oklahoma City, the Moore city council had convened to debate a $20 million risk management bond for city improvements—a new police and emergency dispatch office, a couple of new fire trucks, road construction. At 7:15 P.M., the mayor of Moore, Glenn Lewis, an affable businessman who owned a retail jewelry store in the local shopping mall, asked for a thirty-minute recess, during which time he got a call from Gaylan Kitch, who briefed him about the tornado emergency. When the council reconvened, the bond was passed in what was by all accounts the fastest city council meeting on record.

Kitch was not easily rattled. He'd spent nearly a decade as a police and fire dispatcher, and had seen nearly every sort of situation, every variety of domestic mayhem, criminal violence, and natural disaster that one could see in the middle of Oklahoma. He was a bantam, at five feet four, not the sort to bust up a bar fight or toss a drunk into a cell, but rather one who calmly and efficiently dispatched to the scene those who did such things. Experience and temperament had placed an invisible distance between Gayland Kitch and the rest of the world. He wore the mask common to those who have seen combat in one form or another—on a battlefield, in a trauma room, on the ladder of a fire truck—the mask of people who chose, as he had, to control chaos, to manage emergency.

When asked about the May 3 calamity, Kitch spoke as if he were talking about last week's laundry. He seemed almost impatient with the question: I knew I wasn't the first person to ask it. He even looked as if he might have taken umbrage that I considered May 3 remarkable. For an event to be "remarkable," of course, meant that it at least momentarily fell, however slightly or subtly, outside one's expectations. And as director of emergency management, Gayland Kitch was a master of expectation, of readiness, of preparedness. Being ready for anything, of course, was the key to an earthly form of omniscience—and the key to success in managing emergency. To that end, Kitch had trained his staff, trained and retrained his small regiment of REACT (Radio Emergency Associated Communications Teams)

volunteers, taught them calm, objective radio communication. It was Gayland Kitch who purchased new software, new computers, and other equipment for the dispatch office, who rehearsed systems of emergency response,
attended emergency management conferences all over the country, installed,
maintained, and tested warning sirens. When the time came, as it did on the
evening of May 3, it would be Gayland Kitch who flicked a switch that fired
the sirens that automatically triggered an emergency message that was
broadcast at twice the normal volume over every television set in Cleveland
County, a message of warning delivered as if by some omnipresent, disembodied technological demigod. And the message would arrive in the form of
the recorded voice of Gayland Kitch.

Bob Kaster, a retired Department of Transportation investigator, had
been paged, like all the other REACT spotters, late in the afternoon by Kitch's
lieutenant at Moore emergency management, then dispatched to his assigned
spot, the back parking lot of a Wal-Mart just off I-44, where he had a nearly
unobstructed view to the south, the west, and the northeast. He waited
patiently in his Chevy Tahoe, looking at the horizon to the southwest, which
was unnaturally dark, and listening to his scanner.

At seven, Kaster heard the sound of tornado sirens rising and falling in
the distance. Then he heard another REACT unit calling in a large tornado
on the ground about two miles west. Kaster looked west but saw only the
large black stormcloud he'd noticed before. Then he looked again.

Assistant Fire Chief Jerry Doshier was up on the roof of city hall with
binoculars, looking a mile southwest at the same black cloud. A fire truck
and a medical rescue unit had been toned out a few minutes earlier, before
the local news began sending live images of a massive tornado closing hard
on Moore. Doshier wanted to spot the twister in order to direct his units out
of its path. On the horizon, trailer clouds, long, low, skinny wisps, moved at
speed on the inflow boundary, condensing like dry ice, feeding the storm—
an immense black cloud like nothing he'd ever seen before, a giant wall taking up most of the sky, backlit by a golden horizon. Chunks of hail began
bouncing off the rooftop like crazy Super Balls, so he took shelter under a
big air-conditioning unit and wondered when the tornado would come into
view. Just then, a pickup truck sailed through the air and fell to the ground.
The great wedge-shaped tornado moved quickly. The roof of a house shat-

A mother and child huddle together under an overpass near Newcastle, Oklahoma, on May 3, 1999, as the tornado that leveled much of Moore, Oklahoma, causing F5 damage, approaches. Overpasses are among the worst places to seek shelter. Note satellite vortex to the left of the main funnel. © Used with permission: J. Pat Carter/Associated Press

A tornado of the highest magnitude had begun to form: a wedge-shaped, long-tracking F5, estimated to be a staggering half-mile in diameter, with winds in excess of 300 miles per hour. The Moore/Oklahoma City tornado would be the single-most destructive tornado in U.S. history. © Christopher Duvall, Renee McPherson, Andrew Reader, and Michael Wolfinbarger

tered. More roofs, more debris. Lightning forked inside the funnel and transformers showered multicolored sparks as they exploded. Something was rubbing against Doshier's legs. He looked down for a moment. His pants were vibrating from the pressure changes, as if he were standing next to a pair of gigantic subwoofers. The tornado was a mile away. It sounded like a diesel-electric motor, and it was plowing right through neighborhoods which he knew, in an abstract sort of way, were being leveled. At that moment, the roof of the 2,000-seat auditorium at Westmoore High School was peeling off like the top of a sardine can, sending gravel through the air like machine-gun bullets as dozens of students who had stayed after school for a theater rehearsal cowered in the stairwells. Automobiles were thrown around and stacked up like driftwood. Doshier stood speechless, tracking the tornado through his binoculars, until his neighborhood McDonald's sign came into view, foregrounded against the black of the funnel. Just then he realized he was watching his own house being destroyed.

Moving at a steady 40 m.p.h., the tornado crossed Interstate 35, which was clogged with stopped traffic. People abandoned their cars and ran. If you open a window on a summer night, and the breeze comes rushing through, you are feeling what's known as the Venturi effect: the narrow passageway through the window speeds the airflow. Those who took refuge under freeway overpasses had inadvertently climbed inside the barrel of a cannon that shot shrapnel. One woman was swept away.

Karen Doshier ran into the bedroom closet and piled clothing around her for padding. Joe O'Bryant, superintendent of the Lakeside Golf Course, rushed into the clubhouse, stopped for a moment to watch the tornado—he could see whole trees flying around outside—then ran through the restaurant and dove into the men's bathroom. Mike Pederson was standing in the middle of the dining room of a Cracker Barrel restaurant in Midwest City. From the front window he saw the debris cloud approaching; he fled to the kitchen, where thirty people were huddled under tables. He felt his ears pop. Seconds later, a Penske rental truck crashed through the roof of the dining room, right where Pederson had been standing.

Dana Grimm had already gotten her dogs and her son Adam into a bedroom closet and was watching Gary England, on KWTV, track the tornado's progress through Oklahoma City. "The tornado is at 134th and Penn," England said: this was within a mile of Dana's house. Just then the power went out. Dana raced to the bedroom closet and lay on top of her son. Together in the darkness they heard the sound of hail snapping the wood of the deck outside. One by one, the windows blew out and the rafters began snapping like matchsticks. Very slowly, the walls of the house began to lift up, cold air rushing underneath. Then came a deafening roar and she and her son were tossed around in the darkness like dolls, her mouth filling up with dirt. A moment later, she found herself buried in rubble, looking up through the blades of the family lawnmower. Joe O'Bryant, in the clubhouse bathroom, was pinned down by cinder blocks, hugging a bar stool. Karen Doshier peeped out of her hole and found herself staring into the backside of the tornado as it moved northward.

In Del City, an elderly couple sat down on the couch in their living room and looked out through their picture window at the tornado approaching. When it had passed, the wall on either side of them was intact. The rug under them was missing. The rest of the house was gone, but they remained untouched.

Jerry Doshier jumped into his car and sped home, but so complete was the devastation in his neighborhood that no physical landmark remained. "You go to look for someone in a house, but the house is gone," his friend and colleague Jack Briggs was quoted as saying a few days later in *The New York Times*. "You go to look for the street, but the whole street is gone. Sometimes you go to look and the whole neighborhood is gone." Doshier spent a few minutes looking in vain for the lot where his house once stood. Then, out of the rubble, out of a hole no bigger than a kitchen cabinet, Karen appeared.

Gayland Kitch tossed the keys to an S-10 pickup to Mayor Lewis, who had been answering phones nonstop with other council members at the dispatch office. Fire Chief Charles Stevens had set up a field command center at the First Baptist Church, and he needed the generator.

Lewis loaded the generator along with a bunch of bright orange traffic cones onto the truck and drove up to the north side of town using the traffic cones to bribe his way past the highway patrolmen, who needed them to help secure the area. He crept along a small service road that ran parallel to I-35. The big green signs that hang over the Interstate were twisted and knocked around like so many pretzels. There were cars upside down along the road, houses upside down, piles of debris and dirt. The city truck had EMERGENCY MANAGEMENT printed boldly on the sides and yellow revolving caution lights on the roof, and as Lewis maneuvered carefully through the rubble, people started walking out of the darkness toward the light of his truck and began climbing in—hurt people, bleeding people, crying and screaming people.

By the time he passed his third roadblock, he'd given away all of his traffic cones, and a dozen or more of the wounded were crowded around the emergency generator. Some had broken arms, others cuts. A woman named Julie Rakestraw had part of a two-by-four embedded in the back of her neck. And still the injured came, like an image out of *Night of the Living Dead.* But Chief Stevens was calling frantically over the radio for the generator. There was no room left in the truck. Lewis was forced to leave many of the injured behind.

Boards and shredded lumber, bare nails and metal wire, drifts of Sheetrock, furniture, shards of glass, pink insulation, all were piled high against the back of the First Baptist Church, which was just across the street from Highland Park. The tornado had flattened that subdivision but had just missed the church, which nevertheless sustained considerable damage to its roof. Because it was centrally located and at the top of a hill, the church was the ideal spot for a medical triage site. Mayor Lewis stepped out of the S-10 and put a nail through his foot. He hobbled with the generator to the front of the building, where a field command center had been set up in cooperation with the Norman Regional Hospital. The injured from across the street in Highland Park came hobbling, too, some wearing nothing but pajamas, and when the generator motor started up, searchlights suddenly illuminated the fifty-foot cross on the church's façade. Assistant Pastor Rick Whitaker walked among the hundreds of people flooding across the road from the subdivision, and just kept pointing to the church and saying, "Go to the cross, go to the cross." And for a good long while everyone loaded people into ambulances or onto medevac helicopters, working in the dark except for the illuminated cross. An Air Force colonel stopped Lewis. "Mayor," he said, "I've got seven hundred body bags for you. I'll have probably another thousand in the morning."

THE FORMATION OF every storm represents a fleeting beachhead of sorts, a margin of organization against a generalized chaos of clouds. Some storms are more organized than others, and for reasons we don't understand, sometimes the organization is so complete that the storm leaps into the realm of miraculous paradox. Such was the case with the tornado outbreak of May 3. Out of its faultless order came a magnitude of destruction, a level of confusion and loss, and a degree of frustration and anxiety that was so complete and unqualified as to defy description, even by those who saw it firsthand the next day under a bright spring sky.

The force of the tornadoes, which could only be glimpsed the night before, was staggering. "When we walked out in the streets on Tuesday, it was so overwhelming," said Perry Paterson, a resident of Mulhall, Oklahoma, population 200. Two tornadoes, striking one right after the other, had destroyed 95 percent of the town and pulled down its seventy-five-foot water tower, creating a 400,000-gallon tidal wave that crashed into the front room of Mrs. Katheryn Harris, age seventy-six, who rode out the tsunami in her bed. The Mulhall Christian Church, one of the few buildings left standing, was lifted up and moved fifteen feet off its foundation. Its steeple had vanished. "The debris was as tall as the buildings," Paterson said. "It was too big a job." On Sunday there was no place for any of the three church congregations to meet, so they met in separate facilities seven miles outside of town. "If anybody asks you the proper position to assume for prayer," said Pastor Gilbert Forrest, "it's flat on your face in the hall with a comforter pulled over your head."

The path of destruction could easily be seen from the air, a wide, serpentine swath that stretched across three states. Around the Oklahoma City region, there were half a dozen other swaths just like it. Within each, large trees had been ripped out of the ground or completely denuded, the bark sand-blasted from trunks that bristled with shards of shining metal. Seven cars were pulled out of a Hampton's Inn swimming pool in Midwest City. A woman's cork bedroom slipper was embedded in the side wall of a steel-belted tire. Thousands of two-by-fours, splintered into deadly two- and three-foot shafts driven into the ground, made an elementary school play field look like a bed of nails. Livestock were scattered everywhere: a steer impaled in a tree, others lying in fields or alongside roads, their legs stiffly pointing to the sky, some still alive—a cow limping along with a broken leg, another lowing from the bottom of a well. The grim business of search and rescue was further complicated. Search-and-rescue dogs became confused—human scent was everywhere, on blood-smeared boards, in diapers, in clothing that people had worn. Teams from the Army National Guard waded through thickets, dragging muddy stock ponds and diving into them, looking for human remains. "Take your time, guys," one captain told his crew of Guardsmen, slowly picking through dense underbrush outside Bridge Creek. "Look under things and don't just look down. Look up in the trees."

How to describe the scene through which they moved? Imagine a suburban house with its decades' worth of accumulated heirloom furniture; its heavy kitchen appliances, refrigerators, dishwashers; its bedrooms, its collectible gewgaws and gimcrack; its guns and ammo; its garage crowded with spare tires and Black & Decker power tools and fake Christmas trees, and riding lawn mowers; its gasoline cans and mason jars filled with paintbrushes soaking in turpentine; imagine the stacks of old magazines bundled and tied with twine; barbecue grills, and dollhouses, and box after box of old tax records; imagine the filing cabinets containing all the important documentary evidence of lives lived in late-twentieth-century America—mortgages, car loans, warranties, titles and deeds, stock certificates, birth certificates, passports, diplomas, discharge papers, college transcripts, genealogical records, all painstakingly gathered, neatly alphabetized; imagine the silver-dollar collections, the stamp collections, the sex toy collections. Imagine the photograph albums, the jewelry, the violins and Gibson guitars; imagine wallets and purses left on nightstands. Now imagine putting all of this into a giant blender the size of an office building, dumping in millions of gallons of sod, dirt and water, and pressing "Purée."

The result was a broad, muddy gumbo of personal property entangled, intermingled, impaled, within a melange of shattered building materials, leaking gas mains, sparking live wires. Splinters and cubes and right triangles of collapsed roofs, the lattice of framework, the piles of brick, the kitchen sinks, the busted pipes, the smell of wet lumber, the funk of soggy gypsum board. People returned not to their homes but to a communal wasteland that seemed to be governed by a cosmic irony. Stories accumulated of houses completely erased, right down to the foundation, while the homes next door remained untouched. Sometimes the only recognizable feature on a demolished lot might be, depending upon the story, a bedside table, a kitchen counter, or a file cabinet. On top of these would be some incredibly delicate object—a glass figurine, or a dish rack loaded with dinner plates, or a file folder containing important documents—completely undisturbed. Amid the oddments—here a clothes hamper with shirts and pants neatly folded, over there a wedding dress blown flat against a cyclone fence, all of it written against a backdrop of destruction—the biggest irony might have been found in any wet, mud-spattered copy of *The Daily Oklahoman,* whose forecast for May 3 read, "Partly cloudy today and breezy."

In the Moore subdivision of Highland Park, the big tornado had opened up new, disorienting vistas that reminded many of the Oklahoma City bombing, or photographs of Hiroshima or of the no-man's-land of the First World War. The comparisons strove to convey the blast effect of the tornado, which was astonishing. But unlike those earlier disasters, which killed so many, the effects of the tornado outbreak had far less to do with the numbers killed than with the rending and scattering of community. It was a tribulation of our sense of organization, a reminder of all the things that we take for granted and that tend to hold us together: the electricity grid, the telephone grid, the natural gas grid, the water supply, the lattice of records and deeds and certificates which, shredded and scattered as they were, over dozens of counties, remind us of how slight are the margins that separate us from chaos. The Old Testament God had many tools in his arsenal, and He used each as suited his aims. When a case was hopeless, out came the apocalyptic fire. But it would be a poor pedagogy, to say the least, for God to instruct his more promising creatures by destroying them. To these, He would send some harrowing trial or other—the confusion of tongues to the Babylonians, say; to the Israelites, an extended jaunt in the desert. To the Oklahomans, He sent the Whirlwind. And though his methods may have varied, the lesson in each case was the same: out of a vast confusion came a nearer acquaintance with humility.

In a phenomenon also observed in the immediate aftermath of the collapse of the World Trade Center, the chaos and confusion of the central Oklahoma tornado outbreak brought into the streets people who tested the boundaries between the curiosity seeker, the souvenir hunter, and the thief. And while the impulse of the New Testament was fully engaged in places like the Moore First Baptist Church, where thousands of people wearing little more than wet pajamas were housed, clothed, and fed, most of the early decisions made by public officials in the aftermath of the outbreak came straight from the pages of Thomas Hobbes. At nine P.M. on Monday, just over an hour after the tornado went through, Gayland Kitch dispatched Bob Kaster to guard the entrance of the Moore city hall. It was a rarely imposed precaution, made in the interest of maintaining the integrity of the public records. It was Hobbesian necessity that immediately brought out the state patrol and National Guard roadblocks, that sealed off the damaged neighborhoods even from the storm victims themselves. Officials justified these decisions, made over the strenuous objections of residents, by stressing the issue of safety. There were thousands of natural gas leaks and many thousands of live electrical wires. A multitude of other hazards waited in the darkness—empty swimming pools, razor-sharp metal, nails, glass. But other reasons loomed. Personal property lay scattered for miles, some of it of great value, free for the picking. The interruption in the order of things presented the opportunity, in the minds of some, to address socioeconomic imbalances by a redistribution of wealth. Scattered reports arrived of looting all around the city. With the good fences of the Oklahoma City suburbs blown down, neighbor suspected neighbor. Curfews were imposed, after which even tornado victims picking through wreckage on their own lots were subject to arrest. Gawkers from Oklahoma City clogged the highways, hampering search-and-rescue operations, which, although more than 100,000 dwellings remained without electricity, and many thousands without water, gas, or phone service, was everyone's top priority. Ten people were found, alive and well, trapped by a neighbor's house that had fallen on top of their storm shelter. Many others had been similarly trapped, and the only certain way to find them had been to consult the property assessment records in Moore city hall, which indicated which houses had storm shelters. A list had been compiled and one by one, the lots were searched until the last survivors came, blinking into the sunlight.

Mayor Glenn Lewis, who had worked all night long and still had a nail hole in his foot, was told to wait for the governor to arrive and declare his city a disaster area. At five A.M. on May 4, Governor Frank Keating strode into the Moore city hall, threw down a sheaf of papers, and said, "This is your emergency declaration. I've signed it. Now, I've got to go see Katie Couric." Governor Keating then walked out the door. On Thursday, the last of the dead, a thirty-five-year-old woman, Tram Bui, was found in the mud next to Interstate 35.

There would be time for the armies of young church volunteers—college kids, mostly, up to 330 per week at the First Baptist Church of Moore, arriving from Minneapolis and Mount Kisco and Montpelier to do good—to clean debris fields, to remove bricks, to replace roofs, to pressure-spray trash off the sides of buildings. There would be time for the semitrailer loads of corporate donations, time for chefs to fly in from Dallas to cook round the clock, time for haircuts, time for twenty-four-hour-a-day massages. There would be time for the bureaucracy of disaster relief to slowly gain momentum—time for FEMA divisional director Buddy Young, the former Arkansas administrator who helped Governor Bill Clinton out of a jam, to visit and declare the situation under control. Time for the great noise and caterwaul to kick in, the hauling away of mountains of debris, time for the slow creep of insurance adjusters wading through the wreckage, handing out checks; time to rebuild, to acquire more stuff, and think hard about where one wanted to put it all.

"You think about what you have and what you lost," Jerry Doshier told me from his new house in Paul's Valley, Oklahoma, a beautiful forty-acre expanse of open prairie about fifty miles south of Moore. "Everything I've got now is new. I don't have anything in my drawers, but I've got new drawers." New drawers, new beds, new couch, new chairs, new kitchen, new bath. A new house made of concrete and built right into the side of a hill—a berm house, an underground house, a house built into the ground. Above it, tall grass and the oncoming wind rushing over the prairie. "I don't know if I would have bought an underground house for myself," he said, pausing for a moment. "But I've always admired it as an idea." After the tornado, the idea became the sort of accommodating gesture one makes in a marriage. The Doshiers' dog—a Siberian Husky named Niki—had survived the tornado after being picked up and thrown around. Whenever a storm came up, Niki would lose control of his bladder. Karen was also shell shocked. Any time there was a storm, a breeze, a little rain, Doshier would come home to find his wife hiding behind the bed, the dog cowering. A real estate agent showed them the berm house.

"I remember my wife was holding my arm, and she had these big puddles in her eyes, and she said, 'This house was made for me.'" In the spring of 2003, four years to the week after the great tornado outbreak, a series of twisters again ripped through Cleveland County, plowing through Highland Park again and causing $200 million worth of damage to the town's General Motors plant alone. Jerry and Karen Doshier would watch it all from within their beautiful bunker in the side of a hill. They had moved into their foundation, and the wind could blow as hard as it wanted.

THE YEAR 2003 had been a tough year in Oklahoma, and elsewhere. On December 17, the National Weather Service posted an "Urgent Weather Message" on its website that stated, in part, "The earth has left its orbit and is hurtling toward the sun." It was obviously a joke gone awry, but it took on a life of its own, the way a slip of the tongue can come to seem like a potent sign. But of what? *Harper's* magazine had recently begun a column called "Findings," a kind of list-poem of turbulent discoveries, oddments, and mayhem strung together in a headlong apocalyptic rush, and to which I turned every month, first thing, to get my catastrophilic fix upon the End Times: a Georgia woman's hair spontaneously bursting into flames; parts of Los Angeles covered up to a foot in hail; hundreds of people buried in landslides in the Philippines; 13 million trees damaged in a freak snowstorm in Beijing; a dinner menu from the *Titanic* auctioned for $49,500—on the menu, salmon, consommé mirette, sweetbreads, roast chicken, spring lamb, and golden plover on toast. There was a protean quality to all of this that suggested a world either building or pulling itself apart. So that was it. Perhaps we were in love with endings, including our own.

"The impulse to reach for some transcending meaning is an American impulse," according to Mark Silk, the director of the Leonard E. Greenburg Center for the Study of Religion in Public Life. That impulse was a holdover from a cultural style we'd inherited from the Puritan tradition, of scrutinizing the world for larger meanings of seeing everything as fraught with significance. "You won't find it nearly as much in Europe," Silk said. "We don't take the position that Shit happens. We always want to think, 'Shit happens—for a reason.'"

And the weather had given people a great deal of material by which the shit that had happened might be construed. "There's a formulaic quality of interpreting events—natural or man-made," Silk told me. "When a tornado or hurricane hits a town, you'll commonly hear stories of the miraculous: something about how the only thing that was left standing was the cross— things like that."

I'd spoken to many tornado survivors in Oklahoma—nearly all of them deeply religious people—and much of what Silk said rang true. But if May 3 stories were filled with moments like this—the searchlights illuminating the cross on the Moore First Baptist Church; everyone from the subdivision across the road "going to the cross"—still, I never spoke with a single person who viewed the events as a sign of the End Times. I'm certain those people are out there, especially among Evangelicals, but I never met one. Rather, I found people for whom the crucible of wind had brought a double blessing—a closer walk with the Lord, and a more pragmatic fundamentalism. It wasn't so much that the no-look dunk of fundamentalist baptism of the sort I witnessed at the First Baptist Church had been replaced, rather they had discovered a newfound, hard-won allegiance to storm shelters, for instance—above or below ground—to basements, to berm houses, to well-built homes, and to enough load-bearing brick to ride out the Second Coming, or whatever it was that God, in his infinite mercy, had in store.

ELEVEN

What Would Jesus Drive?

imagined him keeping careful track of mileage and fuel consumption, for starters, entering the figures in a little notebook during a month spent chasing storms, say, and then tallying the totals. If, like us, Jesus had driven his Dodge Caravan, a rental, 6,066 miles, and burned 316.23 gallons of gasoline, then this would make for a 19.8-mile-per-gallon average, which, Jesus would note, while nothing to cheer about, was still at least 1 mile per gallon better than the factory specs. Allowing that 1,700 miles of the above total involved not chasing but some other activity, then Jesus' total chase mileage, both outbound and return, for the month of May would have been 4,364 miles, with 227.5 gallons of nonrenewable, fossil fuel consumed. I imagined him then going to a website maintained by the Environmental Defense Fund and plugging in the figures above to get his "Tailpipe Tally," which told Jesus that in one month he had released into the atmosphere, where it would remain, warming the planet, for the next hundred years, a grand total of 6,324 pounds of carbon. If he then decided to count *only the actual chase miles,* Jesus still would have released 4,551 pounds—over two tons—of carbon into the atmosphere, more than the van's own base curb weight of 4,146 pounds.[1] I'm not sure what Jesus would have to say about any of this, but I am fairly certain that if, for some reason, he had it to do all over again, Jesus would return in a hybrid car, a Toyota Prius, for example, that would reduce the totals above—the consumption of gasoline, the cost, and the total greenhouse gas emissions by Jesus—by over 40 percent. The down side? A hybrid was a little too small to fit *all* the apostles. But hey, Jesus was known for making a sacrifice or two.

This reverie had been prompted by a story in the *Detroit Free Press* about an evangelist minister, Jim Ball, and his wife, Kara Unger Ball, who one year previously, in a new gas-electric hybrid car, a 2003 Toyota Prius, had embarked on an environmental campaign through the Bible Belt, beginning in Austin, Texas, making their fuel-efficient way through Arkansas, Tennessee, Georgia, the Carolinas, and Pennsylvania, sometimes forgetting entirely about gas stations for days, then ending with a press conference in Washington, D.C. The sponsoring organization, of which Jim Ball was executive director, was a program called the Evangelical Environmental Network (EEN), which according to its website was formed because "an evangelical voice was needed in the growing religious consensus that fuel economy and pollution from cars, trucks, and SUVs [were] serious moral issues."[2] The EEN's first major initiative was, of course, the What Would Jesus Drive? Campaign, which had the unmistakable ring of the evangelical imagination, one that routinely sought and found an absolutely breathtaking proximity to the King of Kings. Theirs was an intimately personal Jesus, as reflected in the common homiletic expression "to know Christ as your personal savior." The evangelical mind tended to bring Christ "down home," so that he walked with you as you took out the trash, for instance. Their iconography placed Jesus in up-to-date settings. Sure he still wore a robe, being Jesus and all, but you were meant to imagine him sitting down next to you in your cubicle at the office. The Salvation Army Jesus had it just right—where Jesus looked like a dude fresh out of rehab. While the What Would Jesus Drive? Campaign was merely an application of this proximate Jesus, it prompted more than a few jokes. The *Detroit Free Press,* for instance, offered a riff on the beatitudes with the headline "Blessed Are the Fuel-Efficient," and there were the occasional obscene gestures on the road, as the couple made their way through the South at a steady 64 miles per hour, one mile per hour under the posted limit, in the far right lane, as Jesus himself might have done. I'll confess I had a hard time getting beyond, say, imagining Jesus driving a Cadillac DeVille, or wondering how he might handle afternoon traffic—there were many ways to run with the initial premise—but eventually I had to recognize how simple and effective "What Would Jesus Drive?" truly was for addressing the problem of global warming. For, despite its patent absurdity, "What Would Jesus Drive?" made plain the selfishness at the heart of a culture that was slowly destroying itself and taking the rest of the world with it—and it suggested how this might be amended. The fact was that the world changed, or didn't change, every day, at the level of the quotidian, with Jesus—or the Jesus in all several hundred million Americans—making, or not making, certain basic decisions. The problem of our time, it seemed, was a form of local action decoupled from any guiding principle but self-satisfaction, comfort, and ease. We had confused the pursuit of happiness with the pursuit of entertainment, pleasure, or distraction. Happiness, we had forgotten, was a by-product of a discipline of self-forgetting, self-sacrifice, engagement with the world beyond ourselves. It wasn't a popular idea. I remember looking with pity, for instance, at the weird kids who went trick-or-treating for UNICEF. No grab bag, no candy hoard for them at the end of the night—just a pathetic little milk carton jingling with coins they couldn't keep for themselves. But a republic that thought a little too carefully about the world it was making or unmaking, as the Weather Channel well knew, was bad for business. And the aforementioned "failure of imagination," regarding global warming, if true, cast the problem in the past tense, like some irreparable support beam that had collapsed, once and for all. Now that we were in a position, for good or ill, to answer God's rebuke of Job, to say, in effect, that *we* had changed the climate, and the weather, that *we* were the ones who had something to do with the whirlwind and its frequencies, now that we had in effect usurped God's position, would we prove ourselves unworthy of that new role by choosing every day to remain locked within our own tiny spheres of influence, zooming along at 70 miles per hour? In fact, as Jesus himself would have noted, everyone had the capacity to think globally, to imagine the absolute largest sphere, the one earth we all inhabited, as the only sphere that really mattered.

But let's be clear. For the record, Jesus would probably not drive. He would use public transportation, or walk to work, or, if absolutely necessary, he would rent or perhaps lease a car. Perhaps the part of Jesus that was most like us would at times be captive to the twenty-first-century American predicament of being latecomers, evading what literally loomed in the air, a sense of living in the predicate—of dark things eluded by getting in a car and dreaming the voluptuous American dream of the infinite present progressive. That was the feeling, the fantasy—the temptation—and the payoff one bought every time one got behind the wheel.

By the end of May, I had seen all the storm chasing I needed to see for a lifetime. In my canvas bag I'd packed my daughter's plastic kazoo. I'd picked it up off the floor of my apartment in New York the night before leaving for Oklahoma. Livia had dropped it and moved on to other things. I'd stood there for a moment, all packed and ready to go, my bags bursting with everything I'd need for a month on the road, and I'd looked at that kazoo and wondered whether it might serve some purpose out on the Plains, say, after a spectacular day of encountering tornadoes. It seemed to fulfill some element of whimsy that I thought might be useful. It might surprise Matt, in any case, and prompt him to say something funny. That month I saw more than a dozen tornadoes and funnel clouds, most of them in one magical three-hour period, when on May 24 a storm that Matt had targeted began dropping one tornado after another—twice there were at least two tornadoes on the ground at one time—as they harmlessly augured the wheat fields just south of Belleville, Kansas. We kept following and following, and the tornadoes kept proliferating, but not once did I feel compelled to break out the kazoo. It wasn't because doing so would have been as inappropriate a response as Beethoven's Ninth transcribed for parade float accordions. No, it wasn't that. Rather, it was because Matt was a careful chaser. A responsible chaser, always keeping one step ahead of the circus, and always keeping at least a mile between him and a tornado. Never mind that later in June, driving for Tim Samaras, Matt would get as close to a violent tornado as he'd ever been. It would pass a few hundred yards away, as it tore up a corn field, and it would sound "like a huge waterfall, now and then telephone poles making loud popping noises as they snapped in half." Normally, however, whatever grudge Matt was settling with God by intercepting tornadoes, he settled at a comfortable distance. Thus the feeling I had after our encounter with a dozen tornadoes reminded me of the feeling of returning to home port with my father after a particularly successful fishing expedition off the Washington coast, my father at the helm, riding our little boat on the groundswells all the way to the mouth of the Quilliute River, a catch of iced Coho and King salmon still banging away in the box. In the slant light of an afternoon, one might yawn a great yawn and drink in the ocean breeze and the great green ocean itself, and feel that one had done something. And this feeling, whatever it was, was a long way from the sublime.

Whatever I was after, I seemed to keep getting pointed back to the unlikely town of El Reno, Oklahoma. Back in New York City, climbing out of a subway station and walking through a cyclone of swirling street trash, a bottle cap spinning fiercely at its center, I held in my hands an article I'd found in the library about an experimental filmmaker named George Kuchar, who in 1977, twenty-three years before my own weather journey, was traveling just west of Oklahoma City and decided to take shelter from an oncoming storm. He made a film of the experience, *Wild Night in El Reno,* and began a series of springtime pilgrimages that became the *Weather Diaries,* pursuing the possibilities of the sublime in El Reno, his adopted home away from home, where he seemed to have discovered some sort of harmonic convergence. Instead of chasing storms, Kuchar hung out in his favorite motel and filmed from his doorstep the weather as it blew through town. Using El Reno's mobile home trailer courts and trashy vulnerability like a set of a John Waters film, Kuchar had found a way to outmaneuver the limiting, trivializing effect of the camera frame upon the tornado.

As it happened, so had someone else, it seemed. Near the end of May, I climbed inside Sean Casey's tank. It wasn't something I advertised to my wife, and Matt wouldn't endorse the plan. "That thing is a death trap," he said, but it seemed a fitting thing to do, here, on the cusp of whatever climatic apocalypse we were brewing for ourselves in the years to come, to climb inside a vehicle straight out of a Mad Max movie. I was wary of him, and he of me—with my notepads and my camcorder and pesky questions. And I was a little jealous of him and the life he'd invented. Perhaps it was some East Coast Puritanism I'd absorbed that remained a little awed and jealous of the California Glide, the way, on a given afternoon, I might find him lying around on top of the tank, catching up on some sleep, with his brother Ryan popping the hatch and cranking up the stereo—Metallica blasting away, Ryan playing air drums, young undergraduate meteorologist babes sunning themselves all around him, Ryan saying the only thing that could be said at the moment—*"Steel Beach"*—in a low, imitation "radio voice," a phrase that announced the title of a new summer movie that seemed to be taking place right in front of my eyes.

Didn't I want to be Sean Casey, after all, grease-monkey playboy adventurer, halfway up the TIV, standing on the door ledge, bending over in mock exhaustion onto one of the DOW kids? I would have just returned from the local beauty college, as he once did, where he'd been closely if patchily shorn. He kept feeling around for places that were unevenly cut. Others joined in. Didn't I want to be adored? "It's a patch cut," he said. "You're a true dare devil," someone else said. "On every level, you have no fear." There was a certain new level of intimacy between them all. The ice, long broken, had reached the sea by now. One of the DOW kids, for instance, a stand-offish beauty, allowed Sean to put his head on her stomach while she reclined on the turret housing of the steel beach. They were all snoozing away. Meanwhile, people kept coming up to the TIV as they always did. Sean had tapped into an enthusiasm Americans have for self-taught inventors and mavericks and for large, fuel-consuming tank-like vehicles.

"I came to check this out," a local man said. Nobody on the TIV moved to acknowledge the man. "Quite the deal," he said to me, finally, then walked away.

A pickup truck drove by at low idle then stopped. A woman rolled down her window. "Was this on TV? You guys are famous!" The woman turned to me. "This is pretty exciting, for Fairbury," she said, then drove off.

In the TIV, one always made an entrance. One then had the option of playing it up or playing it down. Sean lying on the TIV, half-asleep, in Fairbury, or Flatrock, or Fact, or Freedona, usually played it down, patiently answering questions of passersby. Another truck came up, this time with two guys in it. "We just wanted to know how fast this thing goes."

One of the DOW kids was petting Sean's back while he reposed with his head in her lap, enjoying this brief moment of rest from the dozens of repair jobs yet to do, his left arm lying over her belly, his right draped over the side of the TIV so that, from a certain angle, it appeared as if he were giving this huge metallic beast a hug. He turned to the two men who asked him how fast the TIV would go, and said, with a beatific smile, eyelids at half mast, "Fast enough, so far."

Eventually we set out and strapped ourselves in. "Welcome aboard," Sean said, with a big plug of Skoal protruding in the side of his mouth. A former student of Ward Davenny named Todd was also along for the ride. Sean slapped a Red Hot Chili Pepper's CD into the stereo and pulled out onto the road. "Please make note of all escape routes," he said. I sat in a bucket seat, both of my shoulders strapped with a complicated seat belt arrangement that released with some difficulty at the chest. My door had to be manhandled open and closed, then a large sliding bolt rammed a few times, to lock me in. I was surrounded by gray insulite padding, silver duct tape, steel, and protruding wires. If you put your finger in the wrong place it came out greasy. The passenger door was the only viable escape route for me, though in a pinch, I might have been able to make it out the front hatch Every time my door opened, it shoved the rearview mirror forward, and since there were no windows to roll down, you either had to stop the TIV, unbuckle yourself, open the door and push the rearview mirror back into position, or just say the hell with it and go without. One had the sense that there were multiple layers of opportunity for wholesale, systemic failure, beginning with the most basic sort of problem, say, that Sean could no longer see what was happening in the right lane because the rearview mirror was pushed forward. It turned out that the windshield wipers didn't work very well, so when it started to rain, the driver wasn't able to see much that was in front of him. It soon started to rain heavily, and the ceiling of the TIV began leaking. I knew it isn't very cool of me to think along these lines, but if, for some reason, Todd, who was now driving, couldn't see through the rain because of the faulty windshield wipers, and somehow drove this seven-ton tank through a guardrail and into a farmer's impoundment pond, well, that would pretty much be the end of us. It was loud and hot inside, smelling of diesel and black waterproof caulking. We soon lost the DOWs and were operating on our own, with Sean, now wearing a pair of ski goggles, standing with his head just barely sticking out of the front hatch, all business, a Rommel of the Plains.

"Okay, everybody," Sean said, "when we start getting cloud-to-ground lightning strikes, make sure you're not touching any metal. And if you're on the radio," he added, "make sure you don't hold onto it for very long."

"Right."

To me, Sean said, "Okay, we'll need to know our dirt road options." I had my De Lorme map at hand. We stopped on the side of the road for a moment, and Todd helped Sean heft the bulky IMAX camera into position in the turret. Then we were back on the road.

"How do you guys feel about getting close?" Sean asked, his head out of the hatch scanning the horizon. I looked at Todd, an art student with shaggy dark hair and horn-rimmed glasses and an off-white T-shirt that had been washed too many times with the rest of his dirty clothes. Todd looked at me, with my map and highlighter pens, my clipboard, my video camera slung around my neck. It was the briefest of exchanges, but we both understood. It said, *Today we will die like men.*

"As long as we don't lift off the ground," I said.

"Ha! That ought to be a good chapter in your book."

Okay, I thought. *Now I've really gone and done it. Enlisted in Napoleon's army, Captain Bly's ship.*

The storms that afternoon had set up west of Oklahoma City, and there was a little bit of chasing in earnest, with Todd leaning forward trying to see through the blinding rain, and Sean barking out orders, and the whole leaking into our laps. Then suddenly we were stopped at a smalltown traffic light. Through my hatch-like window, I watched a couple of guys in the local gas station change the tires of a car up on the rack, listening to Iron Maiden, their air-wrenches *zip-zipping* lug nuts off the wheel rims and dropping with a loud clank into the hub caps. Somehow it all looked familiar. Then I knew—a few seconds before it happened—that I'd been here before, because I had, in what seemed like another lifetime. I wanted to turn to Matt and say, "Hey, wait a minute. Haven't we been here before?" And Matt, would turn to me and say, truthfully, "About a thousand times." But it wasn't Matt. It was an art student named Todd driving the TIV.

Throughout the chase, Josh Wurman and the DOW crew were talking back and forth to each other in a clipped professional staccato. For all the ungainliness of Wurman's operation, when the storms fired up they always seemed to find their best game. Now, however, we were all entering a lull. Sean Casey's massive machine idled away at the stop light, and Josh Wurman came in over the radio. "Anyone have the feeling of déjà vu?"

We were in El Reno, of course. We'd just pass by the Sunset motel, where I'd taken cover from the big storm four years ago—the place that didn't have a basement—and that had set me off on this adventure into big weather in the first place. Four years later I was riding in a tank with a man who, more or less, wanted to get as close as he could to a tornado approaching the town.

Then Josh Wurman came over the radio and announced that the storm had torn itself apart. It was tracking east toward Oklahoma City, and there was a slight chance that it would recycle before it got there, so we continued the pursuit. "It was a gentleman's chase," Sean said over the murmur of the TIV'd diesel engine. People passing the TIV in their cars leaned out their windows and took pictures.

"Last year," Sean said, "the people were just slack-jawed when we passed. This year, though, they're ready with the cameras."

As we approached the city limits of Oklahoma City, Wurman came over the radio: "Anyone interested in their karma should stop wishing for tornadoes now." We all dutifully stopped wishing for tornadoes. The DOW trucks were being followed by a caravan of about twenty cars—support vehicles, hangers-on, teenagers who just happened to notice the big rotating radar dishes—all strung together down the road. Herb Stein, who was driving DOW 2, leading the way, pulled off to the side of the road for a moment, and all twenty cars pulled off to the side of the road, idling there as the wind tossed the wheat fields all around us in the early evening air of the third millennium, and we wondered what was happening. Out came Herb, who leveled his camera at the western horizon to snap a few pictures of the mesocyclone that towered over us and caught the dying light grandly. That was all. He'd just wanted to stop for a moment and take a photograph of something truly beautiful. An epic cloud. We watched him looking at the

Oklahoma sky, an entire train of people looking through their windshields and waiting patiently as Herb stood there watching the clouds, snapping pictures. He then got back into his truck and pulled onto the highway, and the caravan followed in his path. There was still some daylight left. And, warnings about karma notwithstanding, one never knew what might happen.

Notes

One: Becalmed: Dreaming of Yevtushenko

1. Peggy R. Concannon, Harold E. Brooks, and Charles A. Doswell III, "Climatological Risk of Strong and Violent Tornadoes in the United States," Second Conference on Environmental Applications, American Meteorological Society, Long Beach, California, January 8–12, 2000.

2. Robert F. Abbey, Jr., and T. Theodore Fujita, "Tornadoes: The Tornado Outbreak of 3–4 April 1974," in *The Thunderstorm in Human Affairs,* 2d ed., revised and enlarged, Edwin Kessler, ed. (Norman: University of Oklahoma Press, 1981), pp. 37–40.

3. Harold Brooks, "Severe Thunderstorm Climatology: Where and When Do Thunderstorms Occur?" http://www.nssl.noaa.gov/hazard.

4. Matt Biddle is the source for all the terms used herein. One of a handful of researchers who have specialized in tornado risk behavior, Biddle makes the connection between general risk behavior and the human ecology of tornado events in "Format, Utility, and Value Issues for Implementation of Probability-Based Tornado Warnings for Public Use," a Ph.D. dissertation, forthcoming from the University of Oklahoma, Norman, Oklahoma.

5. Mark Fonstad, William Pugatch, and Brandon Vogt, "Kansas Is Flatter Than a Pancake," *Annals of Improbable Research,* vol. 9, no. 3 (June 2003).

6. Lynda Edwards, "Storm Troopers," *Details,* November 1995, pp. 131–80. Matt Biddle says that the *Details* magazine quotes about God were completely fabricated. "I never made any comments to Lynda Edwards about God and tornadoes, or anything about being tested by God." I'm inclined to believe him. This bit of fiction notwithstanding, after coming to know Matt over the years, I can certainly understand why Lynda Edwards would want to nudge the truth of her interview with Matt toward the realm of Melville. For Matt remains a quintessential Ahab-like character, which even Matt himself has acknowledged.

7. WX-Chase posting by David Gold, WX-Chase "From Rags to Riches," 4:45 P.M., Friday, May 7, 2004.
8. WX-Chase posting by Matt Crowther, "Out of the Coffins?" 8:03 A.M., Tuesday, May 4, 2004.
9. WX-Chase posting by Todd L. Sherman, "Friend Going Chasing This Week," 6:52 P.M., Saturday, May 1, 2004.
10. WX-Chase posting by Shane Adams, "Re: Friend Going Chasing This Week," 12:24 A.M., Sunday, May 2, 2004.
11. Alexandra Poolos, "A Poet in New York," *The New York Times,* December 16, 2003.
12. Kevin Chaffee, "Night of Poetic License," *The Washington Times,* April 30, 2004.

Two: Weather Talk

1. Lyall Watson, *Heaven's Breath: A Natural History of the Wind* (New York: William Morrow & Co., 1984), p. 18.
2. *Prymmer or Boke of Private Prayer,* London, 1559, quoted in the *Oxford English Dictionary,* 3rd ed., entry for "chaos."
3. Quoted in Liba Taub, *Ancient Meteorology* (London: Routledge, 2003), pp. 11–39.
4. The ban on the use of the word "tornado," for instance, continued until 1938 and was partially lifted during World War II. Thomas P. Grazulis, *The Tornado: Nature's Ultimate Windstorm* (Norman: University of Oklahoma Press, 2001), pp. 84–85.
5. Charles A. Doswell III, "Tornadoes and Tornadic Storms: A Review of Conceptual Models," Section 3.4. *Fair Weather Vortices.* In *The Tornado: Its Structure, Dynamics, Prediction, and Hazards,* C. Church et al., eds., 1993, Geophysical Monograph 79, American Geophysical Union, pp. 161–72.

Three: Children at Play

1. Climatologies of tornado damage have been done, but to date no climatology of tornadoes based on actual wind speed exists. Telephone interview with Joshua Wurman, director, The Center for Severe Weather Research, January 3, 2005.
2. From *A Comprehensive Glossary of Weather Terms for Storm Spotters,* NOAA Technical Memorandum, NWS SR-145, Michael Branick, NOAA/NWS-WFO Norman, 1996.
3. Matthew 24:29 (Revised Standard translation).

Four: Catastrophilia

1. Annual Report of the Board of Regents of the Smithsonian Institution, for the year 1848, pp. 32–33.
2. *The New York Times,* June 7, 1860.
3. Earnest Lee Tuveson, *Redeemer Nation: The Idea of America's Millennial Role* (Chicago: University of Chicago Press, 1968), p. 232.
4. Herman Melville, *White Jacket,* chapter 36. Cited in ibid., p. 157.
5. Glenn W. Most, "After the Sublime," *The Yale Review,* vol. 90, no. 2 (April 2002), p. 104
6. Ibid., p. 105.
7. Susan Sontag, "The Imagination of Disaster," *Commentary* (October 1965), p. 42.

8. MacLane, Mary, from the story of Mary MacLane, found in *Tender Darkness: A Mary MacLane Anthology,* Elizabeth Pruitt, ed. (Belmont, Calif.: Abernathy and Brown, 1993), p. 89.

9. Ibid., p. 96.

10. Ibid., p. 186.

11. Ibid., p. 3.

12. Ibid., p. 159.

13. Ibid., p. 166.

14. Ibid., p. 200.

15. Ibid., p. 168.

Five: Paparazzi del Cielo

1. For the record, it was at the Yorkshire Motel in York, Nebraska.

2. Pam Belluck, "Get Out Your Boards: Extreme Ironing May Soon Be Hot," *The New York Times,* 2004, Section A, p. 14.

3. Tim Marshall, "Roger Jensen: A Storm Chasing Pioneer," *Storm Track.* www .stormtrack.org.

4. Sandra Coleman and Sam McCloud, "A Brief History of Storm Chasing," National Association of Storm Chasers and Spotters web page, www.chasingstorms.com. And Tim Marshall, "Chase Fever: The Early Years. A Biography of David Hoadley," *Storm Track,* January 31, 1987.

5. From the Warren Faidley website, www.cyclonecowboy.com.

6. From the "Copyright and Legal Notices" section of www.StormChaser.com.

7. When asked upon which bestseller list his book had appeared, Faidley offered that his book was "listed as a 'bestseller' on multiple lists . . . including: Amazon .com (still listed in some old searches as a 'bestseller.')" It was also a bestseller, according to Faidley, on the National Contemporary Science Titles for 1996, and made it into "several educational, book club, and science lists as a 'top ten' or 'bestseller . . . [and] was also a 4-5 star, bestseller for Barnes & Noble, especially around the time *Twister* was released. *The only reason* it did not make any bigger lists was *partly because* the Weather Channel is a privately owned business and they . . . would not release sales numbers [italics mine]." E-mail to the author from Warren Faidley, January 4, 2005.

8. For his part, Faidley states that there never was an officially declared "chaser consultant" for the movie *Twister,* which, according to Faidley, in its earliest conception was to be based on his life. *Twister* was a project, Faidley maintains, for which he was always an early, informal "initial" consultant. Telephone conversation with Warren Faidley, December 29, 2004. Faidley later sent me a letter, dated January 3, 1996, from Warner Brothers to the Weather Channel stating that Faidley had "served as a technical consultant" to the movie *Twister.*

9. Daniel E. Gershenson, "Apollo the Wolf-god," *Journal of Indo-European Studies* Monograph Number 8 (1991), chapters I, II, and III, pp. 1–126.

10. "Wolf is a name for the wind in German, as the studies of Wilhelm Mannhardt showed." Gershenson, p. 6, refers to Mannhardt's *Rogenwolf und Roggenhund: Beitrag sur germanischen Sittenkunde* (Danzig, 1866).

11. Gershenson, Appendix A, "The Stoic Explanation of the Epithet Lykeios," pp. 132–33, points to the work of L. R. Farnell, *The Cults of the Greek States 1–5*

(Oxford, Eng., 1896–1909): "Since 1909 when L.R. Farnell completed publication of his great work, hardly a voice has been raised to claim that Apollo is a light-god. . . . *Lykeios* can not by any means be a light-epithet. There is no doubt that the epithets of Apollo from the root *lyk-* are derived from the name of the wolf, and not from a root meaning 'light.' "

12. Ibid., pp. 6–7.
13. Ibid., p. 7.

Six: Present Progressive

1. The trend at the SPC is to try to provide emergency management officials and other "decision-makers" with quantitative assessments of risk. For example, when the SPC issues a map that includes tornado risk contours, the percentages shown on the map, which can range from 2 to 25 percent, represent a dramatic increase in the likelihood of a tornado touching down anywhere within a 25-mile radius of the contour domain over a twenty-four-hour period. The percentages are always meant to be measured against the overall climatological record for the weather phenomena in question. Thus, if on a given day in May, the SPC placed an area under a 5 percent tornado risk, and the climatological record for tornadoes at that time of year was 1 percent, the risk for tornadoes would be five time greater than normal. Telephone conservation with Stephen Corfidi, Lead Forecaster, SPC, January 3, 2005.
2. The plans for TIV2 have been scrapped in favor of a lighter, more maneuverable vehicle.

Seven: A Citizen's Brigade

1. My account of this incident is based on video, interviews, and e-mail correspondence with David Drummond. In the interests of all concerned, I have decided not to identify the person who was chasing with Drummond on May 22, 2004.
2. "This observation, if true, would suggest that a tornado was very near," observes Matt Biddle. Correspondence with the author, November 23, 2004.

Eight: Good-bye, *Wakan*

1. Andrew Freedman, "Weather Channel Tunes to Changing Climate," *Greenwire,* January 5, 2004.
2. John Seabrook, "Selling the Weather," *The New Yorker,* April 3, 2000, pp. 44–53.
3. "The balance of evidence suggests that there is a discernible human influence of global climate." See Bill McKibben, "Worried? Us?" in *Granta, This Overheating World* (Fall 2003), p. 9.
4. McKibben, op. cit., p. 9.
5. Committee on the Science of Climate Change, "Climate Change Science: An Analysis of Some Key Questions," National Academy of Sciences, May 2001.
6. Freedman, "Weather Channel."
7. The 2004 statement represented a slight revision of TWC's earlier position on global warming, issued in December 2003, which hemmed and hawed about the difficulty and complexity of the climate system, before unloading this gem of sophistry: "It cannot be conclusively stated that humans are completely responsible for global warming." Well, of course not.
8. While it is true that the Weather Channel, alone among networks, regularly addresses the subject of climate change, it is also true, and more to the point, that

this is a recent development. Some observers celebrate the Weather Channel's coverage of global warming. Indeed, it is a promising development—but my aim here
is to counter the self-congratulatory tone adopted by the company for belatedly
taking steps, as the chronology leading up to *The Day after Tomorrow* suggests,
that seem almost entirely based upon the exigencies of market positioning and
public relations strategizing rather than on any purported high purpose. The
movie, the science it addressed, and the spectacular sequence of Florida hurricanes in the fall of 2004, effectively "outed" the Weather Channel on the subject of
climate change.

9. "Climate Change Science: An Analysis of Some Key Questions," p. 4.
10. The seven-gigaton figure is from John Carey with Sarah R. Shapiro, "Global
    Warming," *Business Week,* August 30, 2004. For the water-vapor feedback loop,
    see Peter Schwartz and Doug Randall, "An Abrupt Climate Change Scenario and
    Its Implications for United States National Security," Pentagon Report, October
    2003, http://www.ems.org/climate/pentagon_climate_change.html.
11. "Climate Change Science: An Analysis of Some Key Questions," p. 4.
12. "Climate Change II: Study Finds 'Carbon Sinks' May Actually Generate More
    CO_2," *Greenwire,* September 24, 2004. This article cites two studies conducted by
    Professor Michelle Mack, of the University of Florida, and Professor Tim Moore,
    of McGill University.
13. 55–36 million years ago. CO_2 levels, as taken from ice core samples, are highter
    than they have been in 440,000 years, McKibben, "Worried? Us?" in *Granta: This
    Overheating World* (Fall 2003), p. 8, and Report on Global Warming, United
    Nations Intergovernmental Panel on Climate Change (IPCC) 2001.
14. Dr. Cullen's announcement, a few paragraphs later, also pointed to "strong evidence
    that a significant portion of the current warming is a result of human activities."
    "The Weather Channel Announces Position on Global Warming," *PR Newswire,*
    May 6, 2004.
15. Seabrook, "Selling the Weather," p. 53.
16. Jody Berland, "Mapping Space: Imaging Technologies and the Planetary Body," in
    Stanley Aronowitz, Barbara Martinsons, and Michael Menser, eds., *Techno-science
    and Cyberculture* (New York: Routledge, 1996), p. 124.
17. Andrew Ross, *Strange Weather: Culture, Science and Technology in the Age of Lim-
    its* (London: Verso, 1991). See chapter 6, "The Drought Next Time," p. 242.
18. Freedman, "Weather Channel."
19. "Extreme Weather Hits the Big and Small Screens: The Weather Channel
    'Extreme Weather Week' to Feature Special Programming Tied to Premiere of
    Twentieth Century Fox Movie 'Day after Tomorrow,'" PR Newswire Association,
    May 13, 2004.
20. Telephone conversation with Kathy Lane, Weather Channel public relations offi-
    cer, November 5, 2004.
21. Marita Sturken, "Desiring the Weather: El Niño, the Media, and the California
    Identity," *Public Culture,* vol. 13, no. 2 (Spring 2001), p. 161–89.
22. Ross, p. 241.
23. Ross, p. 242.
24. *Business Wire* press release, April 17, 2003. "Winds of Change Gain Momentum
    at the Weather Channel as 2003–2004 Upfront Season Begins," p. 2. The press
    release quotes an article published in *AdWeek,* but ends, as many Weather Channel

press releases do, with the Weather Channel's demographic stats, which the *Adweek* article did not include.

25. Ibid., April 17, 2003, p. 2.
26. Telephone interview with Wonya Lucas, executive vice president of marketing, the Weather Channel, October 2003.
27. Marc Fisher, "Soaking Up the Atmosphere," *The Washington Post,* May 27, 1989.
28. Ibid.
29. Jeff Klinkenberg, "Music for a Rainy (or Sunny) Day," *The St. Petersburg Times Floridian,* August, 25, 2003.
30. "Am I Watching the Weather—Or Porno," posted by "Monkey" on September 1, 2004, on www.monkeycube.com/article-5.
31. Marita Sturken, "Desiring the Weather: El Niño, the Media, and California Identity," *Public Culture,* vol. 13, no. 2 (Spring 2001), p. 170. Sturken sites Jim Campbell for this point.
32. Most of the information regarding Landmark and the formation of the Weather Channel comes from Frank Batten's memoir, *The Weather Channel: The Improbable Rise of a Media Phenomenon* (Boston: Harvard Business School Press), 2002.
33. Landmark is a 50 percent shareholder, along with Cox Communications, which owns the other half, in a company called Trader Publishing, a consortium of free auto-trader mags. Landmark's nearest rival in this lowbrow but lucrative realm, a company called Community Newspaper Holdings, Inc., with 200 dailies, weeklies, and semiweeklies, including advertising circulars, has revenues in excess of $400 million annually.
34. To this day, it's an issue that plagues the National Weather Service, which suffers the continued harangues of private companies, like AccuWeather, complaining that their patented products—very often software packages and other forecasting tools that have been slightly altered from the original National Weather Service products—are now being "undercut" by these selfsame originals, which the NWS distributes for free. Citing any number of deregulatory laws, including those that reduce duplication of effort between government agencies, private companies have demanded that the NWS eliminate many of its free product lines. The result, many fear, will be something akin to England's laws of enclosure, which privatized land that had been held communally. But in the case of environmental data, what is effectively sealed off from public use is knowledge—climate records, forecasting software—things much less tangible than land. Their privatization would seem a form of weather profiteering for the few, at taxpayers' expense, like putting a surcharge on the air we all breathe.
35. Wonya Lucas offered a picture that struck me as odd. She seemed to refer to a segmentation study that was conducted in 2000, which, she said, identified four basic segments. When asked to clarify whether there was, indeed, a second study in 2000 that broke the viewer segments into the four groups to which she refers below, Lucas, through Kathy Lane, the Weather Channel's public relations officer, gave a one-word response: "No."

> Wonya Lucas: The previous [segmentation study] from 2000 is more along the lines of what you're doing—the segments we came up with were weather enthusiasts, or weather weenies as we like to call them. . . .

> Mark Svenvold: The 2000 segment you came up with were weather wee-nies, or weather involved—
>
> WL: Weather enthusiasts, we had weather commodity people who just want the weather wet-dry-hot-cold, weather planners, people who plan, that's obvious, then weather engaged, between the planners and the enthu-siasts, these are the people who are interested in the awe aspects, the science behind the weather, the inspiration, but they're not hardcore. They wouldn't know all the weather organizations like the enthusiasts would. Those are the main—
>
> MS: Enthusiasts—what were the second ones again?
>
> WL: We'll do them in descending order—enthusiasts, engaged, plan-ners, and commodity. The commodities being people who just want the temperature.

36. Wonya Lucas wouldn't offer follow-up comments on the point I make here, which is, without doubt, an inference, but not a terribly difficult one. I draw it from my telephone interview with Ms. Lucas, in which she mentioned (a) the importance of finding commonalities between segments and (b) that weather-as-"awe" and weather-as-"lifestyle" were two common viewer attitudes. To this I add the Weather Channel's more than evident promotion of awe, as well as the lifestyle ori-entation of "Live By It" and the network's recent "upfront" campaign catch-phrase, "It's not about the weather. It's about life."
37. Tony Case, "Winds of Change," *Adweek,* June 9, 2003.
38. Indeed, in the central Oklahoma weather race, one thing that has given KWTV, Channel 9, an edge over its competitors is its willingness to use both high- and low-tech methods to build its brand. On the low end, four or five times a year, Channel 9 likes to trot out a road show, a catastrophilic severe-weather extrava-ganza, in small-town high school gymnasiums throughout its listening area. Origi-nally called "The Traveling Weather Show," now called "Those Terrible Twisters," it features music, severe-weather film clips, and Channel 9's weatherman, Gary England, perhaps the most popular person in Oklahoma. Three thousand people showed up for a show in Woodward, 7,500 at a recent show in Oklahoma City.
39. Tony Case, "Winds of Change."
40. Michael Taussig, *My Cocaine Museum* (Chicago: University of Chicago Press), 2004.

Nine: Weather Risk and the Great Folly

1. James E. Hansen, "Dangerous Anthropogenic Interference: A Discussion of Humanity's Faustian Bargain and the Payments Coming Due," a presentation delivered in Iowa City, Iowa, October 26, 2004.
2. The $100 billion figure is according to Gerry Lemcke, deputy head of CAT Perils; Swiss Re; and Dr. Robert P. Hartwig, chief economist, the Insurance Information Institute.
3. July 19, 2001, Dyn-O-Mat became the first company ever to take a cloud off of Doppler radar. The company's goal is to "attack large storms and hurricanes, cut-ting a 'pie-shaped piece' from storms so that they lose their strength or disappear all together." See www.dynomat.com.

4. The United States is unique among nations in this regard, giving away the store, as it were, in the interest of open government and the fulfillment of its mandate to encourage economic growth. This policy has led to a private-sector meteorological market with 4,000 employees and 400 firms, generating annual gross receipts of between $500 and $750 million, five times as much as the European private-sector meteorology market. One recent study found that $19 billion invested by the federal government in the National Weather Service has yielded $750 billion in potentially taxable economic activity. Source: Peter Weiss, NOAA Strategic Planning and Policy Office, Silver Springs, Md. The $750 million figure includes two of the big fish in this realm, the Weather Channel, which is more or less a broadcast company making inroads into the commercial forecast market, and WeatherNews, Inc., a Japanese-based firm touting itself as the largest publicly traded weather consulting firm in the world, which is true, perhaps, if by "publicly traded," you mean "traded exclusively on the Japanese Stock Exchange," more than half of whose shares are owned, largely, by one man, Hiroyoshi Ishibashi, and his close relatives or business cronies, "WeatherNews Plans Second Share Offering," Michele Yamada, *Dow Jones Newswires,* December 18, 2003. At $100 million annually, WeatherNews, Inc., tends to skew assessments of the U.S. market. Subtract these two companies and the market shrinks to around $500 million annually.
5. Weather derivative trades are facilitated by brokers who take a point spread, Dodd estimated, of anywhere between 1 and 5 percent of the "notional value" of every deal. Thus, annual gross receipts from the $4.6 billion notional value in derivatives traded in 2003 probably generated up to $230 million.
6. So far, no catastrophic weather event has ever triggered a payout—but, for a few weeks, the four hurricanes that hit the coast of Florida in the fall of 2004, producing over $22 billion in claims, more than the $15.5 billion in claims caused by Hurricane Andrew in 1992, made investors in a $160 million catastrophe bond called "USAA Residential Re" very nervous. The bond had a special "indemnity" trigger that was just high enough to avoid triggering the first payout ever of a cat bond. Christopher McGhee, the managing director of investment banking at Guy Carpenter, Inc., estimated that perhaps $2 billion worth of cat bonds have been issued, a fairly minuscule amount compared with the rest of the bond market, and McGhee gave a rough estimate of what's called the "rate on line" for cat bonds—the amount charged: 5 percent of the issuance, which would bring the total revenues generated by underwriters to no more than $100 million.
7. "Experts: More Intense Hurricane Activity Could Continue in Future Years as Consequence of Global Warming," *PR Newswire,* Oct. 21, 2004. "This past year—in which there were four big hurricanes in Florida, a calamitous Asian typhoon, and [a] Japanese earthquake—was the most expensive in history for insurers. They paid out forty-two billion dollars in disaster claims, and that was less than half of the total damage sustained," James Surowiecki, "The Catastrophe Problem," *The New Yorker,* January 10, 2005, p. 30, and "Experts: More Intense Hurricane Activity Could Continue in Future Years as Consequence of Global Warming," *PR Newswire,* October 21, 2004.
8. Surowiecki, *The New Yorker,* January 10, 2005, p. 30.
9. Andrew Dlugolecki, "A Changing Climate for Insurance," Association of British Insurers, www.abi.org.uk/climatechange.
10. "Insurer Warns of Global Warming Catastrophe," Reuters, March 3, 2002.

11. "Beyond Kyoto," *Foreign Affairs,* vol. 38, no. 4 (July/August 2004), p. 32.

12. "2004 Global Warming Shareholder Campaign," ExxonMobil Shareholder Resolutions, www.incr.com/resolutions/exxon_shr.htm.

13. Inhofe had received more than $500,000 in campaign contributions from big oil and other big energy: www.opensecrets.org. Only one man, Senator John Cornyn of Texas, had received more campaign contributions from energy companies than Senator James Inhofe.

14. Legates is not a paleoclimatologist, nor does his Center for Climatic Research "have anybody on staff presently that does paleoclimatology," according to his Senate testimony. "Climate History and the Science Underlying Fate, Transport, and Health Effects of Mercury Emissions," U.S. Senate hearing, Tuesday, July 29, 2003. Committee on Environment and Public Works, Washington, D.C.

15. According to author Chris Mooney, Soon and Legates had worked as consultants for the George C. Marshall Institute. "Both scientists have collaborated in the past with the George G. Marshall Institute, an organization skeptical of much climate-change science that received $90,000 from ExxonMobil in 2002. . . . Soon was a senior scientist with the institute and received a small stipend for his work . . . and Legates has written a paper and book chapter for the group." "Earth Last," by Chris Mooney American Prospect Online, www.prospect.org, May 4, 2004.

16. Nobody, that is, except for writers like Chris C. Mooney, to whose intrepid reporting on environmental issues I am deeply indebted. "Think Again: False Objectivity in Science Reporting," May 6, 2004, www.americanprogress.org.

17. Testimony before the "Climate History and the Science Underlying Fate, Transport, and Health Effects of Mercury Emissions," U.S. Senate hearing, Tuesday, July 29, 2003.

18. In questioning Dr. Mann before the Senate, Jim Jeffords of Vermont quotes an e-mail from the editor-in-chief of the magazine where Dr. Soon's paper was published. The editor resigned over problems with Dr. Soon's paper. "The paper should not have been published in this forum [the journal *Climate Research*], not because of the eventual conclusions, but because of the insufficient evidence to draw this conclusion."

>Senator Jeffords: What methodological flaws does he mean, Dr. Mann?
>Dr. Mann: Well, I have tried to outline the most severe of those methodological flaws. I believe it is the mainstream view of just about every scientist in my field that I have talked to that there is little that is valid in that paper. They got just about everything wrong. They did not select the proxies properly. They did not actually analyze any data. They did not produce a reconstruction. They did not produce uncertainties in a reconstruction. They did not compare to the proper baseline of the late-20th century in trying to make conclusions about modern warmth.

"Climate History and the Science Underlying Fate, Transport, and Health Effects of Mercury Emissions," U.S. Senate hearing, Washington, D.C. Tuesday, July 29, 2003. Committee on Environment and Public Works.

19. Bruce Barcott, "Changing All the Rules," *The New York Times Magazine,* April 4, 2004.

20. A quick overview of "science abusers" can be found in Chris Mooney's "Think Again: False Objectivity in Science Reporting," May 6, 2004. Available in the "Columns" section of Center for American Progress website, *www.american progress.org.*

21. One of Inhofe's first official acts as chairman was to appoint a coal-mining lobbyist, John Shanahan, former director of air quality issues at the National Mining Association, to oversee clean air legislation. Katharine Q. Seelye, "Senator Hires Coal Lobbyist," *The New York Times,* February 7, 2003.

Ten: How Firm Is Your Foundation?

1. A casual sampling of recent indicators ranks Oklahoma next to last in average teacher salaries, American Federation of Teachers' *Early Estimates of Public Elementary and Secondary Statistics 2001–02,* U.S. Department of Education, April 2003; forty-eighth in the percentage of Oklahomans 25 years or older who hold a bachelor's degree or higher, Oklahoma State Regents for Higher Education, www.okhighered .org/newscenter/broken-promises.html; third in the number of executions since 1977, "Regrets Trouble E-Lawmaker's Soul" by Ginnie Graham, *Tulsa World,* January 2, 2004; fiftieth in all forms of government spending—cities, counties, education, state, etc., Oklahoma Public Employees Association, *OPEA Advocate,* March 2004, p. 3, www.opea.org; first in the per capita number of clandestine methamphetamine laboratories seized, "A Brief History of Methamphetamine" by John L. Duncan, chief agent, Pharmaceutical Diversion Division, Oklahoma State Bureau of Narcotics and Dangerous Drugs Control, from www.daweslane.com; second in the nation for cardiovascular disease, "State of the State's Health," 2004, Oklahoma State Department of Health survey, www.health.state.ok/board/state/ report.html; and near the bottom in per capita income, www.state.ok.us/osfdoc/ pcpi424.html.

2. Kristof, *The New York Times,* August 15, 2003, on the Op-Ed page, cites "For Goodness' Sake: Why So Many Want Religion to Play a Greater Role in American Life," published by Public Agenda and the Pew Cheritable Trusts, 2001.

3. Nicholas D. Kristof, Op-Ed column, August 15, 2003.

4. The World Values Study Group, *World Values Survey,* 1990–1993. Samples consisted of adults aged eighteen and over in forty-five countries. Adults who "completely agree" to "I never doubted the existence of God": United States, 60 percent; Britain, 31 percent; West Germany, 20 percent. Found in *For Goodness' Sake: Why So Many Want Religion to Play a Greater Role in American Life,* A Report from Public Agenda for The Pew Charitable Trusts, p. 54.

5. To prevent heresy, Eskridge mentioned a tradition, dating from the late 1700s, of "church discipline," whereby those who didn't obey church teachings were "disfellowshipped." "They're probably less rigid about things these days," Eskridge said, "but it's a feature of the Southern Baptist Church." Interview with Larry Eskridge, October 22, 2004.

6. All this changed in June 2003, when Tim Samaras successfully deployed an instrument package and a *National Geographic* photo probe, which contained still and video cameras, into an F-3 tornado near Manchester, South Dakota. The event was filmed by an IMAX crew.

Eleven: What Would Jesus Drive?

1. The tally for the other greenhouse gases released is as follows: Carbon monoxide, nearly 90 pounds; nitrogen oxides, about 7 pounds; hydrocarbons, 2.5 pounds. Consult www.environmentaldefense.org to calculate your own emissions.
2. www.whatwouldjesusdrive.org/tour/faq.php.

Acknowledgments

There were many people whose lives intersected with this project and who were open and gracious in sharing their experiences with big weather in Tornado Alley, among them, Ward Davenny, Donald Staley, and Randy and Dana Grimm. Rick Whitaker, Minister of Education of the First Baptist Church of Moore, Oklahoma, was especially helpful in coordinating interviews with survivors of the May 3, 1999, and May 8, 2003, tornado outbreaks. My thanks go out to him and to those who participated in the interviews: Lucy Austin, Brenda Baurey, Naomi Casselman, Linda (Kinder) Miller, Joy Watson, Dorothy and Harry Taylor, Binnie and Jerry Stanislav, Wayne A. Smith, and Sherry Keahey. To the mayor of Moore, Glenn Lewis, and to the assistant chief of the Moore Fire Department Jerry Doshier (ret.) and his wife, Karen, a warm note of thanks and gratitude for your kindness. Thanks go out as well to Gayland Kitch, director of Emergency Management for the City of Moore and to Robert (Bob) Kaster, of Oklahoma REACT. Many people also shared their experiences with the May 22, 2004, tornado at Wilber and Hallam, Nebraska—Cindy Togstad and her son, Will Togstad, as well as Lori and Keith Muller, Susie and Ron Homolka, among other residents of Wilber, Nebraska, including Shawn Kyker, staff member, and B. J. Fictum, coordinator of emergency management for Saline County. A note of thanks as well goes to Reynolds B. Davis, ARRL Nebraska Section

Emergency Coordinator, Larry Ohs of the Lancaster County, Nebraska, Skywarn Network, and to Kenneth F. Dewey of the High Plains Regional Climate Center for their help in explaining the emergency response to the Hallam disaster.

A special note of thanks goes to the many chasers and weather enthusiasts who gave their time or granted access, in no particular order—Charles Edwards, Dave Hoadley, Tim Samaras, Rocky Rascovich, Roger Hill, Bill Hark, Jeff Piotrowski, Jim Leonard, Mark Herndon, Sean Casey, Warren Faidley, Peggy Willenberg and Melanie Metz, aka The Twister Sisters, Herb Stein, Gene Rhoden, David Drummond, Shane Adams, Tim Marshall, and for his insight, humor, and guidance throughout this project, Matt Biddle. There were many scientists and researchers who also helped guide me along the way: first among them, Keith Brewster, of the Center for the Analysis and Prediction of Storms (CAPS), Stephen Corfidi, Sarah Taylor, Dave Imy, and Joe Schaefer, of the Storm Prediction Center (SPC), Joshua Wurman of the Center for Severe Weather Research (CSWR), and Harold Bluestein and Curtis Alexander of the University of Oklahoma Department of Meteorology. Also of great assistance were Peter Weiss of the National Oceanic and Atmospheric Administration (NOAA) Office of Strategic Planning and Policy; David Dowell of Cooperative Institute for Mesoscale Meteorology Studies (CIMMS); and Greg Stumpf and Harold Brooks of the National Severe Storms Laboratory (NSSL). Thanks to Danny Kopelson for answers to musical questions. To all these professionals I extend my deepest thanks for their good humor and expertise in guiding me through the realms of meteorology. The mistakes that remain are my own.

I would like to thank Sarah Chalfant and Jack Macrae for believing in the book. I am grateful as well to the former dean of Fordham College, Fordham University at Rose Hill, the Bronx, Father Jeffery von Arx, S.J., and to Chris Gogwilt, former chair of the Department of English and to Peggy Cuskley, Fordham University at Lincoln Center, for their generous travel assistance. And to Columbia University for its enlightened policy allowing library reading privileges to spouses of alumni, I am deeply grateful. Thanks most of all to my wife, Martha, my best reader, for her support and encouragement throughout.

Index

About the Author

MARK SVENVOLD's first book of nonfiction, *Elmer McCurdy: The Misadventures in Life and Afterlife of an American Outlaw,* was a Book Sense 76 pick and has been optioned in partnership with Bull's Eye Entertainment and the producer Richard Gladstein (*Reservoir Dogs, Pulp Fiction*). The poet-in-residence at Fordham University, Svenvold has won the *Nation/* "Discovery" Award. He lives in New York City with his wife, the novelist Martha McPhee, and their two children, Livia and Jasper.